"In *Will's Choice*, Gail Griffith has told, with a mother's passion, the urgent, necessary story of how her family coped with the devastating shock of a suicide attempt. This is a book about the struggle to supplement love with wisdom in the face of great pain."
—Andrew Solomon, author of *The Noonday Demon*

"[Griffith has] an incredible gift for words, drawing readers in and making them care about not just Will but all those who bravely combat depression."
—*Cleveland Plain Dealer*

"[Will's] story is a strong call for vigilance among parents, even those who may not think their children are like Will—Griffith never dreamed she had a suicidal son, either—as well as a comfort and resource for people of any age struggling out of that pitch-dark place of the soul."
—*Washingtonian* magazine

"*Will's Choice* is actually about two choices: the young man's choice to die, and his choice to live. Griffith's story stands as a heartbreaking and hopeful account that highlights a public health crisis in dire need of attention."
—*Albuquerque Journal*

"I know I'm onto a groundbreaking book when I immediately begin counting up the people in my life for whom it will soon become a must-read. Gail Griffith's story is every mother's nightmare, and her family's battle against the 'intensely unknowable and terrible' disease of depression, using the limited resources of a dangerously dysfunctional mental health care system, is both heartrending and chilling. If this book serves as a wake-up call, it is truly one that could save lives."   —Judith Guest, author of *Ordinary People*

"Gripping, grueling, and entrancing . . . the text never becomes morose, thanks in part to Griffith's light hand as a wordsmith and her often winsome turns of phrase. . . . A knowledgeable guide's revelatory report on a disturbing phenomenon."   —*Kirkus Reviews*

"Affecting. . . . [Griffith's] story will support parents struggling to help their own suffering teens."   —*Booklist*

"Painfully honest . . . heartrending . . . a plea to society to recognize that depression is a serious but treatable illness."   —*Publishers Weekly*

"Stirring prose . . . possibly life-saving advice for parents. . . . Above all, this is a powerful personal story about a young man who finds a way to embrace life again."   —*Library Journal* (starred review)

"In this beautifully written and gripping account, readers learn a great deal about adolescent depression. . . . This account has much to offer adults who may encounter a depressed teenager or teens themselves."
—*School Library Journal*

"Though Griffith is quick to point out that there's hope for the seriously depressed . . . her book never stoops to platitudes or easy answers. . . . Her lucid, honest prose keeps the reader engaged . . . [and] her story provides concrete advice to concerned parents."   —*Nashville Scene*

"A look inside the minds of a patient and his family . . . an excellent teaching tool for clinicians."   —*Psychiatric News*

"*Will's Choice* is a courageous and unflinching chronicle of a mother's battle to save her child from the potentially lethal throes of teen depression. It is a story of fierce love and family in the real world, and, for parents going through this worst of all nightmares, it is a beautifully written handbook of help and hope."   —Emmylou Harris

"Gail Griffith shares so much more than the saga of her family's suffering. With refreshing and helpful honesty, she weaves into her narrative all the latest practical advice and scientific research. Most importantly, she shows how, with time and attention, healing can come and hope can be restored, so that Will can choose life."   —Sen. Gordon H. Smith

"Perceptive and instructive, *Will's Choice* offers a rare look into the minds of a teenage boy and his girlfriend, in their dark and difficult passage from childhood to adulthood. It is a valuable document in the fight for better health care for our mentally ill children, who rarely get the treatment they need."
—Paul Raeburn, author of *Acquainted with the Night: A Parent's Quest to Understand Depression and Bipolar Disorder in His Children*

"This book is truly a gem. . . . Ms. Griffith writes courageously not only about her son's suicide attempt but also about how they worked as a family to renew his desire to live. . . . Highly recommended for all those [who] enjoy reading about the real heroes of our day, those who refuse to accept stigma and who fight for social justice and a far better mental health treatment system . . . simply because it is the right thing to do."
—Darcy Gruttadaro, *NAMI Beginnings*

© Angela Spicer

About the Author

For most of her career, GAIL GRIFFITH worked as an advocate for international humanitarian causes, including the Nobel Peace Prize–winning campaign to ban landmines. After her son's near-lethal suicide attempt, she began writing and speaking to raise awareness about teen depression. She is a member of the National Alliance for the Mentally Ill and serves on the board of the American Foundation for Suicide Prevention. In 2004, she was the patient representative to the U.S. Food and Drug Administration's scientific advisory committee charged with investigating the possible link between antidepressant medication and suicidal thinking in teenage patients. She continues to consult for the FDA and advises the National Institute of Mental Health on suicide prevention research. Visit her at her Web site, www.gailgriffith.com, or for more information on the book go to www.willschoice.net.

WILL'S CHOICE

A Suicidal Teen,
a Desperate Mother,
and a
Chronicle of Recovery

Gail Griffith

HARPER

NEW YORK · LONDON · TORONTO · SYDNEY

Author's Note: Throughout the book, names of the participants, doctors, teachers, therapists, and family members have not been changed, with the exception of Will's friends in Washington, D.C., at Montana Academy, and in San Francisco, whose privacy he wishes to protect.

An extension of this copyright page appears on page 324.

A hardcover edition of this book was published in 2005 by HarperCollins Publishers.

FIRST HARPER PAPERBACK PUBLISHED 2006.

Designed by Nancy Singer Olaguera

The Library of Congress has catalogued the hardcover edition as follows:

Griffith, Gail.
    Will's choice : a suicidal teen, a desperate mother, and a chronicle of recovery / Gail Griffith.—1st ed.
        p.   cm.
        Includes bibliographical references.
        ISBN 0-06-059865-4 (hc : acid-free paper)
        1. Griffith, Will. 2. Griffith, Gail. 3. Teenagers—Suicidal behavior—United States—Case studies. 4. Depression in adolescence—Case studies. 5. Depressed persons—United States—Biography. 6. Depressed persons—United States—Family relationships. I. Title.

HV6546.G75   2005
362.28'092—dc22
[B]   2004059931
ISBN-10: 0-06-059866-2 (pbk.)
ISBN-13: 978-0-06-059866-2 (pbk.)

    10   ❖/RRD   10 9 8 7 6 5 4 3

*For my mother, Duff Witman Griffith,
who never knew a day of depression.
She lived her life expecting wonderful things
to come her way. And, for the most part, they did.*

CONTENTS

FOREWORD

As a psychiatrist, I have been studying the problem of "teen suicide" and its various manifestations—suicidal thoughts, suicide attempts, and, much less commonly, completed suicide—for nearly thirty-five years. My work has required me to read academic papers and books, and to evaluate innumerable statistical tables, looking for flaws and merit. But while an analysis of dry facts, such as age, sex, ethnicity, previous psychiatric illness, and family history, leads clinicians to an infinitely greater understanding of *who* commits suicide, statistics can only do so much; they don't uncover the *why*. Even personal accounts of depression or experience with suicide don't tell the whole story.

In *Will's Choice*, I found an especially helpful account that complemented my clinical experiences in an important way. It is written so graphically and is so unencumbered by interpretation that I found myself quoting it to a research colleague as if it were a case I actually knew. But beyond its clarity as a case study, this narrative offers a special window into the world of the sufferer. Even the most diligent and curious clinicians rarely see how our patients are perceived by others; our information is always learned through the filter of the patient's own limitations and biases. With *Will's Choice* I was given an irresistible look behind the scenes. It was almost as if Griffith were bringing the whole family into my office.

In writing the story of her son, Griffith takes on the role of the investigator trying to fathom Will's perception of his own situation as well as what led him to consider suicide. We see Griffith galvanizing her family to obtain help for her son. She takes us with her while she vividly, often generously (always politely), and, above all, without rancor or polemic, recounts Will's (and her family's) experience with various doctors, therapists, hospitals, and schools. A depression sufferer herself, Griffith was stimulated to find out more. She researched exhaustively, and spoke to experts on adolescent depression and suicide. She joined the National Alliance for the Mentally Ill (NAMI) and the American Foundation for Suicide Prevention and was invited to serve on the FDA committee that reviewed the risks and benefits of SSRI antidepressants.

So *Will's Choice* does more than recount the tale of a sick boy and summarize facts on youth suicide. It paints a picture of a vigorous, intellectually involved American family confronting a problem with determination and energy. They epitomize the healthiest way of coping with a problem—mastering it. Most interestingly, the book draws liberally from the work of two stunningly gifted writers—Will himself and his girlfriend, Megan. Both allowed Gail Griffith access to their journals. Megan's account of her own unusual behavior is unsurpassed, and I, for one, plan to quote it in my lectures to students. Will's diatribe over whether to submit to his parents' and their agents' wishes to stay for more treatment or to follow his instincts and bolt from his therapeutic school perfectly conveys the land of youthful indignation and makes the reader cheer for the hero.

Will's answer to "Why?" was "I just didn't want to be here anymore." End of case? I doubt it. We cannot will our own death through indifference. Fortunately, death requires a formidable injury or effort. By uncovering the thoughts and feelings that led to Will's actions, Gail Griffith, Will, and their entire family, have turned Will's choice into a gift for us all.

—David Shaffer, F.R.C.P., F.R.C.Psych.
Irving Philips Professor of Psychiatry
Columbia University

PROLOGUE

These days my dreams are unnerving flights of fancy, laced with anxiety: my children are always small—somewhere between two and six years old; they are always troubled—there are tears—and they are beset by myriad tiny agonies.

In one dream, a toy block wagon, with primary-colored wooden shapes designed to teach my eldest son, Max, the fundamentals of building, has rolled down a driveway, spilling a chaotic configuration of blocks all over hot asphalt. In another, Max is having a hard time coming to terms with a pillowcase that does not match the Marimekko animal-print bedsheets and he morphs into a clump of Play-Doh while I search hysterically for the matching pillowcase.

In my dreams, my younger son, Will, is sobbing over something he has lost. In my most recent dream, missing were the miniature Spanish doubloons that come with the Lego pirate ship—those tiny gold rounds every parent knows will vanish before the child's next birthday—or, worse yet, turn up in the kid's nose.

In the dreams, Will is inconsolable, as if the toy coins or a missing stuffed bear were all that connected him to his world: the loss of these totems wrecks his sense of wonder, dispatching his innocence somewhere beyond grasp.

Like toxic exhaust from a faulty tailpipe, these dreams vaporize into the atmosphere. Predawn I awaken with a headache from inhaling imaginary particles.

It is now over three years since my son Will's suicide attempt. On Sunday, March 11, 2001, he took an overdose of antidepressants, which nearly killed him. I knew that day that my life's course changed irrevocably and that our family would be defined by the event.

Two years later, I decided to lay bare our experience and Will's struggle with major depression, *because nothing in the therapeutic literature about teens or teen depression prepared us for the battle we waged against this illness.*

This is the story of our journey—a mother and a son—as we struggled to regain equilibrium after a cataclysmic descent into a suicidal depression. It is a story for families who are trying to keep their children from the same terrible abyss, who are challenged by limited resources and poor therapeutic solutions.

Will's Choice offers a candid assessment of what we learned—what we should have watched for, what we missed, what we could have done to prevent Will's suicide attempt, what we did in the aftermath of his attempt, and where we go from here.

Moreover, this is a story of hope: our child survived a suicide attempt and a crippling bout of depression. Although the specter of Will's illness is never wholly obliterated, for now we are back on level ground.

During the autumn of 2000, when it was first evident that Will was depressed, I found it was hard to imagine a more unlikely candidate for the illness. He was popular and athletic; he received good grades and was well liked by his teachers, and he was the easygoing, youngest child in a family who lavished him with love and attention.

He was in his junior year at a Washington, D.C., parochial high school; he had a delightful new girlfriend, Megan, a sophomore at a nearby public school. But what no one realized—not Megan's family, and certainly not ours—was how deeply depressed the two of them were. Neither Will nor Megan was on solid ground as their relationship began in the fall of 2000; their separate descents into depression began months earlier.

For adolescents the desire to bond with peers and experience intimacies on a new level is so powerful that it is not uncommon for kids caught in emotional maelstroms to be drawn to one another—to seek each other out and wrap themselves up in each other's dysfunction.

The stunted relationship becomes a cocoon of pathology and pain, both comforting and hurtful.

Megan was a "cutter"; she routinely took a sharp edge to her skin until she drew blood, opening up scabs, scoring new ones, and collecting scars up and down her arms. Will became so incapacitated by major depression that he decided to take his own life.

It is evident now that during their brief relationship, both Megan and Will had some inkling they were in serious straits, individually and collectively. Each implored the other to get help, talk to parents, take the medication. But in the end, depression deposited them on isolated islands of despair, and separately, independent of an advance signal to each other, they made a run at suicide in the winter of 2001.

How do you explain the suicidal impulses of a child? We give our children life; we think we know everything about them. And why shouldn't we? We tell them what to think and do from the moment they are born. So it comes as a shock to learn that our children have secret lives—and that their secrets may be deadly.

When I undertook to write a book about teen depression, I implored first Will, then Megan to let me tell their stories. Each of us knew I was asking for more than stories: I was asking them to share their secrets and perhaps to revisit recollections too recent to be free from their potential to bruise.

Will was reticent initially; the notion of dredging up recent past was not only painful, it was embarrassing. Megan, whose recovery was swifter and surer, was enthusiastic about disclosing her experience; she had spent a good deal of time analyzing what had happened to her and was eager to write about it.

What I discovered is that both were more apt at telling their stories than I was. So with their permission, I included vast amounts of their own accounts of depression and recovery: Will's journal entries covering his two hospitalizations, his suicide attempt, and the time he spent in a residential treatment program in Montana appear throughout the book; Megan's wrenching and emotionally charged account of her cutting is explored chronologically, as the relationship between the two teens builds and ebbs. I am enormously proud of them for being brave enough to reflect upon and write about that time in their lives.

Teen depression is a national scourge. According to the American Association of Suicidology, one young American (under the age of twenty-four) commits suicide every two hours. Will's story, Megan's story, have positive outcomes. Our families are fortunate. But we are painfully aware the outcomes could have been otherwise.

Roughly two thousand American teenagers between ages thirteen and eighteen *attempt* suicide every day. That is a staggering statistic for a society that, on the surface, has so much to offer its children. Thankfully, suicide rates for teens began falling in the mid-1990s, presumably because of the widespread use of antidepressant medications. Even so, suicide is the third leading cause of death among young people between the ages of fifteen and twenty-four, roughly four thousand of whom will die by their own hand this year alone.

In 1999 the United States Surgeon General issued a report stating that 3.5 million American teens suffered from depression. Yet, a shocking eighty to ninety percent of adolescents suffering from clinical depression go undiagnosed and untreated. If left untreated, depression can lead to suicide.

So why is it so hard to diagnose? When depression strikes a teenager, it often shows up in a confusing set of symptoms that are hard to distinguish from "normal" adolescent behavior—moodiness, irritability, irregular sleep patterns, drug or alcohol use, difficulties at school. Few teenagers reveal their depression to family or friends.

Many teenagers who obtain help are inadequately informed about treatment options and pharmacological choices. Parents of depressed teens are often left to ferret out information about treatment on their own. What you soon discover is that quality mental health care for teenagers is either unavailable on a consistent basis or prohibitively expensive.

Often a parent's first stop is the family pediatrician or managed care gatekeeper—few of whom are expert in diagnosing and treating depression. In addition to finding a competent therapist or psychiatrist to treat a teen (no mean feat), parents need to become educated about the drugs available to treat depression.

Over the last two decades, parents have been flooded with "how-to" and self-help literature and advice dispensed via popular culture. I sense parents today have less faith in their own instincts about their children than our parents did.

Too many theorists compete for the hearts and minds (and pocket-books) of the family members who know their children best. Treatment theories abound, but in reality child and adolescent psychiatry is in its infancy. Only during the last two decades has the field begun to move away from its embrace of psychoanalysis and into a more evidence-based methodological approach to the study of the developing brain and behavior. "Pop-psychology" offers a confusing and sometimes dangerous cacophony of viewpoints and solutions to complex and variable sets of personal problems. The knowledge and certainty with which our parents and grandparents raised us are undermined and often derided for lacking the most up-to-date medical or therapeutic insights.

The conflicting advice of "experts" leaves many of us feeling ungrounded and insecure about our child-rearing abilities. We risk becoming a debilitated, groping, second-guessing group of caregivers, stripped to the bone with worry and fear that our decisions won't be the "right" ones for our children. We need to regain the ability to trust our own instincts. *No one on the planet knows your child as well as you do.* Trust in that knowledge, trust your instincts, and fight like hell for your child's well-being.

In the aftermath of Will's suicide attempt, our family and a set of clinicians came together to try to analyze what went wrong. We began a wrenching process to determine the next course of action—a treatment plan for Will that at a minimum might safeguard against another suicide attempt and at best might conquer his depression.

As we grappled with the situation, we learned a lot about our son and a lot about the limited treatment options for teen depression. We immersed ourselves in the controversy over the growing use of antidepressant medications to treat teenage patients, and weighed the advantages and drawbacks of outpatient versus residential treatment programs. We unearthed the staggering inadequacies of our managed-care system and we discovered that our best hope for helping Will was to become as well as or better informed than the therapists treating him about treatment options. For a family in the thick of a hemorrhagic crisis, it is a lot to handle.

I have watched this public health crisis rip through families and lamented the paucity of ready solutions. I also regret what it is doing to our children—not just to the teens who are ill but to their peers, struggling to understand an illness that still inspires secrecy and shame. A young person sucked into the downward spiral of a friend's depression or, worse yet, the suicide of a peer, is dealt a brutal blow; it zaps their innocence and occludes their sense of wonder and of possibilities for the future. And I have learned that *depression does not need to kill its young victims, but adolescents, whose lives too often hang in the balance between reason and risk, should not be left alone to make that choice.*

In June 2001, shortly after Will was admitted to a residential treatment program for adolescents in Montana, we met face-to-face for the first time with the psychiatrist assigned to treat him. Dr. Dennis Malinak, a bright, warm, engaging parent of two sons, had seen Will every day for the previous eight weeks.

Dennis began our conversation by asking us to characterize our son as a young child, preadolescence. He was looking for a word or phrase to describe Will's personality, something that could be used as a baseline against which we measured his depression. Instantly and without the slightest hesitation, I offered, "Will was joyous."

Will's father nodded in affirmation. I repeated the pronouncement again: "He was joyous." The second time was more a lament than a statement of fact.

As Dennis absorbed this bit of information, his expression changed from matter-of-fact to bafflement—so profound was the dissonance between the adolescent he was treating and the person we knew to be our son.

If we had said "Will was kind of quiet" or "fearful of strangers" or "intense" or "difficult," Dennis could have paired our characterization with the mute and emotionally raw kid he saw each day. But "joyous" was so far out of alignment that even *we* had trouble harkening back to the ease and pleasure we enjoyed as parents raising Will.

I am sure most parents of troubled children have shared a similar moment in the confines of a doctor's office or over the dinner table, as they scratched their heads in wonder and asked, "What on earth went wrong?"

What I *do* know is that over the course of a year and a half, from the onset of his depression to a near-fatal suicide attempt to a residential treatment program, Will lost his innocence and with it the ability to experience joy—or any other emotion beyond the prison of his mental anguish. We watched and held our breath as he struggled to gain back what we all want for our children: a sense of life's possibilities and hope for the future.

Will, and Megan too, traversed a mental inferno most people only experience through books and movies, but in the end, they both emerged from depression intact and optimistic, with more than their fair share of insight and self-awareness.

I am cautiously optimistic the worst is over for Will—and for Megan. And it is not my intention to make either of them a poster child for teenage depression. But, if by sharing this story—our story— I manage to convince countless others, families with teenagers and young people just like them, that there *is* life and perhaps even joy beyond depression, it will be an accomplishment beyond measure.

Oh, where have you been, my blue-eyed son?
Oh, where have you been, my darling young one?

    I've stumbled on the side of twelve misty mountains,
    I've walked and I've crawled on six crooked highways,
    I've stepped in the middle of seven sad forests,
    I've been out in front of a dozen dead oceans,
    I've been ten thousand miles in the mouth of a graveyard,

And it's a hard, and it's a hard, it's a hard, and it's a hard,
And it's a hard rain's a-gonna fall.

            from "A Hard Rain's A-Gonna Fall"
            by Bob Dylan

1

THE BEARS DOWNSTAIRS

10:00 AM, March 11, 2001

A mother's sixth sense is attuned to her child's atmospherics like a cat before an electrical storm. I sensed something wrong the instant I opened the door to his room. Normally, there were heaps of clothing, towels, and books strewn about. This morning it was preternaturally clean.

In the split second before reason takes over from reaction, I felt trouble on my skin. A branch from the blossoming pear tree in front of our Dupont Circle row house scraped rhythmically against the glass, tapping in code: Trouble, trouble.

"Willo, I want you up *now* so you can say good-bye to Jane." I used the tone that leaves no room for equivocation—the tone a mother uses to coax a teenager out of bed.

It was Sunday morning and Will had been up late watching college basketball with his stepsister, Jane, who was home from college for spring break. Usually, I am loath to wake a sleeping teenager on a weekend morning, but I knew Will would want to see Jane off before she and her roommate embarked on the eight-hour drive back to school.

"Will"—I crept closer to his bed—"Jane's about to leave. You need to go downstairs now if you want to say good-bye."

Just as I reached the edge of his bed, he lurched violently to one side. I caught a glimpse of what looked like saliva bubbling around the corners of his mouth. I grabbed his shoulder and rolled him toward me. His skin was clammy, his color yellow-gray, and he was sweating profusely.

"Will?" I tensed and my heart accelerated as I grasped one side of his head. I tried to look into his eyes, to see his pupils. "Will, are you okay?"

He sounded like a recording underwater when he tried to respond. I felt his pulse: his heartbeat was off the chart. He mumbled something about needing to "get out of this bubble wrap." Dread scaled up the back of my neck.

"Oh, God, this is not good," I thought out loud.

Will had been battling clinical depression since fall, but I was convinced he was much better than he had been just months before. That Sunday morning, March 11, 2001, as I geared up to do battle with whatever was afflicting him, my first thought was: encephalitis. Not suicide. En-ceph-a-li-tis.

Certain viruses affect the brain in ways that render patients tangled and disoriented. My son was certainly disoriented. And feverish. He was delirious. It could be a terrible case of the flu. Or how about meningitis?

There were all manner of ailments I knew nothing about. He could have contracted any one of them. That was it. It was the flu. Or maybe it was a drug interaction with an antihistamine; something he might have taken for seasonal allergies was causing havoc with his antidepressant medications.

I tried to raise his head by placing my hand behind his neck; his eyes lolled back in his head and he moaned.

"Okay, that's it!" I said under my breath, and ran downstairs to get my husband, Jack.

On the way downstairs, I bumped into my stepson, John: "Something's going on with Will. Would you go sit by him while I get your dad?"

My husband was loading the last few items into the car for Jane's trip back to college. I grabbed him and took him aside and said, "Something's wrong with Will."

"What do you mean?"

"I mean physically, something is terribly wrong—like a virus or something. He's delirious and foaming at the mouth."

"I'll be right there. Just let me get Jane off."

I raced back to Will's room, where John queried me: "What's up with Will?" John's voice was panicky. He was clearly unnerved by Will's appearance. I saw the fear and bewilderment in his eyes and thought, "No time for guessing—we have to act."

"I don't know, sweetie, but I think we need to get him to a doctor or the hospital quickly."

John and Will were just half a year apart in age and had been close friends since they were preschoolers, long before Jack and I married in 1999, when the two boys became stepbrothers. John leaned over Will's bed and implored, "Hey, Will, do you know where you are?"

Will babbled, "She can wear whatever she wants."

John and I exchanged glances, incredulous. "Huh?"

Jack bounded up the stairs, and I ran past him in the hallway on my way to our bedroom to pull on some clothes. "We need to get him to the emergency room!" I shouted.

I grabbed jeans and yanked a sweater over my head and heard Jack and John in Will's room trying to coax him to his feet. The boys managed to lumber down the hallway, but at the top of the stairs Will balked. He wouldn't go any farther.

"I'm afraid of bears and I won't go downstairs," he uttered. Jack and I looked at each other, perplexed, for half a second.

Will wouldn't budge. He couldn't be coaxed. He repeated the singsong phrase, "I'm afraid of bears and I won't go downstairs, I'm afraid of bears and I won't go downstairs," three or four more times.

The freakishness, the otherworldliness of the utterance propelled our collective anxiety into the stratosphere. There were no family histories of encounters with bears. This imaginary juggernaut, this bear phobia, came from some dark cave in Will's head.

We managed to reach the bathroom at the end of the hallway. Will collapsed on the tile floor. Straining and pulling, we maneuvered him into our bedroom and laid him on the bed.

Jack's ex-wife, Charlotte, had been downstairs helping Jane pack up for school and get on the road. Now, she dashed upstairs to see how she could help us. I passed Will's tennis shoes to Charlotte and she struggled to put them on him, while John and Jack wrestled him onto the bed. I grabbed the phone on the bedroom dresser and dialed 911.

I reached a dispatcher right away. I told her we had a medical emergency, that my son was in dire straits and "we need ... we need ..." Language failed me. I couldn't summon the word "ambulance." I finally yanked it out: "We need an emergency vehicle right away. The one with the lights and siren." An emergency vehicle with lights and siren ... ? I was coming unhinged.

Charlotte, overhearing my disjointed exchange with the dispatcher, gestured frantically, motioning me to give her the phone: "We need an ambulance right away!" She deftly gave the dispatcher our address before returning the phone to me. The dispatcher had a few more questions: his age, approximate height and weight. She asked if Will was "armed."

"Is your son dangerous?"

"I don't think so," I said, trying hard not to lose my grip. I couldn't conjure a situation in which my child might be considered dangerous. "He's only seventeen; he's a little over six feet tall. I think he weighs about one-forty."

It seemed an eternity, but in reality the ambulance arrived within five minutes. The emergency dispatcher sent everything—not just an ambulance but two squad cars and a hook-and-ladder rescue team. I flew downstairs to let them in.

The commotion sent the neighborhood into a freeze frame. Birds stopped twittering and dogs and dog owners alike stood fixed in place and gaped, as if on a theater stage. Four paramedics and two cops barreled through the front door and up the stairs, carrying a stretcher. The medics took Will's pulse and tried to get him to respond to more questions, to no avail. They tried slipping on an oxygen mask, but Will fought it off, swinging like a prizefighter.

"His name's Will," I told them, stifling sobs.

"Will, do you know where you are?" they asked repeatedly. It would not be the last time that day we heard the question.

"Do you know if he took anything?"

"Like what?" I asked.

"Does he use drugs or alcohol?"

"Not often; I know he's smoked marijuana a couple of times, but he's not a drinker."

"Hard drugs, cocaine, Ecstasy?"

"No, never. Not to my knowledge."

The EMT crew moved him onto the stretcher and into the waiting ambulance. I rode with him in the bay, lights flashing and sirens blaring, heading to George Washington University Hospital, about a mile away. Jack followed in our car.

When my kids were little they loved fire engines and ambulances for the noise and excitement. They were raised in the city, so the cacophony tickled them. I thought fleetingly, "Boy, I wish Will knew what was going on. He'd really get a kick out of this."

But Will wasn't Will at that moment. He was pawing the air, grabbing at imaginary bits of dust or bugs or light. Who knows what creatures floated into the web of his consciousness?

Every few minutes, he tried to form a question, but it broke apart into fragments before it made any sense. I grew so frightened that I began to feel nauseous. I tried to stay as close to him as physically possible. I whispered in his ear, reminding him every few minutes, "Willo, this is your mother speaking."

When he was young I used to wake him up in the morning by whispering, "Earth to Will, this is your mother speaking." It always got a rise. But as the ambulance sped through the city, and I tried all of the familiar mother-son connections, Will was unresponsive. "Come in, Will." I might as well have been an alien visiting him from another planet.

Most people I know, in the aftermath of a crisis, describe feeling as though they were operating in two dimensions simultaneously. In one dimension, we are active participants, applying the tourniquet, dragging an animal out of the path of an oncoming car, or diving into a swimming pool after an errant toddler. In the other dimension, we are beset by a voice in our head that says, "This can't be happening," and the crisis unfolds through a surreal lens.

I was observing my son's ordeal on a split screen. An Olympic referee held a stopwatch and suddenly, seeing the tick-tick-tick of the hand, he shouted: "Go!" For me, "Go!" was 10:00 AM Sunday morning. Monitoring my progress from the sidelines, watching and waiting to see how my time-trial would turn out, I was in that other dimension—assessing, critiquing, gawking like a stranger. All cylinders were firing. I was doing what I should do, as best I could: addressing the emergency, calling the ambulance, making a mental list of Will's prescribed medications. At the same time, I was rattled to my core. Oh, my God, I knew my son was in serious trouble and no amount of attention to detail kept me from lapsing into periodic spasms of terror.

We arrived at the emergency room at 10:40 AM. Will was triaged to the front of the line, ahead of Saturday-night drunks, wailing babies, and minor fractures. Despite the rush to get Will from the ambulance onto a gurney and into an examination room, I was stopped at the hospital's entrance by an admissions clerk.

"Sorry, ma'am. You need to register here . . . and we'll need a check or money order for fifty dollars.

You have got to be kidding—a check or money order?! Was it some sort of deposit guaranteeing that I would get my kid back? Did they think fifty dollars was going to be all they needed to fix him? Fifty dollars just to cross the threshold? Why this? Why now? I rummaged frantically in my purse for a checkbook and his insurance card, and at the same time attempted to hold a conversation with Will's stepmother and father in California on the cell phone I clutched in my other hand.

I reached my ex-husband, Bob, and his wife, Melissa, at 7:45 AM, California time. Sunday morning. I did not expect them to be awake when I called, but Melissa answered cheerfully.

"What's up?"

"Melissa, I need to talk to Bob . . . I've got Will here at GW Hospital and it seems that he's got a weird flu or a drug interaction or something." I tried to sound as matter-of-fact as I could. Bob got on the
phone: "Hey, Bud, I've just brought Will into the emergency room.
He's delirious and feverish and I got worried so we brought him here
by ambulance." Just then, the admissions clerk motioned me to cut the
cell phone call and directed my line of sight to a large sign over the
portal of the emergency room, announcing, "Use of cellular telephones
in the hospital is strictly forbidden." Of all the occasions when one
might urgently need a cell phone, this was it, but once I had completed
the admissions paperwork and written out the fifty-dollar check, the
only thing keeping me between the security guard and my son was the
cell phone.

"Look, I've got to go, they won't let me use the cell phone; I'll call
back in just a bit when I know something."

I ducked through the electronic double doors and into the emergency room, filled to the brink with so many people—patients, doctors, and nurses alike—that there were no chairs to sit on. I wasn't
immediately sure where they'd taken Will, but it became apparent he
was behind a cloth partition when I heard a doctor shouting, "William,
do you know where you are?" I pulled aside the curtain and barged in.

Inside the makeshift examining room, the scene was chaotic and
instantly disorienting. I felt as though I'd fallen down a well; voices,
mechanical noise, and lights overloaded my senses like an out-of-
synch motion picture. Will was flailing at the hospital staff's efforts to
apply an oxygen mask and draw blood. He writhed and strained
against any effort to hold him down. When he opened his eyes he
stared blankly, without focus, and after a few seconds his eyeballs
rolled back into his head. He groaned and uttered occasional non
sequiturs, barely intelligible. And every few minutes, amplifying the
surrealism of the scene, he would throw back his head and laugh—a
hysterical, hyena-like screech, mocking and out of control. It was a
scene no parent wants to witness.

Over the din a doctor shouted to me: "Are you his mother?"

"Yes."

"This is how you found him?"

"Yes."

"Any history of drug or alcohol abuse?"

"No."

"Any history of seizures, allergic reactions?"

"No."

"Any major illnesses, disease?"

"No—well, he suffers from clinical depression—but he's recovered," I reported earnestly.

As soon as the word "depression" was out of my mouth, the atmosphere changed. I sensed the hospital staff shooting one another knowing glances. "Goddammit," I thought, "I'm not going to let them go there." But the question was forming in their minds like spray paint on the drab blue stucco of the hospital walls: "A suicide attempt?"

Another line of questioning: "What medications does he take?"

Jack had just joined me in the emergency room. In spite of the rush to get to the hospital, John and Charlotte had had the presence of mind to gather up the multiple bottles of Will's antidepressant medication lying on top of Will's dresser and hand them to Jack in a plastic grocery bag as Jack ran out the door for the hospital. I was grateful for their quick action and foresight; I was too rattled to have thought of it. Having Will's medications in hand would help solve the mystery illness and identify a possible drug interaction.

I tried to recall from memory the medications and dosages, but Jack quickly dove into the plastic bag, doling out transparent orange bottles of Will's medicines to me as I ticked them off for the doctors: "He takes Prozac, eighty milligrams; Concerta, thirty-six milligrams; and Remeron, I think it's forty-five milligrams, but the packaging is missing. And he takes Erythromycin for acne."

I turned to Jack, who was sorting through contents of the bag to make sure we had gotten all of the medications and reported the correct dosages. "Where's the Remeron? I'm pretty sure we just refilled it," I asked.

"I don't know. These boxes are empty. We must have missed them. They've got to be at home." Jack left the emergency room to call John to ask him if he would take another look around Will's room for the missing pills, and I turned my attention back to Will.

"Do you have any way of getting a hold of your son's psychiatrist?" a doctor asked me. I thought, "Oh, no, here we go again." I was edgy.

"Look, I'm not a doctor, but I have a good friend who developed encephalitis and the symptoms looked exactly the same."

"Yeah, well, we need to do a spinal tap to determine that, but we're about to take him down for an EKG to see if there's anything going on there. When we bring him back up we'll do a spinal tap."

I felt lame, I was so obviously out of my element. I could not remember what an EKG is designed to test, but I was pretty sure that if Will was having seizures, the doctors would be able to determine it on an EKG.

Every mother in the world wishes she were a doctor in a moment like this. I had to rely on strangers doing the right thing for my son, and it is a precarious feeling. "God, I hope they know what they're doing." George Washington University Hospital has a stellar reputation. Still, horror stories abound about emergency room disasters.

As an orderly wheeled Will out of the emergency room, I followed the gurney down the hallway, as far as I was allowed to go. Jack brought me a cup of coffee and I headed outside to try to track down Will's psychiatrist, Dr. Alen Salerian.

For several years Dr. Salerian, a gifted diagnostician and expert in the pharmacology of depression, had been medical director of the Psychiatric Institute of Washington (PIW). I had known him for ten years. He had treated Will since the previous December for major depression, and Will spent a week at PIW, under Dr. Salerian's care, in January.

I too was a patient of Dr. Salerian's and had been hospitalized for five weeks in 1991 following a diagnosis of major depression. Alen Salerian and I were on a first-name basis and I trusted him. I figured once I reached him, he would have some insight and be able to help sort this out. But midday on a Sunday is not the easiest day to reach a doctor, even a responsive one, so when I called the main contact number at PIW, I told the receptionist, "Hello, I'm the mother of a patient of Dr. Salerian's, and my son has been admitted to the emergency room at George Washington University Hospital. Could you please ask him to call the emergency room doctor on duty immediately?"

I also gave her my cell phone number, but realized it was unlikely that Dr. Salerian would be able to do anything other than dump a message into my voice mail, given the hospital's prohibition of cell phones. But maybe he could get through to the emergency room personnel.

I scurried back to the emergency room and sat down on the floor of the crowded lobby with my back up against the cinder-block wall and waited for Will to return from the EKG. For the first time in two hours since finding him unconscious in his room, I had a moment to take stock.

Hospital emergency rooms aren't known for their esthetic touches. The colors are not subtle and the lights are invasive. For some reason the drinking fountain wasn't working properly and crumpled paper cups piled up like contortionists all around the base of the cooler.

Patients and their families were not faring much better in the inelegant environment, myself included. As a slice of humanity, we looked off-color and disheveled, haggard and insecure. A young man had been in a bar fight in the early morning hours and was still bleeding from a head wound that needed stitching; a Hispanic family was troubled by their infant daughter's high fever and inability to swallow. You could have measured the anxiety level with a dipstick.

I had not combed my hair or brushed my teeth since getting out of bed, and I had thrown on the clothes I'd worn the day before. I noticed a peculiar smell, something almost feral seeping up through my wool sweater and jeans. Fear. It must have been fear. As the day wore on, the smell intensified, but no one seemed to notice. It blended with the ambiance.

Jack sat down beside me on the linoleum floor. We tried to make ourselves inconspicuous; if we appeared to be in the way, we would be ushered out. Every few minutes an officious nurse darted through the

melee, announcing, "You people will have to wait outside!" which
resulted in shifting postures and much shuffling of feet.

I decided I would be better off taking refuge in the cubicle where
Will had been examined, assuming that the staff would return him,
gurney and all, to the same location. There was a worn-out plastic
chair next to the heart monitor and I took a seat. The same overbear-
ing staffer spotted me within minutes and cast a disapproving glance
my way. "You'll have to vacate this area."

Vacate the area? "I don't think so," I replied defiantly. "I'm waiting
for my son to be returned from wherever they took him for an EKG."
She shot me a withering look, but I was starting to feel like a pack animal who had been beaten once too often and I was not moving.

Jack was performing the dual role of anchor and emissary. In the
fifteen years I had known Jack Brady, first as coach of my boys' soccer
team and as a fellow parent of children at Holy Trinity Elementary
School here in Washington, D.C., I always knew him to be steely and
clear-headed in emergencies. This was no exception. Because of the cell
phone prohibition, he became liaison to the rest of the world, relaying
news, calling family, and fielding queries about Will's status, during
repeated forays outside of the building.

After one such trip, Jack returned to the nurses' station inside the
emergency room to see if they had an update. Initial blood work had
come back from the lab, showing no opiates or alcohol in Will's system. I suppose that was a good sign.

"They're in touch with the poison center to run some data on
overdoses and interactions with his meds," Jack reported.

"What's that mean? Do you think *they* think he overdosed on his
meds?" I could not accept that line of reasoning and my irritation was
careening into anger. This was simply *not* another tragic teen drug
overdose and I resented the implication.

"They have to look into it, as a precaution, kiddo."

The attending ER physician called for the hospital's psychiatric
resident doctor to come down and offer his assessment. The psychiatrist was a young man, intense, but kindly, clean-shaven, with dark

curly hair. He began the standard query about Will's mental health history. These guys were wearing me down like a water torture victim.

"Look, this is *not* what it seems," I told him. "I know my son and in just the past month, we've all seen a steady improvement in his mood. Talk to his doctor," I urged. "He can confirm it. Will's not the kind of kid who would try to kill himself."

"Do you know if he uses drugs or alcohol regularly?"

"God, no. Why do we have to go over this again?"

"No PCP, LSD, or Ecstasy?"

"No. No. No. Wouldn't you see that in the blood work? There's nothing there! I really want you guys to look at what else might be going on. What about encephalitis or meningitis or some other kind of infection in the brain?"

Will was gone from the ER for half an hour. When he returned, it was evident he was continuing to deteriorate. He was ranting an incomprehensible verbal stew and slogging at the orderly who tried to keep him supine on the gurney. He had never been a fighter, never agitated or violent. He had never been in a playground fight or landed a punch on his older brother. Consensus among teachers and family was that he was a peaceable, easygoing kid. Something dastardly had taken over his mind and body.

A nurse screamed at him, "Lie down, William!" I dashed to one side of the bed to try to calm him, imploring, "Lie still, sweetie, please lie still."

I placed my head on his chest and hummed softly (but loud enough for him to hear, I hoped) a half-remembered tune about angels, which Will had learned in kindergarten. ("All night, all day, angels watching over me, Oh Lord . . .") It was a cheery little children's song and I don't know if he remembered it; I'm not even sure why I picked it. Will quieted momentarily and brought his hand up to stroke my hair—just once—before lunging into a sitting position and frantically clawing the air, a look of sheer terror on his face.

The resident psychiatrist bent over him and asked, "Will, do you know what year it is?" Will lay back down.

"1999," Will mumbled, head twitching from side to side.

"What was that?"

Will: "2000."

"Will, who is the president of the United States?"

Will: "Grover Cleveland."

"Well," I pondered silently, "we're not in the right century, but at least we're getting presidents."

As the psychiatrist and a couple of other clinicians tried and failed to elicit further verbal exchanges with Will, the chief ER physician pulled me aside to report: "Nothing showed up on the EKG. His heart rate and blood pressure are highly elevated. I want to do a spinal tap, but first I'd like to get some charcoal down him. It will counter the effects of any poisons he might have in his system—just in case he took something."

"So, what do you think is going on, doctor?" I prayed he had an inkling of an answer.

"I don't know." The doctor looked down and momentarily avoided making eye contact. I detected a nervous uncertainty.

"Have you seen anything like this before?" I was almost afraid to ask.

"No," he admitted reluctantly. I was stunned.

"It's a teaching hospital," I tried to console myself. "These guys are young and they don't know everything. There's got to be someone here who knows what to do."

"Doctor, should I ask his father to fly out—he's in California?" I was testing. If he said, yes, then I would know we were in real trouble.

"I think he needs to get here as soon as he can."

"Oh, Jesus, this can't be happening," I thought. I began to shake uncontrollably. "They must be exaggerating. They just need to cover their bases. *This just can't be happening!*"

I covered my face and started to weep as a nurse shoved me aside so she could try to intubate Will, forcing liquid charcoal through his nose and down his throat. Will shrieked and flailed and swung at the nurse. An orderly pinned Will's arms to his sides. He looked like a terrified animal—I had never seen anyone, let alone my child, look so frightened. I was beyond panic.

The hospital staff went into overdrive. Everything was speeded up, louder, more frenetic, and for the first time that day I was forced to consider the possibility that Will might not make it.

The nursing staff insisted that I step out of the enclosure while they continued to struggle to get a tube down Will's nose. Finally, after sounds of thrashing and stifled roars, I heard someone say, "William, you have another option here. If you drink this liquid, we won't force it down your nose."

I held my breath.

There was an eruption of gagging and spitting from behind the curtain. I wanted to know what was happening, but at the same time, I thought I might lose it if I had to watch the nurses force thick black fluid down Will's throat.

"Swallow all of it, William!" a nurse commanded. More sputtering and gagging. I peeked behind the curtain. What looked like tar was splattered all over the floor, all over the bedding. Some of it had hit the wall beside the gurney. It streamed down Will's chin, neck, and chest and came out his nose. The gurney was now soaked with sweat and urine. An orderly propped Will's head up as the nurse tried to force more of the charcoal down his throat. His eyes were closed and his skin was a ghastly shade of yellow-white, streaked here and there with black ooze.

I ran outside and called Will's father in California.

"Bud, the doctors think you need to get here right away." I delivered the news in a voice as calm as I could muster, but there was no mistaking the message.

Momentary silence on the other end. I could visualize Bob's face. We were thinking the same thing: "There's only one reason for urgency."

There is a scene in the movie, *Terms of Endearment,* in which the mother, played by Shirley MacLaine (she is harried, wears no makeup, her dark roots are exposed), is outraged by the hospital staff's inattentiveness to her daughter (Debra Winger), who is in excruciating pain and dying of cancer. MacLaine vaults over the nurses' station and flies into the face of the head nurse, demanding immediate action. She screams at the nurse to give her daughter the painkillers she needs.

That cinematic moment accurately portrays every mother's clarion call. I identified with the instinct to throw some verbal punches on behalf of my kid. I was the Shirley MacLaine character—a mother who feels betrayed by a system that should be working *with* her, doing the best for her child. Were we moving closer to resolving the crisis? The medical team didn't seem to know what to do. My confidence was sinking as my anxiety mushroomed.

Will was hooked up to a monitoring system. Every few minutes he tried to detach the wires crisscrossing his body. The doctors were watching for the first signs of organ failure, possible cardiac arrest, or renal failure.

I was anxious for them to perform a spinal tap, but the staff's initial attempts to roll Will onto his side and lie still were exercises in futility. Whether Will was reacting to the cold of the cleansing solution applied to his back where the needle would be inserted, or the rough handling by the orderly who tried to keep Will on his side, he could not be stilled—at least not still enough for them to perform a spinal tap.

I tried, once again, to calm him by whispering in his ear, "Willo, it's your mom, sweetie. You need to lie still. It's going to be okay." This time he reared up and began swinging in all directions. I choked back tears and struggled to keep from becoming hysterical.

At 2:30 PM, the doctor in charge decided to inject Will with doses of Haldol, assuming that once he was sedated, it would be easier to move him into position to do the spinal tap. One dose; fifteen minutes later, another. Half an hour passed and yet another dose of Haldol.

"God, I hope they know what they're doing." I wondered how much sedation his system could handle in this state.

Still no abatement in Will's violent thrashing.

A stranger stumbling onto the scene might have surmised that Will was possessed by demons and that we were engaged in a high-tech exorcism. Indeed, we had crossed over into a netherworld where reason and control were beyond our grasp. I was not quite ready to surrender my meager authority to a higher power, but I was getting close.

The Haldol did not calm Will down initially. Despite the repeated doses he forcibly aborted two more attempts to do a spinal tap. Now we were stuck. It was 3:30 PM.

The ER staff decided to move Will upstairs to the critical care unit as soon as a bed could be found. The medical team would attempt a spinal tap once he was settled on the unit.

Bob boarded a flight for the East Coast at 11:00 AM Pacific time. He would transfer midway across the country and land around midnight in Washington. He planned to call when he changed planes in Dallas. Before he left San Francisco, Bob called our oldest son, Max, who was in his first year of college at Berkeley. Bob told Max that Will was in the hospital but did not let on that the situation was grave. Max, who was prone to worry and had always been close to his brother, sensed he wasn't being told everything. But what was there to tell? We knew nothing for sure.

But as the day wore on and no diagnoses were forthcoming, even I had to confront the possibility that Will's condition was drug induced. I would accept the notion that he took an overdose intentionally. But a suicide attempt? No way. It had to be accidental. Still, the staff was resolute in their efforts to force charcoal into his system; the doctors assumed they were dealing with an overdose. Charcoal, with its toxin-absorbing properties, is standard fare whenever accidental or intentional overdoses turn up in emergency rooms. Another doctor on staff continued to scour the Poison Control database, researching the symptomatology and antidotes for all of the medications Will was taking.

4:00 PM: A burly orderly transported Will to the fifth floor of the hospital. I trailed behind, hauling Will's jeans and tennis shoes and the bag of his prescription medications.

There was a minor flap when we reached the fifth-floor nurses' station about which room Will should occupy; the staff wasn't quite ready for him, but after five minutes he was rolled into a semiprivate room and onto the bed closest to the door. An elderly man lay unconscious in the bed next to the window, and his wife watched our arrival with disdain. She didn't like what she saw—a ranting, writhing, out-of-control young man. I cannot say I would have welcomed this intrusion into the hush of the hospital room either, but her displeasure turned ugly. "Get that animal out of here!" she demanded of the orderly, rising out of her chair in protest.

"Ma'am, calm down, we'll handle this." The orderly gestured her to stay away.

"You can't put that creature in here with my husband!" she glowered.

The orderly tried to ignore her and struggled to bring some calm to the tumult by binding Will's wrists and ankles to the bed railing with canvas restraints. Will, still flailing away attempts to hold him down, gyrated in every direction, blindly swatting away the attendant until both of his hands were secured by the side of the bed.

"You take him and put him somewhere else!" the woman ranted. "He's an animal!"

The scene was too much for me.

Every time I thought the day couldn't get worse, it did. To see my son, his lips stained black from the charcoal, soaked in dirty linen, arms and legs tethered to a steel bed frame—to have a stranger charge that my child was violent or vicious—this was too much. I was living an unholy nightmare. The moment called for compassion, not a verbal barrage from a stranger.

I stood in the hallway with my back against the wall and sobbed, while the orderly tried to usher the indignant harpy back to her side of the hospital room. A nurse, hearing the commotion, rushed in and rescued us from further abuse.

"We'll move him to a private room," she directed the orderly. She put a hand on my shoulder as if to say, "I'm sorry. I know this is a lot to handle." Her small kindness gave me a measure of hope: maybe we could get things back on a different track. At least now we were out of the chaos of the emergency room.

But was I wrong.

Will's step brother, John, had been diligent in his investigations to determine whether there were any empty bottles of medication lying around Will's room—any we missed in the hurried search before we left with the ambulance. John talked with Jack by phone late morning to report that all he came across was one empty container in the trash, but no pills.

But, with his suspicions aroused, John looked further and discovered a slew of empty bottles under Will's bed, and, lying next to them, a stack of handwritten notes—suicide notes.

John drove to the hospital in a fury, not knowing where to find us and angry because we were not answering our cell phones. By coincidence, Jack was in front of the hospital just as John raced up in his mother's car, the fistful of notes in his hand, tears streaming down his face.

So Jack received the news before I did. He walked briskly back into the ER and approached the doctor in charge of Will's case.

"Could I talk to you for a moment?" The two men huddled in a corner and Jack reported, "My son found Will's suicide notes; he left them under his bed."

The game plan shifted. Further attempts to do a spinal tap or other tests were abandoned. The doctors went to work ferreting out information on a massive overdose of the antidepressant drug Remeron.

Jack waited until Will was moved from the ER to the critical care unit upstairs before coaxing me away from Will's bedside.

"Come out in the hallway, I have to talk to you," he urged gently.

I must have known what he had to say, because I refused to move or look in his direction.

"Gail," he said, placing his hands on my shoulders to steady me, "John found notes under Will's bed. They're suicide notes. Will left notes."

My world blew apart in an instant.

We are so accustomed to witnessing the public grief of strangers that it is hard to adequately characterize that same emotion when you are at the heart of the catastrophe. I have watched scenes from a great distance of bus bombings in Jerusalem, or earthquakes in China, and wallowed in the instantaneous media transmissions depicting bereft widows and bloody victims.

Until now I was only peripherally acquainted with personal tragedy and I was utterly unprepared for the depth of emotion I felt. It is the overwhelming force of grief; none of us is ever adequately prepared.

A sound that I can only describe as primordial surged up from the base of my throat before it burst forth into a baleful, foreign wail. The noise was accompanied by a noxious taste in my mouth. I wanted to vomit. I was trapped in someone else's bad dream.

A nurse moved us to a "quiet room" down the hall, and there I sat doubled over and wept uncontrollably until I was numb. Jack tried to comfort me, but I withdrew to such a sorry place, not even he could reach me.

After a short while, Will's suicide notes in hand, we reentered his hospital room like soldiers returning from a bloody military defeat. There he lay, twitching and mumbling. Perhaps the Haldol was finally beginning to grab hold, or maybe he finally wore himself out; at last he was starting to wind down like a busted toy.

I stared at him from the foot of his bed, arms folded across my chest, face swollen and wretched from crying. "How could you have done this, Will?" I whispered. "How could you have done this to us?" I knew he couldn't hear me. Just as well—my voice was full of reproach. And even though I was engulfed by a profound sorrow, I sensed the oscillations of competing emotions—anger and relief—germinating somewhere down deep.

Now we knew. Now the medical team could work to make sure we didn't lose him.

The overdose triggered a condition called serotonin syndrome, the result of Will's ingesting an estimated 1,300 milligrams of the drug mirtazapine (trade name: Remeron). One of the newer classes of anti-depressants, mirtazapine is akin to serotonin selective reuptake inhibitors, or SSRIs, a cluster of drugs assumed to be less toxic in an overdose than older antidepressant medications.

Nonetheless, complications of serotonin syndrome include seizure, coma, hypotension, and metabolic acidosis (a disruption in the normal alkalinity of blood and body tissues), which can lead to organ failure or cardiac arrest.

If I thought about any of the negative outcomes for too long, I became catatonic with fear. So I turned to the task at hand: it was time to make the calls—a telephonic chain letter of bad news.

"Could you please get in touch with so-and-so [grandparents, uncles, aunts, family friends] and let them know?" It was a mournful undertaking, each person reacting to the news with a mixture of shock and grief.

Will's father was somewhere in the air, winging his way across country. My heart ached for him and I realized he must've been overwrought in transit limbo. He checked with Jack between connecting flights and learned about the suicide notes.

Jane, Will's stepsister, was on the road, halfway to her college in Charleston, South Carolina, when she got the news. She wanted to turn around and come back, but Jack talked her into sticking to her journey. "I saw him really late last night," she sobbed. "He was just joking around with me and I thought he was writing stuff in his journal."

Doctors and nursing staff continued to come and go. Every few hours a new clinician would be on the scene and we were forced to replay the episode—what happened and how we got here. No one at this juncture engaged in prognostications. The physicians in charge were in touch with the National Poison Control database and researching the literature available on overdoses of Remeron. But there was no reliable information on the drug's lethality—it was too new, we were told. And from what they knew of mirtazapine, Will's reaction to an overdose was atypical.

Will's vital signs were stabilizing, but the staff was still on alert for any sign of organ failure or hyperthermia. It was too early to assess whether or not he would suffer permanent damage to his body or his brain as a result of the overdose. So we sat there, in the dimming light of early spring, in his hospital room, communicating in hushed tones with various anguished family members who called via the hospital switchboard as soon as they got the news. We were wretched and spent.

At around 6:00 PM, Will's aunt and uncle, who live in the nearby suburb of Silver Spring, Maryland, joined Jack and me. Will's cousin Stephanie, their fifteen-year-old daughter, was one of three friends with whom Will spent Saturday night bowling.

Saturday night, Will had come home just before 11:00 PM, reported that he had a good time, and appeared to be in good spirits in the hours leading up to his overdose. My in-laws told Steph what had happened on Sunday afternoon; my poor niece was devastated. I was anxious to ask her what had gone on Saturday night. Did something wacky or unpleasant happen that would have prompted Will to try to kill himself? Did he and Megan have a fight? Nothing in Will's behavior the night before indicated he was feeling awful. Like the rest of us, Stephanie was utterly stupefied. Will had fooled us all.

As he lay unconscious in the hospital bed next to my chair, I decided to open his suicide notes. I counted on them to offer clues.

Will wrote four notes: one addressed to his father and me, one to his brother Max, one to his girlfriend, and one addressed to "friends and family." He was thorough and meticulous, ticking off all of the relationships he valued. I opened the letter he wrote to Bob and me first. After my first read-through, I was astonished. The note was shocking—not because of what it said, but because of what it *didn't* say.

Will wrote that we were the "best parents in the world," and that he couldn't have been happier. He thanked us for all we had done for him and signed off with love and a postscript asking us to give the monies in his savings account (a total of nine hundred dollars) to Harry, the wasted vagrant who hung out next door to our neighborhood Safeway.

Feverishly, I opened the others. They were identical in tone. To his girlfriend he wrote, "Don't worry, there'll be blue skies around the corner" and "I'll always be there for you—watching you from somewhere up above," and he instructed his older brother, "When you have cute little kids of your own, Max, be sure to tell them about their uncle Willy."

My God, he had written the frigging Hallmark card version of suicide notes. The writing was sentimental and flowery—and not the least bit revealing. They were surreally horrible. What made him think these would be an adequate apology for his exit? I was disgusted and disturbed. "How could he have done this without a good reason or a clue?" It was chilling. Did he think that was all there was to his life?

He even went so far as to write a blanket acknowledgment for "all of you I may have not mentioned by name," in the note addressed to "friends and family." "This isn't the Academy Awards ceremony, Will," I chided him mentally. "These are suicide notes!"

I shared the letters with Jack and Will's aunt and uncle before I stuffed them into my purse. Their reaction was the same. "What on earth was he thinking? There's nothing here."

It was 7:00 PM. We hadn't eaten all day. My clothing reeked and I didn't know what to think anymore. Will lay unconscious, but his breathing sounded normal and his heart rate had gone down. Hospital protocol in the aftermath of a suicide attempt required a duty nurse be stationed in the room to monitor him twenty-four hours a day. We could break away for a while without leaving him alone. And there were details we needed to attend to.

It was 2:00 PM on the West Coast when my son Max phoned his father and heard the news of Will's suicide attempt from Melissa. He immediately rang me on the hospital phone in Will's room. Gagging on sobs, Max pleaded me to allow him to fly to Washington immediately. "I'll even pay for it myself," he implored. Since he was in the middle of midterm exams in his first year at Berkeley, I hesitated momentarily before consenting. It was devastating to hear him so torn apart. The boys were very close; it would do Max good to be able to be with his brother—and it might do Will some good, too.

Max had plenty of time to pack and hitch a ride to the airport for a red-eye flight from San Francisco later that night. I called United Airlines, explained the situation, and drained my frequent-flyer account to cover a round-trip ticket, but of all things: now we needed to rush to the United Airlines counter at National Airport before closing time so that they could issue the ticket in Max's name.

Details of modern life were beginning to mingle in the midst of our grief—frequent-flyer accounts, conversations with airline agents, where to lodge family and how to feed and transport them, hastily assembled plans—going through the motions as though it were a death in the family, a funeral.

Bob was due to arrive at our house sometime after midnight and Max would arrive at Dulles Airport at 7:00 AM Monday morning. Both sets of grandparents were deliberating whether to fly out from Southern California; John would spend the night with Charlotte, at her house in Glover Park, but he wouldn't be going to school the next day. Jane made the eight-hour drive back to Charleston, South Carolina, shaken and distraught, and we decided it best that she remain at school for the time being.

Wearily, I gathered up the debris scattered about Will's hospital room—empty Styrofoam coffee cups, orange peels, a half-eaten bag of Fritos from the vending machine, a section of Sunday's newspaper, and hospital admission forms. I kissed my son on the forehead and tried to smooth his hair.

"I love you, Will. You *have* to know I love you," I whispered. He emitted a low growl and struggled briefly against the wrist restraints.

I glanced back one last time as Jack and I crept out of the room. It was dark outside now. The bile-green numbers emanating from the heart monitor were all that lit the hospital room. Tubes snaked in and out of Will's body, weaving their way into the stringy, worn fabric of the cerulean cotton blanket. Here was my child, my son. *Any* mother's son.

7:00 PM, March 11, 2001

Only nine hours measured in real time, but, oh my . . . I had traversed a galaxy's worth of light-years from the sobering instant when I opened the door to Will's room. The cataclysmic events of the morning and afternoon settled over me like a thick, wet mantle. I felt heavy, dirty, cold, and slow.

Will's suicide attempt forced me to reevaluate all of the fundamental precepts: love and family ties, parenting and relationships, wellness and treatment. I had trusted my instincts and, boy, I could not have been further off the mark. Would I ever feel grounded again? Would any of us?

Jack and I trudged up the iron stairs, up to the deck and the back door of our townhouse. Odd, everything looked just as it had when we tore out of there for the hospital at 10:30 AM. Since my life had been rearranged during the course of the day, shouldn't we have been returning to an altered physical structure? Same pictures on the walls, same houseplants in need of watering—even dirty dishes the kids deposited in the sink sat collecting soap grunge and caked egg yolk from breakfast that morning.

I plopped down at the banquette in the sunroom off the kitchen with a cordless telephone and address book open in my lap, but I could not bring myself to make another phone call. Here, at this table—not even twenty-four hours ago—Will and I had our last conversation.

"We should eat something," I murmured, and Jack asked if I would eat a pizza if he ordered one.

"I don't care. Go ahead." I poured myself a glass of red wine and went upstairs to take a bath.

As I lay in the bathtub I was roiled by recollections of the previous evening: Will left the house at around 6:00 PM to go bowling with his friends. When he returned, I heard him park our Jetta in the carport off the alley and climb the back stairs of the deck. I was sitting at the banquette off the kitchen, reading. He opened the back door, flashed me a smile, and folded his gangly limbs into the banquette and sat across from me. I put my book down and we chatted for a few minutes while he fiddled with a laminated salt shaker that needed refilling. His voice was even and upbeat. With evident glee, he boasted that he bowled in the hundreds two games in a row.

I gazed across the table at him and it struck me what a great-looking kid he had become. At six feet and still growing, he might have evinced the awkwardness that comes with that age, but his usual demeanor was one of quiet confidence, and his steady, clear blue-eyed gaze made him appear open, honest, and older than his seventeen years.

He was an easy kid to love, an easy kid to be proud of. Still, after the hellishness of the last few months and his struggle with depression, I watched him with the intensity of a feral cat, always looking for signs of vulnerability, points of weakness—tiny markers that would point to depression.

I threw out a cautious line of inquiry: "You seem like you're feeling better, sweetie. How are things going for you?"

In the last ten days his mood had improved visibly and I was hopeful that the antidepressant medication was finally bringing him some relief.

"Yeah, no . . . I *do* feel better. Yeah, I really do," he offered with a reassuring smile.

I beamed at him and he kissed me on the forehead before joining Jane and her friends in the living room to watch the NCAA Tournament. A few minutes later, I went upstairs to bed buoyed by our exchange and his apparent progress. I thought he was on the road to recovery.

How do you recognize a suicidal teenager? What are the characteristics of an adolescent at risk? There are a surfeit of markers, and for better or worse a teen who may be actively contemplating suicide exhibits the same indicators as a teen who is diagnosed "depressed." Depression symptoms include

- change in eating and sleeping habits;
- withdrawal from friends, family, and regular activities;
- violent actions, rebellious behavior, or running away;
- drug and alcohol use;
- unusual neglect of personal appearance;
- marked personality change;
- persistent boredom, difficulty concentrating, or a decline in the quality of schoolwork;
- frequent complaints about physical symptoms, often related to emotions, such as stomachaches, headaches, and fatigue;
- loss of interest in pleasurable activities, not tolerating praise or rewards.[1]

Similarly, according to the American Academy of Child and Adolescent Psychiatry's Teen Suicide Fact Sheet, a teenager who is planning to commit suicide may

- complain of being a bad person or feeling "rotten inside";
- give verbal hints with statements such as "I won't be a problem for you much longer," "Nothing matters," "It's no use," and "I won't see you again";
- put his or her affairs in order, for example, give away favorite possessions, clean his or her room, throw away important belongings;
- become suddenly cheerful after a period of depression;
- show signs of psychosis (hallucinations or bizarre thoughts).

If you are parenting a teenager and reading these lists for the first time, you will be confounded by how many of the symptoms listed—not all, perhaps, but a fair number—are manifestations of "normal" adolescence. Low self-esteem? Disregard for authority? Mood swings? No kidding. These characteristics go with the territory of adolescence.

How does a parent determine when a child is depressed or just behaving "age-appropriately"? Are these lists of indicators helpful? Are they even accurate predictors of suicidal impulses? If you were attentive to all of the indicators, symptoms, and markers, would you have enough information to preclude a son or daughter's suicide attempt? I am not so sure, but it is a start. And that, in and of itself, is disturbing.

Noted adolescent psychiatrist Dr. Harold S. Koplewicz, in *More Than Moody: Recognizing and Treating Adolescent Depression*, goes deeper and explores the "factors" underpinning a suicide attempt. Koplewicz looks for

- an impulsive personality;
- biological factors such as neurochemical imbalances;
- lack of strong family ties;

- social factors such as social isolation, a recent suicide by someone close or in the same community, or absence of strong taboos about suicide;
- easy access to and familiarity with guns
- agitated mental state.[2]

But Koplewicz reminds us, "Little can be said about diagnosis that is hard and fast. There is no gold-standard medical test for depression."[3] The same can be said for a teenager on the verge of suicide.

Parents are left in a precarious limbo, forced to evaluate a sweeping range of qualifiers, weighing "normal" adolescence against the slight deviation that crosses the line into "pathology." And we are forced to undertake this analysis bereft of solid guidance or support from the experts and institutions best qualified to come to our aid.

Wounded heart

I cannot save you from yourself

Though I wanted to be brave

It never helps

'Cause your trouble's like a flood

Raging through your veins

And no amount of love's enough

To end the pain.

If you listen you can hear

The angel's wings

Up above our heads so near

They are hovering

Waiting to reach out for love

When it falls apart

When it cannot rise above

A wounded heart

from "Wounded Heart"
by Jude Johnstone

2

PULLED FROM THE WRECKAGE

"What the hell happened?" I puzzled. I lay immobilized by exhaustion and despair in tepid bath water. A cloud of suspicion floated to the surface of my consciousness: Could Will have disguised the depths of his depression, horded his meds, made peace with friends and family, and plotted a permanent escape? Or maybe this was the dreaded "rollback phenomenon" psychiatrists see in some patients, who, in the early stages of recovery, experience a sudden surge of renewed vigor and energy—and, perversely, an uptick in suicidal thinking. As bizarre as it sounds, a person previously incapacitated by major depression and lacking the energy to act on suicidal impulses suddenly feels good enough to commit suicide.

"Suicide euphoria"—a term bantered around in the therapeutic literature—characterizes this sudden mood shift, which transforms a person in the throes of a serious depression, making him appear brighter, calmer, and more positive in the days or weeks leading up to a suicide attempt. A "tip" for families concerned about a suicidal teen on the American Psychiatric Association's Web site offers:

> Teenagers who are planning to commit suicide might "clean house" by giving away favorite possessions, cleaning their rooms or throwing things away. They may also become suddenly cheerful after a period of depression, because they think they have "found the solution" by deciding to end their lives.[1]

Yes, indeed, Will had straightened up his room before taking the pills on Saturday night. I remember being unnerved by how tidy his room looked—it was my first impression when I opened his bedroom door Sunday morning. According to Megan and his cousin Stephanie, Will was calm, even cheerful, Saturday night. And he seemed sure-footed and positive about the future ever since his decision weeks earlier to drop out of high school, get his GED (General Equivalency Degree), and go to work full-time.

How could I have missed what was really going on? If he harbored thoughts of killing himself, he never mentioned it to anyone—not his closest friends or girlfriend—and no one suspected it. Nor did he drop a hint of it to his psychiatrist, Dr. Salerian, or Dr. Vaune Ainsworth, the psychotherapist he saw twice weekly.

I faced the stark realization: *I could have prevented this.* At the very least I was naive, and in moments when I feel particularly guilty about what happened, I think I was downright negligent. Here is a lesson every family with a depressed teen should take to heart: *Never allow your son or daughter to administer his or her own medications.* It is a no-brainer. And yet, neither of his doctors—not his psychiatrist nor his therapist—suggested this simple precaution should be followed. Were we all that dense? Did his doctors assume the drugs were too benign to represent a real threat? Did they assume I would know better than to allow him to dose himself?

I thought I was a good parent, caring and insightful. My children, my stepchildren, and I have had a strong bond and open communication. If Will had had a history of serious drug or alcohol abuse, I never would have allowed him to manage his own meds. But Will *did* have a history of depression. He was just as out of control as any drug- or alcohol-abusing kid. How many ways had I failed my son? Or should I fault him for not reaching out to me, to anyone, in the predawn hours Sunday morning, when, as he later claimed, he was "overcome by a black wave." I owed it to Will to remind myself repeatedly that depression is an illness, that "the suicide attempt isn't really who he is."

Suicide is not a rational act. It is not a reasoned choice. Thoughts of killing oneself—or "suicidal ideation"—are to clinical depression what paralysis is to polio: *the worst possible and sometimes unavoidable consequence of a serious illness.* As Will's mother, I was staring at the challenge of untangling his impetus and motivation. There is no sense denying that I was confused and bitter because I felt he had rejected me, rejected all of us, and coveted life without us over death. But it just is not that simple.

Throughout Will's young life he had tried to please everyone, family, friends, and strangers alike. He aimed to be consistently even-tempered and "good." I can understand his reluctance to confess the resignation and despair that led to his suicide attempt; he had crawled too far out on a limb and didn't want to come back. I had been caught in that trap before myself: "I don't want to alarm them [friends and family]"; "They'll get along just fine when I'm gone." Nothing could be further from the truth. As I said, suicide is not a rational act. There would be no good answers and no logical explanations—not for us, the family that loved him powerfully—and the logic of his act would surely elude Will himself once he regained his health further down the road.

It is completely unjustifiable to lay blame upon the individual who is suffering, as the author William Styron reminds us in his masterful depression exegesis, *Darkness Visible: A Memoir of Madness:*

> The pain of severe depression is quite unimaginable to those who have not suffered it, and it kills in many instances because its anguish can no longer be borne. The prevention of many suicides will continue to be hindered until there is a general awareness of the nature of this pain. Through the healing process of time— and through medical interventions or hospitalization in many cases—most people survive depression, which may be its only blessing; but to the tragic legions who are compelled to destroy themselves there should be no more reproof attached than to the victims of terminal cancer.[2]

At the end of the day, what more was there to say? I descended into a black hole of guilt and anxiety and the miserable sense that I had failed Will. Will was not in control—I should have been. He was battling a severe illness; it fell to me to protect him. I should have anticipated all of the possible twists this disease might take. I should have taken every precaution—no matter how foolish it seemed—to make sure that he didn't have the means to make a run at suicide. The overdose of pills. For the remainder of my life, I will feel unassuageable guilt about the pills. The drugs were within his reach all along. Right there waiting, no less dangerous than a loaded gun.

Late at night, Jack and I huddled together on the couch. We ate cold pizza and tried to watch a little mind-numbing Sunday-night television. What a dastardly limbo to be in.

I must have dozed off. When the doorbell rang, I was startled to discover it was already 1:00 AM. Will's father had finally arrived. Time to head back to the hospital, just Bob and me: two heartsick parents preparing to keep a doleful vigil next to our badly broken son.

Letter from Will's stepmother in San Francisco:

March 12, 2001

Dear Will,
I have never written a letter quite like this one before, though I probably should have when my younger sister Marie tried to commit suicide twice in her early twenties. At the time, all I could think to do was be there for her, physically. But I didn't really know what to SAY to her. I feel more comfortable with mental illness now, and I need to say some things to you.

Like everyone else in our family—the entire conglomerate of your parents, stepparents and siblings—I was stunned that you were so full of despair and that your medication had so thoroughly failed you. For the past many weeks, every night, when your dad came home, I would ask, "How's Will?" On those days that he had talked to you, he would say you sounded OK or Good or Really Good, depending on how he thought you sounded and what you had said to him. We wanted to believe you were getting better, but now we know better—and fortunately, we still have the opportunity to try and help you get better. But I know it's not as simple as that.

My sister says, remembering her own despair, that no matter how close and supportive your family is, when you are in the throes of mental illness you don't think anyone on the "outside" can understand what you are going through. For her, what helped over time were good medication, a great psychiatrist and an amazing support group. She still relies on all of that, and she's more than OK with that.

Being depressed may not be a life that you can envision for yourself, but please don't jump to conclusions so early in the battle. And please, if you can't talk to your family, please talk to your doctors. And if they aren't the right doctors for you, please tell your mom or your dad, so we can find the right doctors. They can't help you if you don't help them.

I'm sure what I am saying will be said again and again this week. And it probably sounds pretty obvious. But I wanted to add my voice, as much for me as for you.

I feel fortunate that my sister survived in spite of our lack of communication. My life and my family's life would have been very different if she had not survived her suicide attempts. But, more importantly, she conquered an illness on her own. That's pretty amazing.

I can't help but believe that if Marie can win that battle then Will can, too.

I will see you soon, I know.

Until then, you have all my love.

Melissa

7:00 AM, March 12, 2001

It was going to be a horrendous day. I opened my eyes, steeling myself for another round of doctors' interventions and analyses—all of which, I knew, would provide no answers, no certainties. There would also be, I knew, a series of interminable and agonizing conversations with family and friends. But there you have it: I opened my eyes reluctantly and faced the day.

Washington was experiencing an unseasonably mild spring and I felt sucker-punched by brilliant yellow light and birdsong. The previous twenty-four hours had swallowed us up in an emotional maelstrom. What an affront to be further tested by an exuberant spring day! I was woozy and numb. No one in the household had slept enough—or well.

Will made it through the night. When Bob and I left the hospital at 3:30 AM, doctors monitoring him closely for any signs of organ failure promised to call if he took a sudden turn for the worse. Thank God—no phone call. Our last conversation with the hospital staff before leaving was about what to expect the next morning. The doctor who had followed Will's case throughout the day Sunday warned us Will might be unconscious for as many as three days—a disheartening prospect.

We were nearly certain that Will had overdosed on Remeron; two of his bottles containing roughly sixty pills were missing. Remeron was one of the newer, less lethal antidepressant medications, only on the market for a few months, and there was no data to predict the outcome of an overdose. Since we were not certain how much he took or if he mixed Remeron with any of the other antidepressants prescribed for him (Concerta and Prozac), we were in uncharted pharmacological territory.

Moving to the front of our line of fears was the possibility that Will's drug overdose might render him physically or mentally impaired. Today was only Monday. Waiting another two days to find out whether he was going to be all right was a diabolical joke. I tried to push the notion aside. I was too distraught to entertain the possibility of a brain-damaged Will.

I arrived at the hospital just before 8:00 AM and crept into Will's hospital room unobserved by the staff at the nurses' station. He was still a jungle of tubes and wires and I found the bleep of the heart monitor unnerving. There was an empty urine bag dangling from the side of the bed, the catheter snaked under the sheet. Then I noticed the restraints were off his wrists and ankles. This was a good sign. It had to mean he had stopped his wild gyrations. I got closer and I could see his lips were raw and stained black from the charcoal mixture the emergency room doctors had administered the day before. He reeked of sweat and urine, but he was sleeping peacefully.

I prepared myself for what we believed would be the long wait for Will to regain consciousness. I tried to picture what it would mean to have Will live but be seriously brain damaged or physically impaired. I could not contemplate it; it was just too hard. My body hurt all over and my mind was static. I could only process the bare necessities. Up to now, our family had been spared the withering trauma of a life-or-death tragedy; nothing I had ever dealt with prepared me for any of these eventualities: suicide, drug overdose, brain damage. What about families whose children are victims of horrific car accidents? They must wait for the outcome with this same mixture of dread and unfounded hope.

Somehow, this was worse. This was not an accident. This wasn't fate or happenstance. To the outside world, my son brought this on himself—he did this on purpose. If he were to suffer permanent damage, would the reaction be "Look, he tried to kill himself; he has only himself to blame"? Parents who find themselves struggling to cope in the aftermath of a child's suicide attempt shouldn't have that slapped on them. Society's ignorance and lack of understanding about depression may lead others to that conclusion, but as a parent, you do not have to accept it.

Still, as much as I knew about depression, and as familiar as I was with the awful depths of the illness, I confess I fell victim to feeling periodic waves of betrayal and rejection. No matter what the circumstances, it is hard to come to terms with the idea that your child has rejected the life that you gave him. It is natural in such a situation to be shaken by conflicting emotions.

What I wanted now was for someone to tell me what the future held and how we walked back to "normal" from here. But no one did. There were no inspirational missives from doctors or therapists, no hope offered by interested parties, no pamphlets, primers, or textbooks on what to do next.[3] I assumed that the professionals observing us, the ones who would write such texts, were already making judgments—and were inclined to presume that I had failed as a parent. Or, perhaps, they figured that my kid, my Will, was damaged goods and had turned to (pick one) drugs, alcohol, or outrageous behavior because he was "deviant." He was just another angry teen out to "punish" his family and the world.

Of course, none of this was true. The people tasked with Will's care, with saving his life, did not know me and they did not know my son. It is possible that they were beyond drawing conclusions. They went about their business courteously and efficiently, all the while walking in and out of Will's room as though they were tripping over a breathing corpse. Everyone spoke in hushed tones and cast sidelong glances at the family members gathered around Will's bed. And I knew that in addition to my own conflicting emotions about what Will had done, we were about to go up against society's preconceived dicta about suicidal behavior.

Since Will was still under twenty-four-hour observation, a duty nurse sat reading by his bed. The nurse, a soft-spoken Jamaican woman, said he had spoken to her a little earlier. "What? Are you sure?" I was astonished. She must have been mistaken.

"Hey, Willo, it's your mom." No response from Will—not an eyelid fluttered; not a muscle moved. I nuzzled up against his ear and whispered his name again, gently, tenderly. I sat down next to his bed and took his limp hand in mine.

Until that very moment, I hadn't really thought about what I *would* say to him once he regained consciousness. The emotional deluge of the last several hours had left me spent. What I needed was inspiration, but instead what I felt was guilt, anger, hope, and anguish.

What does a parent say to a child after he or she has committed an act so shocking and so incomprehensible? If your teenager wrecks the car, or gets busted for drugs or flunks out of school, you are devastated, but you pick up the pieces and go on. You look for ways to help him make a new start and you move on. But nothing I'd ever read in books on parenting offered guidance on how you talk to your child after he has tried to kill himself. Where do you begin? What are the first words you say?

I sat and watched him breathe. I desperately wanted to climb onto his hospital bed and wrap myself around his spindly, seventeen-year-old frame, but he was hooked up to so many tubes and monitoring systems, it was impossible. I put my ear to his chest. It was a comfort to hear his heart was no longer racing; his pulse and respiration remained normal. Maybe there really was cause for hope.

What would Will's first conscious reaction be? Assuming he had not suffered injury to his brain, would he comprehend instantly he was still alive? Would he be relieved or would he be angry his suicide attempt had failed? Would he understand how terribly hurt we were or how wretched we felt? Should I be gentle or reproachful? I didn't have a clue. All of my parenting skills had been upended.

His hospital room was infused with a buttery morning light. As I stared out the window, I was crushed by memories; a kaleidoscope of recollections: Will's goofy little kid giggle; Willy, the happy baby and impish, easygoing kid; the no-fuss teen. All of us—his family and friends—were captivated by Will's guileless charm and keen sense of humor. Perhaps it would make sense to try a bit of humor to ease Will back into our world and our family's embrace.

We are not a devoutly religious family. Will's father was raised as a Roman Catholic and we decided to raise our children as Catholics, too. I was not Catholic, but I have a strong, faith-based spiritualism. Will had attended Catholic schools ever since nursery school. But our faith—Will's and mine—digressed years earlier toward a nontraditional view of the afterlife. I would be surprised if Will had counted on communing with legions of angels when he took the overdose of drugs on Saturday night.

So, at 10:00 AM that Monday morning, when he opened his eyes for the first time in over thirty hours and glanced around the room, trying to assess his whereabouts—*before he had a chance to speak*—I whispered to him, "Yes, Will, you *are* in heaven; *I'm* an angel, and boy, are you in trouble, you little jerk!" Will looked at me, startled. Then he got the joke. He gave me a feeble smile and a weak thumbs-up and murmured, "Hi, Mom," before he closed his eyes again. I was so overwhelmed, I cracked with relief and wept openly. I was pretty certain he was back on Planet Earth and we had escaped a calamitous tragedy.

Will startled us all by regaining consciousness on Monday morning. He was groggy and confused, and drifted in and out of sleep, but the medical team examining him uncovered no signs of brain damage. To say we were relieved is an understatement. I did not know how to handle this new emotion: joy and grief intertwined like a bad marriage.

The rest of the morning went by in a blur. Too many people coming and going, Will in and out of sleep, family arriving on the scene laughing and weeping; well-intentioned friends stopping by to show love and support. And the medical team, always there, evaluating, probing, asking the same questions of us, of Will, again and again and again.

In some ways, the dynamic paralleled a wake: lots of touching and memorable stories about the loved one commingled with a sense of sorrow and loss. We were exhausted. I didn't know whether I should offer refreshments, cheer everyone up, and play the good hostess or send the visitors home and post a sign on the door saying, "Will's family appreciates your kind concern and we'll get back to you after we've cleaned the place up and undergone some serious attitude adjustment."

Ultimately, I crept along and rode with the chaos; there were too many people who needed to see Will and touch him and be reassured.

Max and Bob arrived shortly after 10:00 AM. "He spoke to me," I whispered to them, with tears in my eyes. "He's all right." Bob exhaled a galactic sigh of relief and Max climbed onto Will's bed and said, "Hey, Will, it's me. Wake up, man." Will roused and responded, "Hey, Max." They shared a powerful embrace before Will drifted off again.

Will's cousin Stephanie and her younger sister, Kate, arrived with their mother. Again, a flood of tears of relief and whispers of reproach. Megan, Will's girlfriend of five months, entered the room with trepidation, not knowing what she would find. Will seemed genuinely glad to see her and I left them alone for a few moments so they could talk privately. Will's stepbrother (and best friend), John, who had found the suicide notes, was understandably edgy and anxious and didn't leave Will's bedside for hours. Family friends brought gifts of food and consolation.

I had been on the phone for the last twenty-four hours trying to speak in person to Dr. Salerian. When we finally connected around 3:00 PM, he had already spoken to the hospital staff and was businesslike and confident in setting a course of action: Will would be transferred back to the Psychiatric Institute of Washington as soon as the hospital team was willing to release him, perhaps as early as Tuesday, and we would go from there. "The Plan" wasn't exactly swimming in details; it offered little comfort. But I had to admit that we were stumped and didn't know what else to do.

Late that afternoon we were visited by the hospital's chief of psychiatry, Dr. James Griffith, who brought a retinue of psychiatry interns along with him. He seemed knowledgeable and caring, but for parents seeking answers, it seemed we were going over the same old tired ground: "How long has your son been depressed?" "Any history of drug or alcohol abuse?" "Depression in the family?" And so on.

Dr. Griffith left the room momentarily to take a call, and one of the interns who remained behind to continue the assessment remarked offhandedly, "You're lucky all your son took was the Remeron. If he'd taken it in combination with his Prozac or Concerta, it would have been much more lethal."

"Oh, great!" I uttered sarcastically. This young intern had just done something jaw-droppingly idiotic. With Will present in the room, following the discussion, she had just given him the formula for his next run at suicide. Bob and I exchanged horrified glances.

The chief psychiatrist stepped back into the room and asked us to leave so he could conduct a private consultation with Will. We repaired to the corridor. As the doctor recounted it, Will admitted to making an earnest attempt to kill himself. "I didn't want to die," he confessed, "I just didn't want to live anymore." When I heard that I thought: "God, I know that feeling."

The psychiatrist asked Will to write down what had led him to attempt suicide. Will completed the task, but what he wrote was an outlandish account of the events as he remembered them from the time he got to the hospital on Sunday until he regained consciousness Monday morning. His written recollection was detached from what he had done and full of oddball characterizations. He began the piece with "On Saturday night I took my pills . . . all of them. I emptied two bottles of Remeron, a sleeping medicine/antidepressant, onto my bed (probably about 50 or 60 pills) and swallowed them in two handfuls with a sip of Snapple Iced Tea." His account ended with "And then came the visitors. Wave after wave of disappointed, yet relieved family and friends."

Like Will, I too was overwhelmed by the "wave after wave of disappointed, yet relieved family and friends." Word of our crisis spread quickly. I didn't discount the innumerable acts of kindness and hopeful wishes channeled in our direction, but *we* were now the car wreck from which you can't avert your gaze. I couldn't explain what happened to us; how could anyone else make sense of it?

If I knew then what I know now, I would have handled the immediate aftermath of Will's suicide attempt differently. You are so emotionally raw in this period that you need to husband your resources. Obviously, Will was raw, too. I would recommend that visitors be strictly limited to immediate family—and even then, you should place limits on the amount of time allotted to each visit. There will be time to acknowledge the wellspring of kindness at another time.

And I also concluded that the best thing you can possibly say to a parent or family member of a child who has survived a suicide attempt is, "How wonderful your child made it! He (or she) survived and now you have a chance to fix the problem."

What we needed to do now was turn our attention to the next step, to figuring out the appropriate medical treatment for Will's depression. This would prove to be a formidable challenge.

Will's journal account of his suicide attempt written on March 13 at the request of the doctor treating him at George Washington University Hospital:

These are the events as I remember them: On Saturday night I took my pills . . . all of them. I emptied two bottles of Remeron, a sleeping medicine/antidepressant, onto my bed (probably about 50 or 60 pills) and swallowed them in two handfuls with a sip of Snapple Iced Tea. This was definitely an attempt to take my own life, yet I went to bed calm . . . unfazed by the idea that I was killing myself. I thought about what I had done, not with regret or relief, but rather with a strange indifference, as if it didn't concern me at all. I do not remember waking up the next morning.

I was in the hospital, though I did not fully realize it. I was half asleep, half conscious. And half extremely agitated. I can remember hearing doctors yelling at me to stay in my bed or to leave the i.v.'s in my arm, which I was constantly trying to remove. I don't know why exactly I wanted to leave my bed, but I think I wanted to get my shoes and pants out from under the bed, articles of clothing which my parents did not even bring into the hospital until the next day.

They did not know exactly what was wrong with me (until they found the suicide notes I had left on my desk) and wanted to do a spinal tap to see if this would give them any clues. I was not going to let this happen. I am in no way a violent or even uncooperative person, but if you were to ask the medical staff at George Washington University Hospital, they would testify that I am at least 95% pit-bull. They sprayed some kind of cleansing fluid on my back to prepare me for the spinal tap. This did not make me happy. I complained that it stung and burned, although I was told later that it was just the cold, which shocked my skin. After several minutes of trying to hold me still so they could clean my back, they realized that there was no possible way that I would be still and calm enough [for them] to actually perform a spinal tap, a procedure which involves very large needles and very still patients.

Luckily, about that time my stepbrother found the notes, which I left behind explaining my actions. They came to the conclusion that by no coincidence were my two full bottles of sleeping pills entirely empty. I had definitely overdosed, and I had definitely done it on purpose. I'm not sure what time all of these events took place, although I imagine it was mid to late Sunday afternoon, as my mom did not find me until about ten o'clock Sunday morning.

When they realized that I was clearly suffering from a drug overdose they came up with one solution: charcoal. Now, there are few aspects of this whole experience which I remember as clearly as the charcoal, simply because swallowing twenty ounces of liquid charcoal is not easily forgotten. I later learned that charcoal is common in cases of drug/alcohol overdoses and accidental poisonings. As one might imagine, gagging down cup after cup of liquid charcoal is not the high point of anyone's day, least not an unsuccessful 17-year-old suicidal boy's. So it goes without saying that I was not terribly pleased about this.

Realizing that they would be hard-pressed to get me to take in the charcoal myself, they tried to pipe it into me through tubes in my nose. This turned out to be extremely painful, and Lord knows I would not stand for that. I was in no mood to tolerate any kind of pain and therefore was forced to get the charcoal down on my own.

There are few things quite like swallowing nearly a liter of liquid about as thick as tar and probably quite similar in taste. To this very moment, nearly two full days later, I am afraid to move my bowels for fear of shitting charcoal briquettes.

I got through one cup, spitting out much of the liquid into a small bucket held by the nurse, then a second cup, and half of a third to make up for what I left in the bucket. It was one of the single-most unpleasant experiences of my life and I feel extremely lucky that I was only half conscious throughout it.

With the charcoal in place to settle my stomach and hopefully absorb the excesses of the Remeron, they moved on to questioning if there was any kind of permanent damage to my brain. They gave me a CAT-scan, something which has always interested me, but which I can't describe here simply because I remember practically none of it.

All of the events, which I have just described, occurred in what seemed to me like a very short period of time and are still very fuzzy in my mind. I was filled in on most all of the details the next day. I was expected to stay under for about three days, starting on Sunday night. I woke up at 9 a.m. Monday morning. Pretty fucking tough if you ask me, but then again, who did?

When I woke up, I found my arms held down in restraints to the sides of the bed, a precaution, which was taken to keep me from removing the i.v.'s and needles from various parts of my body. I imagine it was also a precaution against leaving the doctors open for me to hit, which seems extremely out of character, but not all together impossible, considering my mental state.

I also awoke to find my penis painfully attached to a tube, which led to a thick plastic bag. This, I was told, was to enable doctors to take a urine sample without me even being conscious to give one. Oh, the technology! I was about as happy as one might expect a suicidal boy to be when he wakes up to find a tube attached to his penis.

When the nurse who had been assigned to sit with me as I slept noticed that I had woken-up, she offered to remove my arm restraints, to allow me to get up to wash my face. She would have let me get up to use the bathroom, but as she said, I was "all hooked up" and could feel free to "let it go." I found peeing into a tube while lying in bed extremely uncomfortable and declined to do so. When she realized this (apparently the lack of visible urine traveling through the tube into the bag) she offered to remove the tube, although [she] admitted that it would be uncomfortable, translation: painful.

I agreed to this since I really did have to pee quite badly. In describing this process as uncomfortable, that nurse had never been more 100 percent correct in her entire life. In fact, it was so uncomfortable that I might go as far as describing it as REALLY FUCKING PAINFUL. The moment she removed the tube, I was so surprised by the pain that I was almost tempted to scream, "Jesus Fucking Christ, why don't you just cut it off Goddamnit?" but thought better of it since she literally had my balls in her hands.

And then came the visitors. Wave after wave of disappointed, yet relieved family and friends.

*   *   *

Consultation Record
The George Washington University Hospital
Psychiatry Attending: Dr. James Griffith
Date: 03-13-01; 9:00 AM

Patient Interviewed. He made a low/moderate risk, but low-rescue
suicide attempt, intending to die. He has a partially treated major
depressive disorder and his suicide attempt represents more his
fatigue in living with chronic emotional pain than a wish to die.

I recount the events of those two days and I am traumatized all over
again. I sit staring in front of the computer screen, biting my nails and
rocking back and forth methodically. The rocking is unconscious, self-
pacifying; I drift into it without being aware of it initially. I associate it
with bouts of depression, and I have seen it in others—that strange
hyperkinetic motion that flags us as mentally ill.

Writing this story is like writing from the bottom of a well. I am
struggling to bring these recollections, these insights, to light, but more
often than not, dredging the memories is like swimming through black
ooze. And any attempts to array them in a rational chronology or place
them in the context of medicine and healing is, well . . . downright
depressing.

I am no stranger to mental illness. I have battled severe depression
all of my adult life. It is a chronic illness, not unlike diabetes or hyper-
tension. In theory my approach has been: You deal with it and you
move on. Although, if you were to ask me if it's *really* that simple, in
the midst of a bout of depression, your question would elicit an ugly
response. I hate the illness not just because of how it makes me feel,
but because of who I am when I become depressed.

Depression is the great medical misnomer of our epoch. Too
often, the illness carries a mystique propagated by the misguided
notion that those who suffer are touched with artistic gifts above and

beyond those bestowed on the rest of the population. The illness is cloaked in a veneer of undeserved glamour.

I have spoken to friends—musicians, artists, and writers—about their depression. Some lean into it unflinchingly; "My mental anguish is my gift," or "I create through my emotional suffering." Maybe for them. Not for me. If my depression is a gift, I want to return it. The illness dismisses me from the ranks of the living, and rather than reaching an apotheosis through it, I become incapacitated, immobilized. I become a useless shell.

According to historians, Winston Churchill referred to his depression as "the black dog," but he drew on his moods for profound oratorical inspiration and painting. Comedians Robin Williams and Jonathan Winters both battle depression but consider the illness a wellspring for their electric humor. Writers, painters, politicians, and poets—the list is legion with famous people who contend with depression.[4]

Does the public benefit from reading or hearing accounts of celebrity depressions? Perhaps it serves to make the illness more visible, and thus the public is more comfortable discussing depression, but I do not think so. By attributing the illness to celebrities, we tend to instill it with a whiff of magic so far off the mark, it does everyone a disservice.

More typically, depression hits mainstream folks living ordinary lives. Depression is capable of incapacitating the plumber, the schoolteacher, and the banker and those among us who are least able to cope: the working poor, single mothers, the physically or mentally disabled, and the elderly. And if you take into account the legions of drug- or alcohol-addicted individuals, driven to addiction as a means to quell serious depression, you have to include in the tally the homeless and the destitute who live on the street, or in state institutions and prisons, much like the mentally ill of a century ago.

In an August 2004 interview, the director of the National Institute of Mental Health stated that clinical depression is the *number one* medical cause of worker disability for workers between the ages of fifteen and forty-four.[5] That's a staggering fact. Very few Americans realize that there are almost twice as many suicides as homicides in our country.[6] I have been open and forthcoming about my own bouts with major depression. Mental illness is still regarded with superstition and shame, and that disturbs me profoundly. By being up front about depression, I aim, in small measure, to counter the stereotypes of the mentally ill. For depression to be recognized and treated as the bona fide illness it is, it must be destigmatized.

I understand depression. And I even understand *suicidal* depression and the hypnotic trick suicidal fantasies play on a depressed brain; I have suffered their blandishment myself. But suicide is not a choice made by a healthy person. Suicide is where the mind goes when the brain chemistry is altered to the point of nihilistic fatalism. *Depression is a suicide illness.*

Forty years ago, the medical community assumed that adolescents were too young to suffer from depression; a teen suicide was an anomaly, an act so far off the charts that it was seldom reported and often covered up by the family. Is teen depression and teen suicide more common today than it was in the middle of the twentieth century or have we simply become more adept at recognizing the signs?

Dr. Kay Redfield Jamison's comprehensive study of suicide, *Night Falls Fast: Understanding Suicide,* suggests that because the average age of the onset of puberty has dropped sharply over the last several decades, it is possible that "the age at which depression first occurs has also decreased."[7] But maybe our society's changing dynamics play a part as well.

In a provocative book, *Liberation's Children: Parents and Kids in a Postmodern Age,* social critic Kay Hymowitz argues that we live in a culture devoid of moral clarity, leaving children yearning for deep connections to family and traditional values. She argues that two powerful forces distinguish our generation from that of our children: absentee parents and a "sexualized and glitzy media-driven marketplace."[8] Could these factors lead to an increase in the incidence of teen depression?

A 2004 Rand Corporation study published in the journal *Pediatrics* (funded by the National Institute of Child Health and Human Development) demonstrated empirically that watching sex on TV "predicts and may hasten adolescent sexual initiation"[9]—the first time a teen experiences intercourse. By their measurements, two-thirds of all television programming contains sexual content and the study suggests that

> reducing the amount of sexual content in entertainment programming, reducing adolescent exposure to this content, or increasing references to and depictions of possible negative consequences of sexual activity could appreciably delay the initiation of coital and noncoital activities.[10]

You would have to be an alien to be surprised by these findings. What is surprising, however, is that the study showed that even though intercourse among adolescents is commonplace, the majority of the teens wish they had waited longer to have sex. The study concludes: "[This] suggests that sex is occurring before youths are prepared for its consequences."

Today more American children are raised in families with two working parents than in any time in our history. Often the necessity of having two wage earners leaves parents with no choice. But some social critics suggest that we—in particular, women—are beholden to measures of success that value what we achieve in the workplace over the family and home.

Around the country, often the first question you get is, "What do you do?"—the benchmark of your contribution to society. I never hear anyone respond, either male or female, "I am raising a family." Are kids suffering because of these changed dynamics? Hard to argue that they have no impact.

And you would have to be living in a remote corner of the planet to miss the rapid changes in technology and marketing that aim an increasingly dumbed-down, sexed-up media to young people, with all of its superficial absolutes.

No discussion of depression and mental illness is complete without

taking into account the role played by genetics. During the nineteenth
and early twentieth centuries, vast repositories of the mentally ill were
homeless, destitute, or confined to asylums. Stories about a "crazy" aunt
or uncle locked away in a closet upstairs wound their way through family
lore. Almost every family had one such tale. By the middle of the twentieth century, effective treatments became available for people suffering
from debilitating mental illness, and for the first time the mentally ill
began leading more normal lives. As lives improved, so did attitudes
about the mentally ill. But not entirely.

Today, people with chronic mental illnesses, such as bipolar illness
or major depression, anxiety disorders, and even schizophrenia, are
marrying, raising children, and living productive lives—*and* passing
genetic predispositions for mental illnesses along to future generations.

Much more work will have to be done by scientists and the medical establishment, along with a more concerted effort by parents and
educators, to build support for a rigorous public policy debate to
determine why we are seeing an increase in major depressive disorder
in teens. It is a horrific problem with far-reaching consequences and it
is not going to vanish in our lifetime. The causes may indeed be physi-
ological or biological; illness may be a function of genetics or it may be
the social ecology. I argue *it is no one thing;* it is an anomaly: depression
is a combination of all of these factors and it will require monumental
and collaborative efforts on the part of the medical and therapeutic
communities, the government entities charged with protecting the
public welfare, and educators to come up with dynamic new initiatives
to tackle the problem.

Identifying and diagnosing teen depression presents an entirely
different and more complex set of challenges than diagnosing depression in the adult population. Adolescents' inclinations toward impul-
sivity, volatility, and delusional thinking (particularly about death and
their own mortality) challenge conventional depression treatment
regimes designed for adults. And initiatives designed to preclude suicidal teens from taking their own lives must be tailored to adolescents
with a natural predilection for engaging in risky behavior.

In order to reduce the number of teen suicides, a number of steps must be taken, but first and foremost among them is accurate diagnosis.*

I have watched family and friends struggle to ferret out what is really going on with their teenagers, and I have concluded that parents today are ill-equipped to steer their children through the rugged terrain of mental illness. Worse still, we have so little confidence in our judgment about what is best for our children that our anxiety over doing the "right thing" often results in doing nothing at all.

In a 2003 survey of American families, ninety percent of parents indicated they were "confident in being able to tell if their child was depressed or thinking about suicide."[11] But in reality, the findings go on to state that "only one-third of teens with mental health problems are known to parents or any adult."[12]

Sometimes families of troubled teens refuse to accept the overwhelming evidence pointing to a child with depression when it is right in front of them. Drugs and/or alcohol abuse, risky sexual behavior, truancy, petty larceny, and self-mutilation (including eating disorders) are all in their own way a cry for help; take two or more of the behaviors together and alarm bells should go off.

Often, parents confronted with the challenge of handling a troubled adolescent see the problem as a reflection of their own parenting skills—or lack thereof. They worry they will be judged harshly by the community if they own up to a "failing" kid. Some families worry that if they tag a child with a "mental illness," the label will stick and preclude the teen from reaching the heights the parents envisioned before the illness struck.

How can a parent, who professes to "want the best" for his or her child, believe the problem is better ignored than tackled head on? Maybe, by denying it exists, you hope it will just go away of its own accord. All of

---

* The American Psychiatric Association has an alphabetical listing of psychiatrists who work in schools, at www.psych.org/public_info. The National Mental Health Association, in partnership with *Psychology Today*, offers a searchable database by region of therapists, psychologists, and psychiatrists at www.nmha.org.

us engage in a bit of denial when it comes to raising our children, but as most of us have learned the hard way, the problem almost never recedes on its own—and it usually gets worse before it improves.

Even parents adroit at intuiting the magnitude of their child's malaise would rather wish the problem away, but if you suspect your teen is depressed, doing nothing is a luxury you cannot afford.

Look at the statistics on teen suicide and they paint an ominous picture. Over two thousand American teens, aged thirteen to nineteen, commit suicide each year.[13] Include young people up to age twenty-four and the number of suicides doubles. Of the approximately 2 million young Americans who attempt suicide in a given year,[14] girls are two to three times more likely to attempt suicide than boys, but teenage boys are four times more likely to die from an attempt than teenage girls.[15]

All suicide attempts should be taken seriously. Each year almost seven hundred thousand teens receive medical attention for suicide attempts;[16] but there is a presumption among the medical community that suicide attempts by girls are more often a "cry for help," whereas boys' attempts are riskier, more impulsive, and hence more lethal. And it is telling to note that nearly sixty percent of completed suicides committed by young males are carried out with firearms or explosives.[17] Is it any surprise that in the United States firearms are the most common method of suicide for both genders and all ages and ethnic groups?[18]

If you break the statistics down by gender—how adolescent males versus females approach suicide—the facts speak to the fundamentally different ways in which we raise boys versus girls in our culture. Despite the fact that the suicide rate for young males is higher than for girls,[19] over the last two decades we have seen a marked increase in self-destructive behavior among adolescent girls, initially showing up as eating disorders or sexually risky behavior. Most recently, depression in teenage girls has taken shape in the form of self-mutilation, or "cutting."

You do not need to be a member of the psychiatric establishment to presume that these grotesque manifestations of self-loathing stem from low self-esteem. Our teenage daughters are struggling to calculate their worth in a society replete with mixed messages.

It also reflects poorly on our society that gay, lesbian, and bisexual teens are more likely to attempt suicide than their straight counterparts. This group is subjected to a multitude of risk factors (depression, substance abuse, sexual victimization, family conflict, and ostracism at school).[20]

But here is the clincher: whether male or female, gay or straight, a teen who has made a previous attempt at suicide is "100 times more at risk of completing a suicide than one who has not made an attempt."[21] Often the second attempt follows in close proximity to the first and is much more serious.

This last statistic is particularly worrisome for parents of depressed teens. In 1999, roughly one of every thirteen high school students in the United States reported making a suicide attempt the previous year.[22] Dr. David Shaffer, of Columbia University and a leading authority on teen suicide, suggests that roughly twenty percent of high school students will have contemplated suicide in any given year.[23] Given that there is sufficient anecdotal evidence to suggest that only a fraction of teens report making a suicide attempt, how are we to know whether or not a child has made a previous attempt—or two or more?

There is yet another and perhaps more troubling pattern among suicidal teens. It turns up more often, but not exclusively, in adolescent males, and has been underexamined and underreported. I call them the "stealth" candidates for suicide—the kid next door who appears to be doing just fine, the type of kid my son Will appeared to be.

How often have we seen media reports of the "star athlete" or "president of the student council," or the kid voted "most likely to succeed"—the teenager with everything going for him—who comes home on a Saturday night and with no warning loads a gun and shoots himself? If there is a suicide note, it is vague in the extreme—"Sorry for the inconvenience," or "I just couldn't handle stuff anymore."

This type of kid typically closets emotions, while aiming at goals and self-imposed standards that are impossible to meet; he is a "high-achieving, anxious, or depressed perfectionist," writes Kay Redfield Jamison. She concludes:

It may be difficult to determine the extent of such a child's psy-chopathology and mental suffering, due to the tendency to try to appear normal, to please others, not to call attention to oneself.[24]

While one category of depressed teens resorts to angry, explosive, oppositional behavior or demonstrable self-abuse, another masks feel-ings and emotions. Both pose challenges to proper diagnosis and treat-ment.

Finding a doctor, a psychiatrist, to treat a young person is a huge challenge. The reality is harsh: psychiatry is the poor cousin of the medical establishment, and within the practice of psychiatry, few doc-tors sign up for child and adolescent specialties.

Beyond four years of medical school, it takes a doctor at least two or more years to be trained in psychiatry. But once qualified to prac-tice, psychiatrists are constrained by the health care system from achieving financial parity with their peers in pediatrics, or gerontology or other specialties, because of a punishing insurance reimbursement schedule biased against the treatment of mental illness. It is no surprise that so few doctors elect to practice adolescent psychiatry.

Adequate mental health care for families and adolescents will only be achieved by forcing insurers to treat mental illness on a par with physical ailments. Bipartisan congressional legislation to address insurance parity is slowly making its way through the U.S. Congress. Although the legisla-tion does not stand much chance of passing in the near term, there is an ever-growing recognition by our politicians that health plans need to cover the treatment of mental illness.

Statistics vary, but the mental health community argues that only ten percent of depressed adolescents receive proper diagnosis and treatment. When parents suspect a child is crossing that fine line between "normal" adolescent behavior and something more troubling, their first stop is often the family doctor or pediatrician. Some general practitioners are excellent at diagnosing depression in children; others are not. It takes skill and practiced observation, which I argue comes after years of practice in the field of mental health.

If the family is lucky, the general practitioner will refer the child up the food chain to a specialist to render an accurate diagnosis—and prescribe a course of treatment. But again, because of the contractions in the health care system, which have occurred over the past decade, younger patients are rarely seen by a mental health clinician or psychiatrist. Unless a parent directly requests a referral, most doctors are too busy or lack the skills to pick up a signal or symptom.

Oftentimes parents are dissatisfied with the care their teenagers receive from mental health clinicians. More often, the teenager mistrusts the intervention of a psychiatrist or psychologist. But since it's much harder to track recovery from mental illness than, say, a broken collarbone, patients and parents who don't see immediate improvement often fault the doctor.

Clearly, if your child refuses to communicate honestly and openly with his or her doctor, and after six or more months your child shows no signs of a recovery, there is a problem. And a good doctor knows to keep an ongoing dialogue with the parents, too. If you're not receiving regular status reports on your child's progress (or lack of progress), do not hesitate to demand more frequent communication. For treatment to succeed, everyone—the child, the doctor, and the parents—needs to be on board with the treatment regime.

Movement is afoot to allocate more government funds for accurate diagnosis and treatment of young people in an effort to reduce the number of teen suicides.

One ambitious new program that will benefit from the congressional funding is Columbia University's TeenScreen, developed by Dr. David Shaffer and his colleagues working in the field of adolescent depression and teen suicide. The program, run by Laurie Flynn, a leading children's mental health advocate, works with state and local communities to promote and provide a "mental health checkup" for high school–aged kids. By the end of 2004 TeenScreen was active in nearly three hundred communities nationwide.

Unfortunately, mental health screening has run into a buzz saw of criticism from conservative elements who characterize screening as an unwarranted breach of family and privacy rights by federal and local officials. But if we screen school-age children routinely for vision, hearing, and physical well-being, why shouldn't we screen for their emotional well-being as well?

TeenScreen's model involves a two-step test, *administered with parental notification and parental consent*, that includes a prescreening questionnaire followed by a computerized interview program. Because studies show that young people are far more willing to submit to a computerized probe of their emotions than a face-to-face interview with a counselor, TeenScreen's interactive methodology finds teens are more inclined to answer the computer questions honestly.

The initial concern that screening adolescents for suicide was harmful and would lead to an increase in suicidal thinking among suggestive teenagers was examined by a team of child and adolescent psychiatrists. Their findings were surprising and counterintuitive. "High-risk" teens—kids with symptoms of depression or a prior suicide attempt—who were asked outright whether they were harboring thoughts of killing themselves "were neither more suicidal nor distressed than high-risk youth in the control group; on the contrary, depressed students and previous suicide attempters in the experimental group appeared less distressed and suicidal respectively, than high-risk control students."[25]

As a parent, it's hard to know what to make of these findings. Perhaps by broaching the worry head-on and asking your child directly, "Are you thinking of killing yourself," you are breaking the shell of taboo and discomfort—for both of you. Perhaps it provides an opening or even a measure of relief that allows the depth of the pain to be expressed bluntly, directly.

After scrutinizing suicide awareness programs for teen populations, Dr. Shaffer concluded that programs designed to counsel and educate adolescents about suicide often fail to address the root cause of the problem: undiagnosed and untreated depression. In fact, research shows that school-based *suicide* awareness programs (as opposed to programs designed to teach adolescents how to recognize depression) are not always beneficial.[26] Opening up the classroom to a general discussion of suicide "makes some kids more likely to try to kill themselves."[27] Since "suicide clusters" or copycat suicides often follow a single tragic incident that subsequently receives excessive media or community attention, a thoughtful dialogue between students and educators (and/or health professionals), emphasizing the markers and triggers for teen depression over suicide, better serves our children and helps prevent susceptible adolescents from being sucked into the vortex of suicide.

Programs are underway to develop curricula[28] for family practitioners and pediatricians that will help sharpen their tools for diagnosing and treating young people at risk of suicide. But if we really hope to save the lives of children and adolescents, everyone in the community—school counselors, teachers, clinicians, public health and welfare agencies, and volunteer organizations—will have to pitch in and collaborate.

In 2004, a landmark funding bill was enacted, allocating $82 million over three years for mental health screening at the state and local level. Monies are being distributed through the Center for Mental Health Services of the U.S. Department of Health and Human Services. Compare $82 million to billions spent on military spending and disaster relief. It's a drop in the bucket, but it's a start.

If there is a hurt more wrenching than watching your child suffer, I do not know it. There is no doubt that we are raising our kids in a difficult time—we are in uncharted territory. But there is "normal" adolescence and there are teenagers who suffer from depression. The two are very different.

Time is the antidote for the bruising volatility of adolescence. If your teenage children are safe and relatively content, chances are by the time they're in their early twenties you can begin to relax. But if your child were battling cancer, you would not sit by and wait for the disease to run its course. And if your teen is depressed, he or she is up against a life-threatening illness and you need to seek help. Immediately.

See what you lost when you left this world

This sweet old world . . .

The breath from your own lips

The touch of fingertips

A sweet and tender kiss

The sound of a midnight train

Wearing someone's ring

Someone calling your name

Somebody so warm

Cradled in your arm

Didn't you think you were worth anything?

The pounding of your heart's drum

Together with another one

Didn't you think anyone loved you?

from "Sweet Old World"
by Lucinda Williams

3

TUNNEL VISION

Three days after his suicide attempt, Will was admitted to the Psychiatric Institute of Washington for the second time in two months. I sat next to him on a couch in the dreary, dimly lit lobby with his four suicide notes in my purse, ready to turn them over to Dr. Salerian. The letters were the hard evidence linking him to his "crime," and for his transgressions he would pay the price: involuntary commitment to a mental hospital. As a society, we are notably lacking a better solution to treat a suicidally depressed person—either an adult or a child.

I have thought long and hard about how this setting—any institutional setting for the treatment of mental illness—could be improved upon. Shouldn't there be generous amounts of natural light and pleasant music? Certainly. Something pleasing to look at, such as an aquarium, an aviary, or a garden, instead of a droning television in a common room? Exercise, meditation, and fresh air? Maybe a cruise ship with no specific destination, just blue sky and water? Bed linens that don't imprison you in the smell of institutional detergents? Perhaps even little chocolate mints on the pillows? (Please, *no* Enya tapes.) A staff that radiates kindness and good health and a knowledgeable kitchen chef adept at preparing meals people actually want to eat? And, while I fully understand the need to protect suicidal individuals from doing harm to themselves with sharp objects, how many of us really enjoy eating with plastic utensils unless we are required to do so by aviation authorities while airborne?

I realize that my fantasy treatment setting is more likely to be found at an Elizabeth Arden day spa than a treatment facility for the mentally ill. But I am convinced that some subtle changes could be introduced to the institutional trappings of most mental hospitals, which would enhance patient well-being and, I dare say, reduce the length of stay required for most everyone. It could be a win-win: happier patients, less frazzled health care providers, less ruthless HMOs and more solvent insurance carriers.

Hospitalization, however, addresses a single urgent need: security. The psychiatric hospital offers a family in crisis a giant time-out. I would hesitate to say I was "parking" my son at PIW after his suicide attempt, but with no other viable options, I was counting on a team of professionals to have eyes and ears on him 24/7 for as long as it took to muster the next steps. No family, not even a family with supernatural coping skills, is adequately prepared for the challenges following a child's suicide attempt.

The minutes ticked by as we—Will, Bob, Jack, Max, and I—waited for the intake personnel to process the paperwork. A palpable gloom bounded off the surroundings. Will was being admitted to the same unit in the same hospital where I had spent five weeks for the treatment of clinical depression ten years earlier, in 1991—one of life's ugly little ironies. For me, it was eerily disturbing to have him in this environment. So little had changed in the decade since I'd been there: the mauve and ivy-green color scheme (decor reminiscent of late eighties Marriott hotels), bland floral prints hung on the walls, functional hardwood furniture with shredding upholstery, and a constant shuffling population of severely dysfunctional people.

Will too had already marked time in this facility. Following his first weeklong hospitalization at PIW two months prior, Will returned to see a staff psychotherapist, Dr. Vaune Ainsworth, twice weekly, as well as Dr. Salerian, a medical doctor, who monitored and administered Will's medications.* Dr. Ainsworth, a lovely, lithe, fair-haired

---

* At this time, in the United States a psychiatrist is the only mental health professional licensed to dispense medication, except in a few states where nonmedical doctors (psychologists) also are allowed to issue prescriptions.

woman who looks twenty years younger than her age, exuded warmth and tenderness and had engaged Will in cognitive behavioral therapy (a form of "talk therapy") for the previous two months, to delve into the issues and stressors in Will's life that might have triggered or contributed to his depression. This two-pronged approach, medication plus psychotherapy, has been shown to produce the best results for depressed teenagers and children.[1]

Dr. Ainsworth's tiny office was down a corridor off the dim lobby. She spotted me as I was signing all of the family into PIW as "visitors." We hugged, and the two of us cried.

"I am *so* sorry," she lamented. "I didn't see this coming."

"I know. Neither did we; no one did." Her evident guilt over misreading Will's emotions and intentions made me want to comfort *her*.

"You know," she said, "the burden is on us [Drs. Ainsworth and Salerian] to figure out what went wrong with Will, how we missed this." I appreciated her candor and empathy. Clearly, she was shaken by Will's suicide attempt.

Dr. Salerian entered the lobby doors and approached our little family cluster with a pained expression. Without words, I handed him the stack of suicide notes. He glanced through them briefly and turned to Will.

"We'll get to these soon, Will," he said gently. Embarrassed and guilty, Will stared at his feet and Dr. Salerian disappeared through the security doors.

The admission process dragged on. Volumes of paperwork needed to be completed before we could move Will upstairs and onto the ward; the insurance carriers' narrow view of what constitutes a "mental health crisis" required submitting detailed histories before Will's admission could be guaranteed coverage. The hospital's business office made repeat phone calls to insurers, arguing the medical urgency of Will's case.

While we waited in the lobby, the police escorted a woman in the company of her adult child through the doors. The woman was agitated and angry and clearly did not want to be handled by either the cops or her daughter and battled with both.

We sat on the aging couch, with its busted coil springs, and watched the passing scene with a mixture of resignation and dread. I desperately wanted to find a way to connect to Will so I could have a serious conversation with him about depression and about my own struggles with the illness. I strained to reach for a positive note, a tiny inspiring missive. Will wasn't buying it.

Will asked me if I ever wanted to kill myself.

"Oh, God, sweetie, probably a thousand times over. Some years, not a day went by when I didn't figure the only way out of the misery was to end it," I confessed. "Do you remember when I was here when you were little? You were only seven. I was here because I was so depressed and suicidal your dad and Dr. Salerian thought I was a serious risk to myself, and I checked myself in voluntarily."

"So, Mom, what kept you from doing it?" Will asked.

"I couldn't do it because of you and your brother. I wanted to end the pain—just like you do—but I couldn't abandon you. It would have been a betrayal of everything I believed about mothering you guys—and I loved you so much. Even when I'm depressed, I know that the two of you are what matters most in my life." Such is the redemptive power of motherhood. At my lowest moments, the thought of my children kept me alive.

I had my arm around Will and stroked his hair while we spoke in hushed tones; I was trying to soothe him, trying to soothe us both. I had never seen him look so dejected, so sad, and so trapped. He did not want to be back at the psychiatric hospital; for the past three days the entire family had been handling him with kid gloves, soft-pedaling our opposing emotions of hurt and relief, but these emotions were outsized and I am certain Will was able to intuit our despair over the course of action he chose—and I am also sure he felt guilt and shame. Moreover, now he was back in this pathetic institution, in psychiatric limbo, with no clear end in sight.

"Will, it's too early for you to appreciate this insight, but, I know you *will* recover from depression—it's a stupid fucking illness, but there *are* cures." I told him that I had gleaned some knowledge of depression, which caused me to think more positively about certain aspects of the disease.

"Oh, right, like what?" His skepticism was warranted. Depression isn't an illness you would wish on anyone, nor would you suggest it offers ancillary benefits in ways the medical establishment has yet to define.

"Well, in my experience, I think I am able to see things differently from other people. I don't know; this seems a little vague, but I think over time, depression has allowed me to sense things with an intensity I don't think I had before. Do you understand what I'm saying?" I asked. He didn't look at me, but his body language suggested that he was trying to absorb the conversation.

"Maybe because you're more exposed, more raw—more open," I continued. "I *do* think I'm a more compassionate person because of the depression. You will be too, Will. I don't want you to think of this as a total loss. I honestly believe there are some colorful bits to the experience that you can't get anywhere else. Maybe a better understanding of who you are."

Will resisted making eye contact, but his head relaxed on my shoulder.

"You don't see it now, Will, but there *is* a light at the end of the tunnel." At this, his posture shifted. I could tell he was spinning the metaphor. Several seconds passed, then: "Mom, if I thought there was a light at the end of the tunnel, I wouldn't be depressed."

His insight hammered me. "My God, he's right," I thought. *That* is the crux of depression—how do we conquer the sense of futility that becomes the disease's inescapable mantle? How do you crawl out of the breach when there is no incentive to do so? A first-time sufferer of depression doesn't have the inventory to know, "This will pass, I will recover." And what about a teen, whose limited experience of life consists of a catalogue of expectations about the future? Will was wise beyond his years, but it would be a long time before he learned there is life after depression. But how on earth did he get to this point?

* * *

Recently I was at my local bank branch making a routine withdrawal when I was invited by the branch manager to discuss ways to optimize my meager certificate of deposit. The bank manager was a man I'd never met, who I estimated to be in his mid-forties, vital-looking and confident—the ideal personality profile for sales. After pitching the bank's new products, I reluctantly confessed that I was not in the market for new accounts, that I was husbanding the small amount of cash in the certificate of deposit, as it gave me the liquidity I needed while I took the year off to write a book.

"Really, what about?" he asked cheerfully.

I always wince slightly when asked and try to gauge how much information to reveal. It's not like writing a book about historical figures or politics—as everyone is wont to do in Washington.

"I'm writing a book about teen depression and teen suicide."

He sucked in a breath. I had caught him off guard. His posture and demeanor shifted noticeably.

"My daughter's fifteen," he said, slowly punching out the words. "She's been diagnosed bipolar and she cuts herself."

"Oh, my God. I'm so sorry," I empathized.

We spoke for several more minutes about his daughter and he unfurled a familiar litany—evaluation, testing, and misdiagnosis; academic failure and poor high school counseling, discovering his daughter's self-destructive behavior; slogging through the maze of therapy and medication; the effects on the rest of his family; and even, he confided, the toll his daughter's problems was taking on his marriage.

We swapped names of doctors and programs and I wished him and his family well before I headed out of the bank, unnerved by his confession and evident pain.

I do not often elicit casual confidences; I am not that sort of person and Washington is not that kind of town. But I have found over the past year that whenever the topic of this book comes up in conversation, among friends or with strangers, it dredges a bed of sorrows I did not know was out there. Those who are touched most directly morph into atoms of anxiety as they recount a son, daughter, or grandchild who has been caught in a similar downdraft. Not only does the subject touch an exposed nerve, but almost everyone I meet has a story to tell of a teen in serious trouble. And it causes me to ask the obvious: What is happening to our children? What changes has our culture wrought over the past thirty years to precipitate this cataclysmic shift in our children's well-being?

I can only surmise that *it's no one thing:* it's not just more drugs, more alcohol, violence on television; it's not the heightened emphasis on consumerism or the rapid pace of communications; it's not the surge in single-parent families; it's not the failing schools nor the lack of community or sense of shared values. Some or all of these factors play a part, but *it is no one thing,* and to suggest otherwise is both disingenuous and delusional. And as I struggle to make sense of my own child's history, sorting for clues and causality, I find it is as tangled as a batch of crossed computer wires.

You look back at your child's brief history and it is as though you are viewing it through a kaleidoscope; the recollections are fluid and mutate into several variations on one particular episode you thought you knew by heart. If your child is struggling, you are looking for markers from the past: Was it the time we laughed at him when he told us a flying saucer had landed on the playground? Or the time you called to say you missed your flight and you weren't going to make it back in time from a trip out of town to be there for a birthday? Was it an overly harsh reprimand or changing schools in the seventh grade?

And then there are the gut-wrenchers, the seismic traumas: You announce to the children that you and your spouse are getting divorced. Or that a sibling is seriously ill or that you are moving halfway across the country and they will be forced to leave friends and family. And if you and your children are still intact by the time they are ten or twelve, their kaleidoscopic histories split into multiple fragile splinters and spin away from you.

If your teenage child falls ill, or is hurt or traumatized by forces you think you might have handled better when he or she was a child, inevitably you wonder, "What did I do wrong?" But like depression, the answer is that it is probably no one thing—no single event but a combination of events, mixed up with biology, genetics, and social pressures. Nonetheless, parenting today raises the bar on self-inflicted guilt.

My son was elfin. He had light-brown feathers for hair that flew away from his scalp in opposing directions, and with saucer blue eyes and a Cheshire cat grin, he was impish and adorable. And he played tricks on us from the get-go.

With all due respect to the medical establishment, everything we learned from our doctors about the baby we were expecting in the fall of 1983 proved to be wrong. First, there was the matter of Will's sex. Repeated sonograms led our bright young team of female obstetricians to pronounce that the baby in utero was a girl. Baby Susanna.

We announced the news to Max, who began to divvy up the toys for his little sister-to-be (trucks would be all his; she could have some of the stuffed animals), and I began to contemplate how to introduce a pinkish cast into our household hitherto dominated by brown- and green-hued guys.

Midway through the pregnancy, our obstetrical team began to show concern because I was carrying higher than normal levels of amniotic fluid. Max had been delivered by a lovely Dutch obstetrician in her sixties, whose vast experience and claim to having brought thousands of babies into the world were a perfect match for a first-time mother. But her practice had expanded to meet the demands of Washington's baby-boomer moms; she hired a new team of well-educated, eager young doctors and she retired from the practice of obstetrics. The fresh crop of obstetricians rotated in and out of my pregnancy, depending on who was on duty on any day. When flags were raised signaling possible trouble, the prospect sent the obstetrical team into overdrive, but not in a patient-friendly way.

Given their limited experience, an anomaly—a pregnancy with risks and challenges—was something to get excited about. For them, my atypical pregnancy was intriguing, a medical mystery, and we were sent home from frequent checkups with flyers about spina bifida and hydrocephalus and other developmental abnormalities. The team could not agree on a plan of action. At five months, with a viable pregnancy in the works, termination was no longer an option. Some highly experimental in utero surgical interventions were posited and then taken off the table. As the parents, we were both frustrated and profoundly anxious.

By the seventh month, I was so unhappy with my doctors and with their lack of clear guidance that I sought out my first obstetrician, the Dutch doctor. With her vast wisdom and experience, she quickly downplayed the risks that I'd been led to believe were evident and reminded me, "My dear, there are no guarantees in pregnancy." She continued, "These days everyone expects—no, *demands*—beautiful, healthy, perfect babies. I wish it weren't so, but pregnancy and birth always carry risk. That's why we call it 'the miracle of childbirth.'" She was right. Risk is a given. Bringing new life into the world is the ultimate roll of the dice.

At the next appointment with my medical team, I announced, "Look, you haven't given me enough evidence to conclude that we're up against an elevated risk of a severe abnormality, so we're not going to entertain the possibility anymore. I'm going to bank on the odds that this baby will be well." I closed the door to further discussion and awaited my baby's birth.

Will was due on November 22, a few days before Thanksgiving. My mother flew out from California and began baking and lavishing attention on Max, our earnest and intense two-year-old. December 1 came and went and still no new baby. In profile I looked like a Volkswagen beetle. I was massive, sluggish, and impatient for the event to be over.

My doctors and I had agreed that if it appeared we were dealing with a large baby—a baby weighing over eight and a half pounds—we would resort to a caesarean section. Going into the last two weeks of the pregnancy, several members of the medical team assured me that this baby was at most eight pounds. Once again, our Will fooled us.

The doctors decided to induce labor on Wednesday, December 7—a full two weeks after the due date. I was exasperated; they were increasingly concerned about the baby's status. Nothing was going according to plan. My mother was scheduled to return home on the tenth. Unless the baby came soon, she would have come and gone without ever having set eyes on her new grandchild.

In retrospect, once we were past the due date, I wish I had lobbied harder to induce sooner. December 7, Pearl Harbor Day, "a day that will live in infamy." If dates of birth bestow symbolic meaning, I should have argued for the sixth, the Feast of Saint Nicholas, a jolly sort of day, rather than a day marked by a bloody American humiliation.

The birth did not go well for either of us. A chemical drip designed to trigger labor guaranteed that contractions went from zero to sixty—full throttle. No gradual warm-up, the way nature likes it to happen.

"God, I remember now how this feels, and I remember I didn't much like it the first time," I told Bob. "Lock me up if I ever bring up the subject of more children."

By 7:30 PM, I had demanded and received an epidural, which took the edge off the seismic contractions—but only temporarily. The team doctor assigned to see me through the birth voiced concern that the baby might be larger than gauged earlier. I thought, "Dammit, here we go again. Why can't they get this right?" There was talk of a caesarean, but at 9:00 PM, we were wheeled into the delivery room to see if a combination of pushing and forceps could manipulate the baby through the birth canal.

At 9:30 PM, Will emerged—partially. His head exited, but his shoulders were stuck. The doctors had badly misjudged his size. He was a huge baby. The obstetrician wrenched him free by extricating and then yanking his right arm out of the birth canal. There was a snap and what sounded like a small animal gargling. She had broken his collarbone in order to extract the rest of his body.

At 9:35 PM, we delivered a badly battered infant boy—not a Susanna—bruised from head to toe the color of ripe eggplant, weighing an astonishing ten pounds, eight ounces. On the spot we decided to name him William, after Bob's father.

I held my breath and prayed as the doctors conducted a swift but thorough examination. The pediatrician on duty in the delivery room called out, "The baby's just fine. Shut down the ICU." And through a distillation of drugs and exhaustion, I heard the medical team let out a cheer.

President Dwight D. Eisenhower's insight into the nature of war is applicable to the birth of a child. Eisenhower reflected, "Every war will surprise you." The same is true of a newborn. You can plan, fantasize, make outlandish predictions (become immobilized by fear), but every child enters life setting off a serendipitous and unpredictable chain of events. Maybe *that* is the miracle of childbirth.

Will surprised us all—his sex, his enormous weight—and best of all, he confounded the doctors' dire warnings of a "severe abnormality." He was battered and bloodied after the rugged birth, but so was I. And wasn't it fitting that after all we had been through together—the traumatized pregnancy, the anxious and overextended wait, the botched delivery—he and I trumped some serious odds? We were a team! We had won a primal struggle. He was just my kind of kid.

September 1992
"My Family"
by Willy D. (8½)

I have a mom, a dad, a brother, a turtel, and two fish. Thay are all nice to me. My fish east fish food. My turtel eats turtel food, grownd up beaf and ledis.

My dad's favrit contre is Italy. He was born in Hollywood, California. My dad likes Christmas the best. We got him a bike for Christmas. He was born in the year 1949.

My mom is nice too. I love her choclet chip cookes. She is very biyudifol. She is a good cooker. I love my mom. She's the best.

My brother picks on me a lot but I stil like him. He is very funny. It is relly his turtel but I call it mine.

That's my famly.

*   *   *

I recently invited Will's former kindergarten teacher to meet me for tea in a local café. Will started attending a parochial nursery school in Washington when he was almost three. Max was ready for kindergarten, so we enrolled both boys at the same time at Holy Trinity Elementary School, a small Catholic parish school, run by a principal with a reputation for fostering a sense of community and values.

At a time when many public school systems were agonizing over moral relativism and whose values to impart to students, I was impressed by the confidence with which Holy Trinity defied the wisdom of the times and promoted standards of compassion and decency that I believed were hallmarks of common sense.

Although Bob was educated in Catholic schools and the boys were baptized in the Roman Catholic Church, we had not assumed that we would send the kids to parochial schools prior to deciding on Holy Trinity. But we looked around and liked what we saw. We decided that if we were going to pay for private education, at the very least the boys would receive a well-grounded, values-based education in exchange for our tuition dollars. It was money well spent.

Trish Bickford (now Trish Petty) was Will's kindergarten teacher for two years, from September 1988 to June 1990. He loved her and she took a special interest in him. She followed his progress at the school through sixth grade, and for years after he left Holy Trinity, she kept track of his whereabouts through parents and friends. We were as fond of her as she was of Will. With that in mind, I wanted to talk to her about how she remembered Will as a small child.

Trying to uncover the origins of your child's depression is like peeling an onion. You shift through thin membranes of recollection, small incidents and large, looking for clues. Maybe there was something there at the beginning, something glaring that we missed in those early years.

Trish arrived for our late-afternoon get-together looking as youthful and buoyant as I remembered her. As a brand-new teacher in the mid-1980s, she was a dimpled, athletic, chipper young woman from upstate New York who sported clogs and striped kneesocks. Just a few years out of college, she impressed us with her enthusiasm and insightfulness about her students. Eighteen years later, she had shed the clogs and kneesocks, replaced them with a pearl necklace and a classy sweater set, but she still looked much younger than her years.

Still teaching kindergarten at Holy Trinity, she talked about the early years of her career with fondness and nostalgia. I had to ask her, "Trish, what do you remember about Will when he was little?"

"He was adorable, Gail. He seemed like one of the happiest little kids I've ever taught. He was a little shy, but playful, and I can still remember hearing his giggle across the room when he and one of his buddies would be huddled in a corner of the class, telling each other stories."

"Will's giggle—yeah, I remember that, too. It was definitely a distinctive giggle." I too was succumbing to the nostalgia of the moment.

We sat in the light of a late-autumn afternoon on a bench outside of a Dupont Circle tea parlor. It felt good to be in the company of someone whose judgment about children I valued, telling me what I wanted to hear, no less.

Trish and Holy Trinity epitomized the kind of educational experience that few families have nowadays. She and the school held an institutional memory, a kind of road map to our children's early lives. As I try to piece together a puzzle, a portrait of my son, albeit biased and incomplete, where better to start than his kindergarten teacher?

"You know, Gail," she continued, "what you guys have been through with the kids, with Will, I don't get it. If there was something there early on, I'd like to think I would have seen it."

"How do you spot a kid who's clearly showing signs of mental illness that early, Trish? Does it turn up in your classroom as something you recognize immediately?"

"Nowadays it does. Now you see kids starting school—remember, this is just kindergarten—and they're already worried. They're only five and they're worried. I see fewer happy kids than ever before and it really bothers me. I think if you had kids in elementary school now, it would be a very different experience than the one you had twenty years ago."

"What do you think explains the change?" I asked.

"Parents are driven, children are driven; the parents are so anxious for their kids to succeed, some are making themselves sick. The kids, even the young ones, are under a lot of pressure. And it makes for seriously unhappy children."

I believe her.

In the spring of 1989 we met with Holy Trinity's principal, Ann Marie Crowley, and Trish Bickford to assess the results of Will's standardized testing, which the school administered to all of its students at the end of kindergarten. Will had tested in the ninety-ninth percentile across the board. But with a December birthday and the school's policy of holding back boys whose birthdays fell after September 1 for a second year of kindergarten before they advanced to first grade, Trish and Ann Marie weren't sure what to do with Will. Should he remain with Trish for an extra year of kindergarten despite his high performance on the standardized test, or should we advance him to first grade, where he would be the youngest kid in his class? Would a second year of kindergarten bore him silly?

Ann Marie argued, "You know, Holy Trinity might not be the right fit for Will. He's a child with exceptional skills; he might just be better off in a more tailored program that could offer him more individual attention."

"Oh, God, Ann Marie, I don't want him in a 'gifted and talented' program—I don't really want him anywhere but here at Trinity." Bob agreed.

"Look, he's a happy kid. He's got great friends here. Our goal is a *happy* kid. I mean, I've known a number of kids who were singled out as gifted and talented, and from what I've seen some of them thrive but some of them become downright miserable. Do you really believe that he'd be better off somewhere else?"

Ann Marie thought about it and said, "No, I think we can work with him here at Trinity, but I'd recommend that we use the extra year of kindergarten. All of the boys benefit from the added maturity, and let's let Will be a kid a while longer." Trish offered to augment his kindergarten routine with special programming designed to keep him interested and challenged. Bob and I left the meeting content with our mutual decision. Will was slated to spend another year in kindergarten with Trish Bickford.

At the end of his first year of kindergarten a number of Will's closest friends were promoted to Mrs. O'Connor's first grade. Most of the kids in the tight-knit school had been together since they were toddlers in the nursery program. We had to break the news to Will that he would be staying behind. We told him he would still be able to play with his old friends; they were all going to be on the same playground at the same time, and he could still spend time with them on weekends, whenever he wanted to. And, we insisted, he would make new friends with the new group of kids coming into kindergarten in the fall.

But in spite of our sugarcoating the transition, Will was troubled by this turn of events—the first bump in an otherwise blissful childhood. He seemed confused as he struggled to make sense of the decision. We tried, unsuccessfully, to get him to talk about it. I waited a few days and thought it best to let the news sink in. On a June day, at the end of the school term, when I picked Will up at school, I decided to broach the topic again.

"Willy, you *do* know why you're going to spend another year with Ms. Bickford, don't you? Do you understand why it's not time for you to go to first grade yet?"

"Yep," he said matter-of-factly. "It's 'cause I'm dumb."

I was floored. I scooped him up in my arms and twirled him around.

"No, you little goofball!" I laughed, hoping to lighten his angst. "It's 'cause you're *too* young. You are *one smart cookie*. Everyone says so. Ms. Bickford says so. Mrs. Crowley says so. Ms. Bickford wants to keep you with her so you and she can work on special stuff. Just for you, when the other kids are napping. You're a smart guy, sweetie. And if anyone tells you you're not, I will eat them up."

The answer seemed to satisfy him; at least it was not an issue again until the start of the new school year, when friends from last year's kindergarten class turned up on the playground dressed up in the simple gray and blue uniforms worn by first-graders—the first outward marker that you were moving up the elementary school hierarchy. If he was troubled by the shift, he did not let on, and he quickly acquired new friends in his second round of kindergarten.

In retrospect, was keeping him at Holy Trinity the right thing to do? Was holding him back for an extra year of kindergarten wise? Did we fail to seize an opportunity to challenge an extra-bright kid to live up to the full measure of his potential? I still place a higher value on a "happy child"—as hard to define as that may be—over a "gifted and talented" one. We can all be faulted for lapses in judgment when it comes to raising our children, but I trusted my instincts about Will and I am still pretty certain we made the right choice for him.

Will was five years old in the spring of 1989 when he joined the Blue Sharks soccer team, coached by Jack Brady, father to Will's closest buddy, John. In the early years, the Blue Sharks team was made up of five- and six-year-old kids from Holy Trinity—tiny kids, just a couple of feet taller than the soccer ball. Will was a natural, a tenacious little runner who played forward and sometimes goalie. John had talked Will into signing up; the boys had been best friends since nursery school and they were inseparable. Their friendship had far-reaching consequences we hardly would have forecast at the time.

As personal histories go, my own trajectory intertwined season after season with the lives and fate of the Blue Sharks (who huddled for team cheer, "Ha! Ha! Ha! Ha! Ha!" at the beginning of each game). Both of my boys continued to excel at soccer well into their teens, and by the time they moved on to high school and other interests, Bob and I had separated and I had fallen in love with Jack, whom I married almost ten years to the day after Will's first soccer game.

Besides sports, one of Will's unique gifts was—and is—his facility with language. As soon as he was able to string a phrase together, he demonstrated an ability to capture visuals with a clever or fantastical description. "Wow! Look, a bird race!" was how he described, at age three, a triangulated flock of geese migrating south. Squirrels chasing one another across an electrical wire strung between utility poles became a "squirrel circus"; blinking red and green Christmas decorations were "having a light party."

He was barely able to read and write when he began making up fanciful stories about spacecraft and monsters, and on long car rides, we could count on Will to keep the driver awake by spinning a never-ending yarn, linked with the absolute segue to end all segues, ". . . And, you know what?" Later in life Will would use his writing skills to expose some of his darkest moments.

My Big Fish

My big fish
Just floats around
Slowly moving
Without a sound.

The seasons are changing
Outside it's snowing
But my fish just sits there
Wading and growing.

My fish is no dummy
He just likes to swim.
And if that's all he wants
I think I will let him.

Willy, age 6

If I were tempted to measure my children's development by a psychologist's checklist, I'd have to believe that Will sailed through early childhood without major mishap, no horrible catastrophes—just standard everyday fare. We even had a classic "oedipal" encounter one afternoon, when Will, age four, suggested that we take steps to find Bob a new place to live so that he and I could marry. Whoaaa. He caught me off guard, but I tried to handle the moment with the sensitivity and aplomb of a female Fred Rogers: "Sweetie, that just won't happen. Dad and I are already married and you will get married one day too to someone you love."

He furrowed his brow, his lower lip jutting out, as he glared at me, unconvinced and clearly dissatisfied with my response.

"And," I continued optimistically, "she'll cook all of your favorite foods and she'll smell wonderful," assuming these attributes were central to the limited scope of his desire.

"But, why can't we find Dad a new wife and *then* I can marry you?" The endearing little nitwit was really pressing his case and I wanted to get out of the conversation before it became any more surreal.

"Well," I proposed, "since we're all pretty happy right here—you, me, Dad, and Max—why don't we just live together for a while and see how things work out?"

It was logic fit for a four-year-old. "Okay." He seemed satisfied with the notion and ran off happy as a clam. The subject never came up again. His childhood was about as untroubled as a kid's could be: Max doted on him, his dad adored him, and he was my happy-go-lucky good-luck charmer.

Thursday morning, March 15, 2001, found us—Jack, Bob, Max, Will, and me—in an overcrowded patient conference room on the fourth floor of the Psychiatric Institute of Washington. With us were Dr. Vaune Ainsworth and the psychiatric social worker assigned to Will's case. We assembled in a chaotic little cluster around a speakerphone on a side console and placed a call to Melissa, in San Francisco, so she could be patched into the family meeting.

Max, who had been with us since early Monday morning, needed to get to the airport later in the day; he would return to the West Coast and college and to midterm exams he had asked his teachers to postpone.

The space was so cramped that Will sat hunched up on the floor, looking uncomfortable and distant. There are times in your life when you are happy to be the center of your family's attention, but for Will, this certainly was not one of those times.

Dr. Vaune Ainsworth began by suggesting that Max be given an opportunity to express any thoughts he might have before he left Washington and said good-bye to Will.

"Is there anything you'd like to say to Will, Max? I know you have to get back to school and I thought you might want to convey your feelings about Will's suicide attempt before you leave today."

Max stared unabashedly at Will, who reddened with humiliation and guilt before deciding to fix his gaze on a coffee stain on the carpet directly in front of his feet.

Silence.

"Is there anything you can say to Max, Will, that might make him feel better about leaving today?" Vaune prompted.

"Yeah, well, you know I love ya, buddy, even if you're a jerk most of the time," Will offered in an attempt to defuse the tension.

"Max?" Vaune probed expectantly.

Another several seconds, then, "Yeah, Will . . . you broke my heart. You really . . . broke my heart."

Stunned silence. And then tears. Hot, irrepressible, noiseless tears made their collective slide down each of our faces. Leave it to Max with his intensity and unflinching honesty to lob a charge so bald and raw. And true.

Max struck a note so true—and tapped the feeling we each fought hard to keep under wraps for the past few days: we hurt horribly. What good could possibly come of this awful event? We were all broken and vulnerable—and Will more so than anyone.

No one in my family thought I would take to mothering. I had a reputation for taking myself a little too seriously, and my notions about work and career were a little overvaunted in their minds. My younger sister, Suzy, was married and had two children before I was shoved in the direction of motherhood by a hormonal surge, which whacked me unexpectedly in my thirtieth year. Suddenly I saw infants everywhere, like spring bulbs pushing up cartoon shoots in fast motion. I followed toddlers out of the corner of my eye with the concentration I had once reserved for shoe-store windows; I smelled babies in my sleep. I was hooked. I wanted babies.

Since I had made plain my ambivalence about motherhood in my twenties, my family was naturally skeptical when I announced that Bob and I were expecting. My sister kiddingly questioned me, "Frankly, Gail, are you sure you're mother material?" borrowing a famous turn of phrase my mother had coined.

"You know, I'm just not mother material" was our mother's way of explaining away occasional maternal lapses and an allergy to all things mandated or participatory, such as PTA, Brownie Scouts, graduation ceremonies, and mother/daughter teas.

My family's doubts about my commitment to motherhood were needless, and although I was beset with concern for the kind of world into which I was bringing new life, I never doubted my ability to be a good mother.

I loved my infant children with intensity and ease, it was like discovering a latent talent for the cello, or waking to discover that overnight you had mastered the Italian language and that you spoke it with elegance and fluency. My children made me a person of substance: finally, I *was* somebody. Motherhood made me a take-charge kind of person; it was my personal charter cruise into a Jules Verne voyage of discovery.

That is not to say I was never challenged. I was, as all parents are. Challenged constantly, mercilessly, and unwittingly.

If I thought I should be overly concerned about one of my children, it fell to my wonderfully intense, sometimes cranky, oldest child, Max, to ratchet up my anxiety on a regular basis.

The first time I ever held my newborn son Max, he stared at my face with a focused intensity that pierced my inner core. He screwed up his tiny worried brow and sent a penetrating stun-gun glare my way, as if to say, "Oh my God, Mom! It's you . . . I sure hope you know what you're doing." I hooked him up to my right breast, we revved up our engines, and off we went on our dizzying adventure.

As the firstborn, Max fulfilled all of the requisite birth-order postulates. He was serious and occasionally fearful. He was a demanding little perfectionist who insisted upon strict adherence to a rigid routine with regard to all things elemental: same bath time and bedtime, one favorite pair of pajamas, the standard-issue sweat suit (an inconspicuous navy blue jersey with a hooded sweatshirt, hood tied under the chin at all times), and the same children's book at bedtime every night for a year, Maurice Sendak's beloved and quirky *Where the Wild Things Are*.

When Max was two, Bob bought a kiddie seat and attached it to the back of a bicycle. We thought Max would enjoy cruising around our Capitol Hill neighborhood with Bob. Before Bob pulled up with the bike in front of our house, I strapped Max into a yellow child's bike helmet, twice the size of his head, making him look like a bumblebee on steroids. Max loved the helmet, but as soon as he laid eyes on the bike, with its mounted child seat, he backed away, eyes widening with terror as he sputtered, "Ooops! No thanks. Too scary for me!" and scurried upstairs to hide under his bed. And Max asked the deep, difficult phenomenological questions like "Whose mother is this pea?" or "What if Willy pops?" or "Why is the airplane teeny-tiny in the sky and big on the ground?" He constantly challenged me to explain precepts about the natural world I thought I'd left behind in high school physics class.

Even though Max entertained each new encounter as though approaching a potentially explosive lab experiment, he could be as stubborn as a wino with a lottery ticket. He compensated for his timidity in public by morphing into a hard-to-handle terror at home. He famously graced family reunions with such outrageous behavior that after one such gathering, my mother remarked, "Gail, you're going to have to do something with that child." Yes, I conceded, it was true, but what to do? Is there such a thing as a Jesuit military academy for four-year-olds? Classically, when Max was good, he was exemplary, and when he was bad . . . what a monster! He never managed to find a middle ground.

With Max staked out at one end of the family behavioral matrix, it came as no surprise that Will gravitated to the polar opposite. What was exceptional, however, is the way Max welcomed Will into the dynamic.

At age two, Max was the center of his own universe, but he met Will's arrival with awe and delight: he thought that Will was *his* baby, a gift lovingly bestowed by his parents. As Max said the first time he saw and held Will in his arms, "This is *my* little tiny, tiny Willy, Will." Who is to argue with the logic of a two-year-old? We decided not to disabuse him of the notion.

Will, in Max's eyes, was the gift that kept on giving. Will was there in the morning when Max woke up and throughout the day to amuse or fuss over. Max behaved like a mini-parent: "Mom, Will needs a new diaper," "Mom, Will doesn't like those little peas," "Will needs a nap," or "Did you give Willy his vitamins?"

Max tore up the household and threw tantrums; Will looked on beatifically. Max careened through the "terrible twos"—and threes and fours—like a power mower; Will rolled along as cheerful as an ice cream truck. Will could do no wrong.

But I am sure he could have—or, more appropriately, I am sure he should have. Being the "good kid" in a family, constantly teetering at that end of the seesaw, can be a burden. There is a price to pay when you are "adorable," the kid everyone holds up as an example, when you are sweet and friendly and make no enemies on the playground. And later, when you make the honor roll (almost always), and make your friends laugh and your parents proud—all of the time.

I carry an indelible memory: We were in Jack's Volkswagen van with all four kids on the way to visit the Baltimore aquarium. It must have been spring break, 1992 or 1993; Will was about ten years old. As our van pulled up to a stop sign, a vagrant wobbled into the crosswalk. The old man was decidedly drunk. He stopped in the middle of the crosswalk, turned and faced the car, and began an incoherent rant. Cars behind us began honking ferociously.

I remarked, "That poor old drunk guy better find a safer place to give a speech than the middle of the street." The kids were hanging over the back of our seats to get a better look, waiting to see what would happen next, when Will remarked, "Yeah, or he's gonna be a old dead drunk guy soon."

Jack and I exchanged a sideways glance. "Was that Will?" Heads swiveled and all eyes were on Will. We were stunned, and slightly amused. It was such an uncharacteristically caustic remark for Will.

"Whoa, Willy! That's a little harsh, don't you think?" I exclaimed.

"Uh-oh, could this be a new, leaner, meaner Will?" Jack teased.

"Yeah, it's the New Will!" the rest of the kids chimed in.

Will looked mortified and stung by everyone's reaction. His was a harmless remark—nothing really out of the ordinary for a ten-year-old boy, but the rest of us jumped on it, half jokingly, suggesting that Will was finally exhibiting an age-appropriate, edgier side to his unassailably sweet nature.

"Ooooh, ooooh, the New Will," the kids chanted tauntingly. As I recall, we didn't hear much from Will the rest of the day.

In the intervening years, when any one of us teased him about some minor transgression and suggested that it was further evidence of the "New Will," he took umbrage. He made it plain that he did not appreciate the reference.

"Don't say that 'New Will' thing anymore, okay?"

"Okay," we agreed.

Will never managed to own up to his failings—normal, everyday, universal human failings. How big were these tiny lapses anyway? He was only a kid—he never grabbed an opportunity to be outrageously over the line. But the die was cast: he was a "good kid." In his late teens, his sense of who he was would crash headlong into who he thought he had to be—for his own sake and for ours—and the consequences would be calamitous.

If Will had a difficult time coming to terms with failure, he had an even harder time dealing with pain or anger. He never appeared worried. But all kids worry. According to the U.S. Surgeon General's office, roughly thirteen percent of children between ages nine and seventeen are troubled by worries that border on full-blown "anxiety disorders."[2] I was a worried child; my son Max was a worried child. But not Will; Will never seemed worried.

I had anxious, hideous worries, bedtime worries that, by age seven, developed into a nightly ritual of tears. One night the worries would be prompted by a scolding (unjustified, of course) by my first-grade teacher; the next night I was beset with terror about the atom bomb. I can't say that I've ever successfully conquered "the worries."

Max also worried big worries and small. But over time Max and I developed a routine for confronting and managing his worries. Before bedtime, the hour in which most children's laundry cart of worries tips over, Max and I would take inventory. And then we would walk the worries back: "If that [dreadful thing] were to happen, then what?" "And what would we do about it [the diminished dreadful thing] then?" "And then what would happen?" until we stripped away all of the dastardly possibilities and were left holding on to each other and anchored to the rock of family.

"Max, you will always have us, your mom, your dad, your brother, your family." "We will always take care of you." "We love you, and we have each other." This technique (which I later discovered mirrors some of the fundamentals of cognitive behavioral therapy) worked most of the time. But Will never participated in our "soothing ritual"; he never seemed to need to.

Will did, however, have a habit of falling victim to stomachaches on Monday mornings. On average, he missed a Monday every month or two. I didn't think it was particularly significant. After all, not many of us are eager to go to school or work on Monday morning. Perhaps we should have taken it as a warning.

Just recently, I came across an article that suggests, "In the prepubescent child, depressive symptoms are commonly expressed as physical complaints, such as stomachaches."[3] Well, for heaven's sake! Like so much else about successful parenting, I missed that signpost.

Will never worried overtly, but he did tell fibs, particularly when it came to schoolwork. He went to lengths to cover up missing assignments and overdue homework.

"Will, do you have any homework?"

"Nope."

"Did you finish all of your assignments?"

"Yep."

Often, a call or a note from a perplexed teacher forced him to ante up the truth. When presented with the evidence, he showed terrible remorse and embarrassment. He claimed he lied because he got in over his head and he didn't want to disappoint us. Perhaps so. I don't believe Will was lazy. Most educators refuse to apply that characterization to children, insisting that *all* children can be motivated to learn if given the right stimulation.

Bob and I suspected Will did not know how to manage his time, so we collaborated with his teachers to help him organize his schoolwork while he was still in elementary school. But in middle school and even into high school, Will fell victim to his own charm: teachers cut him slack because he was likable, and when he fell too far behind he made matters worse by covering it up. So what of "the good kid" moniker? When, in his teens, Will became ill, seriously depressed, he fell behind in all matters both crucial and insignificant, and he tried to cover up the depression, too.

It is important to talk to your kids about depression. Openly. Candidly. And at intervals as they grow up.

Since depression showed up in generations of family members on both sides, it was apparent that we were at risk of handing down a genetic predisposition for the illness to our children. It is chilling when you think about it in retrospect: As a person with depression, had I known that my children would inherit a fifty percent chance of being struck down with major depression, would I have decided to forego motherhood?

Knowing our genetic heritage is important because it tells us where we came from and who we are. It also provides a rough guide, a biological treasure hunt, mapping out who our offspring may be.

Researchers are getting close to identifying the "depression gene," or genes. Although the "nature versus nurture" debate still occupies sizable bandwidth in psychiatry circles, there is enough evidence to suggest that depression begins with an underlying biological risk. The results of findings published in July 2003 were heralded as changing "the paradigm for how we think about genes and psychiatric disorders," according to Thomas R. Insel, director of the National Institute of Mental Health.[4]

Researchers focused on the gene, identified and designated 5-HTT, in studies carried out on a group of nearly nine hundred New Zealanders, tracked from age three to twenty-six, to measure which of the subjects were beset by depression and which were not, given the same set of life experiences, tragedies, and setbacks.[5] The study demonstrated that the long variant of the gene 5-HTT provided "emotional resilience";[6] the subjects with two long genes did not fall victim to depression after suffering adversity or tragedy, whereas the subjects with one short gene and one long gene, or two short genes, were more likely to become ill in the aftermath of a stressful event. Renowned psychiatrist Dr. Peter Kramer, author of *Listening to Prozac*, reports:

> It made no difference whether the subjects had been mistreated severely in childhood, nor whether they had encountered deaths in the family, ill health or financial losses. But among subjects with one or two short genes, adversity, whether early or recent, led to an increase in depression at age 26.[7]

These findings were replicated in a U.S. study, published in 2004, which demonstrated that infants with the same variants of the 5-HTT gene identified with depression in adults, and who were reared in settings where documented child abuse had occurred, suffered an increased risk for psychopathology due to "environment interaction between experiences of stress and the serotonin transporter gene."[8]

As I said earlier, depression is the result of no single thing, but what we can surmise at this point from the scientific investigations is that several things must go wrong at the same time. Or as Dr. Kramer concludes, "Depression has a firm basis in harm to the brain. Liability to that harm arises not only from pertinent events but also from inborn vulnerability."[9]

After my own diagnosis of depression, I thought it was important to begin coloring in the outlines of depression for my children, filling in the details and providing information regarding family members and their different experiences with the disease. As they moved from childhood to adolescence I wanted them to be able to discern the difference between feelings such as "sad," "angry," and "discouraged" from "hopelessness," "despair," and "resignation." We talked about symptoms and signals to watch for and what they should do if and when symptoms turned up.

If I were a betting person, I would have placed money on my irascible, temperamental, intense, and challenging son, Max. *He* was the one I watched for signs of depression. *He* was the one I thought had been tapped with the "at risk" genetic marker. But not our insouciant, lovable Will. Not Will. Never would I have imagined Will would be the one to take the hit.

Oh, oh deep water

Black and cold

Like the night.

I stand with arms wide open

I've run a twisted line

I'm a stranger

In the eyes

Of the Maker.

from "The Maker"
by Daniel Lanois

4

LIKE MOTHER, LIKE SON

Three months after Will's suicide attempt, Will's father and I found our-selves face-to-face for the first time with Will's principal psychiatrist at Montana Academy, the therapeutic boarding school in which he was enrolled for ten months. By the time we met Dr. Dennis Malinak for a cup of coffee in the lobby of a Hampton Inn in Kalispell, Montana, Will had been in Dennis's care for six weeks. Although we had spoken with Dennis dozens of times by phone, this was our first family visit since Will began the program on May 1; I didn't know what to expect.

I was pretty certain I spotted Dennis as he strode into the lobby at the appointed hour, 10:00 AM, Saturday morning, June 16. He had the carriage and demeanor of a man on a mission and he glanced around the reception area trying to figure out which of the many hotel guests congregating in the lobby might be Will's parents. I judged him to be in his early forties, tall, handsome build and thinning brown hair, and he was dressed casually in jeans and a flannel shirt.

"Are you guys Bob and Gail?" We exchanged pleasantries and staked out a quiet corner of the lobby where we could talk privately. Soon enough we would be able to see Will and take him off campus for an overnight visit, but beforehand, it was clear that Dennis had a num-ber of questions he wanted to put to us. He had seen Will every day, individually and in group settings, for the past month and a half, but it was obvious that the shards of information he was gleaning from Will, scanty offerings by therapeutic standards, didn't add up in Dennis's

mind, and he was hoping we could demystify certain fragments of
Will's emotional history.

"So tell me about when you and Bob divorced," Dennis probed.
"How did Will react to the news of the divorce?" Bob and I tried to
remember the details.

There is no such thing as a "good divorce" for a kid. The effect of
divorce on children is the medical equivalent of infecting them with a
flesh-eating bacteria: they may, over time, become resistant to its
effects, or it may savage them.

Academics have been investigating the effects of divorce on children
since the late 1950s, but until recently, no one had undertaken a long-
term look at the issue, tracking children from youth to adulthood. Over
twenty-five years ago, psychologist and recognized authority on divorce
Judith Wallerstein initiated the Children of Divorce Project, and documented her findings in the best-selling book *The Unexpected Legacy of
Divorce: The 25-Year Landmark Study* (Judith S. Wallerstein, Julia Lewis,
and Sandra Blakeslee, Hyperion Press, 2000). One of the study's most
significant findings suggested that long-term emotional well-being of
children depended more on what happened in the aftermath of the
divorce than on the family dynamics at the time of the breakup.

Nevertheless, Wallerstein reported:

> For children and adolescents, the separation and its aftermath
> was the most stressful period of their lives. The family rupture
> evoked an acute sense of shock, intense fears, and grieving which
> the children found overwhelming. Over one half of the entire
> group were distraught, with a sense that their lives had been com-
> pletely disrupted. Less than 10 percent of the children were
> relieved by their parents' decision to divorce despite the high inci-
> dence of exposure to physical violence during the marriage.[1]

In June 1992, Bob and I sadly but resolutely moved to dissolve our
marriage of fifteen years and an intimate relationship that stretched

over two decades. There was no shouting. There had been no fights and hardly any real arguments or major disagreements. The slide began after the children were born, and over the course of ten years the interlocking fibers of our relationship disintegrated as if they had been dipped in a slow-acting chemical solvent from an undetectable source.

My former husband is a good and kind man; he was the sort of father people held up as an example. Trying to explain why a relationship goes bad forces you to conscript all of the small differences, moments of alienation, and petty grievances and amass them in front of the reviewing stand: "See, this is why we lost the battle for the union." And, like the root causes of depression, the factors leading up to divorce are hardly ever attributable to any one thing. Looking back on it now, however, I am certain that my depression played a role in the dissolution of our marriage.

I came of age at a time when women had more choices than ever before. I was well schooled and opportunities unfolded. I was at home in professional settings that were largely the province of men. By the time my children were school age, I returned to work part-time and we were comfortable financially. It should have been perfect. But I was hideously, deeply, secretly depressed.

Divorce is public admission of a failure. We sought remedies—counseling, time apart. The core of our existence was the boys. We went to lengths to protect them from the pain of a family wreck. In the end, Bob was determined to see us remain together; I was not.

A close friend recounted telling her mother that she was divorcing her husband and giving up on their marriage of ten years. She had two children roughly the same age as my own. Her mother chided her, "Why would you leave a man who is willing to make changes for you?" "Because," she remembered thinking to herself, "I have already moved on—and there's no going back." I don't think her mother understood. My mother and women of her generation would not have understood either.

It is my impression that women in my generation have been more willing to risk pulling up the stakes of an unsatisfactory marriage. For most of us, the dissolution represents a financial setback; the battle for income parity wages on. But for many of us, with skills and education, independence from a spouse is no longer out of the question.

For me, divorce was driven by a potent mixture of flawed identity, poor self-esteem, and, most of all, persistent and debilitating depression. Granted, there were times when I was angry with Bob for what I perceived to be an intentional unwillingness on his part to initiate or offer "a plan," be it who we might invite over to dinner or how we were going to spend our vacation. He, by nature, "went with the flow," and complained that whenever he suggested a plan, I would steamroll right over it; hence it was futile for him to even try. There was some truth to that.

We also had different styles of parenting—an issue that bedevils many a couple. He was easygoing and more tolerant of minor infractions, such as bad table manners or an intentionally rude remark; he was quick to dismiss them as "just a phase" and often suggested that I was overreacting. But I was just as quick to react to small bits of bad behavior on the assumption that these minor infractions would be harder to tackle later on. So, in the end, I became the stricter, more authoritarian parent, clearly the less fun role to play in the family dynamic.

Sometimes I felt shut out: there were "the three guys" and there was "Mom." And as the boys grew from toddlers to youngsters, from tiny people who needed all my love and protection to boys who rightly doted on their dad and aspired to emulate him, I felt a sense of diminished purpose. Odd mom out.

I know now that the impact I had on my children never changed, it simply changed character as they grew older. But as they naturally gained independence from me, I felt I was approaching a precipice. I had thrown my entire identity into mothering them, and if they were changing the rules of the game, then I would have to change, too. But I loved them with such ferocity that I didn't know how to change. I needed to figure out who and what I had become, apart from a wife and a mother. What emerged was a completely separate, albeit broken, spirit.

If you are raising children, if you are working and involved in a marriage and family, you know there isn't even enough time in the day to pick the dirty laundry off the floor before all of the domestic elements, demanding their fair share of attention, conspire against time for quiet reflection. When illness, especially an illness like depression, intrudes on family and makes its own demands, most families are poorly equipped to bear the burden. I wanted to extract my illness from the family; in the end, the illness remained, but the family fell apart. The failure of our marriage was, in large measure, my own, and I am forthrightly sorry that I was not able to manage better.

It was a Sunday. School was over for the year. It was late June, already hot and clear, foreshadowing a long, drawn-out summer. After church we sat the boys, ages eight and ten, at the dining room table. Will sat with his elbows on the table, hunched over a place mat; Max fidgeted with a chain of paper clips. We began cautiously, sketching out the rough outlines of a proposition allowing that Bob and I would be spending more time apart—that "we love each other—as friends," but that "we are going to stop being a couple."

The phrases, disguised to be reassuring, spilled out like an odorless poison gas and filled the room with an invisible cloud of small terrors. How could I be so cruel as to torture my children this way? Maybe there is no "right way" to tell your children about an impending divorce. It was one of the most difficult moments of our life as a family. It was unthinkably painful.

The boys were quiet. I could hear a vein in my temple pulsing in time to the wall clock. Words were spoken slowly, hesitantly, not in a torrent of anguish, more like a tape recorder on playback at too slow a speed.

"Does this mean you're not our mom and dad anymore?" Will began to cry.

"No way, guys. We are a family. We will always be a family. Nothing changes that," Bob bolstered them.

"So what's gonna happen?" Max asked.

"Well, nothing really, except that someday Dad and I won't be married."

I couldn't believe I had uttered such an abject absurdity, "nothing really." How ridiculous to make it sound like a day at an Orioles game!

Perhaps ambiguity is *not* the best policy. We wanted to be as gentle as possible, but I could see our approach caused confusion and consternation. And after this feeble beginning, Bob and I decided we had best bring the conversation to a close. The boys had absorbed as much as they could for the moment. We distracted them with routine Sunday fare, an outing to the park, a trip to the market, casual events we performed all together, as though nothing had transpired.

That night I put Will to bed. We talked about the much-heralded appearance of the first firefly of the season in our backyard earlier in the evening. Will slept on the lower level of a red tubular metal-frame bunk, surrounded by a flotilla of favorite books and Ninja Turtle action figures. A few weeks prior at soccer practice, a hefty teammate had landed hard on Will's left arm, breaking it in two places. I slid a pillow under his cast as he struggled to find a comfortable position on his stomach. I rubbed his back and his little body began to quake with muffled sobs.

"This is hard, Mom."

Of course he meant the split.

"I know, sweetheart. It's one of the hardest things you'll ever have to think about. But it won't stay hard. It will get easier."

"But it hurts."

"I know. But Dad and I are going to do everything possible to make sure it's easy on you guys. It won't be as bad as it sounds. It just sounds really scary when you first hear about it."

Nine years later Dennis Malinak was trying to mine the effect our divorce had had on Will. We had spent the better part of an hour in the Hampton Inn lobby spinning the threads of Will's young history.

"Every kid, in my experience, remembers where they were the moment they got the news that their parents were splitting up. It's like remembering where you were when you heard President Kennedy was shot. They remember where they were and how they found out."

For a child, learning that your parents are about to divorce is, in Dennis's opinion, a nuclear first strike in the battlefield of childhood.

"Will insists he doesn't recollect when you got divorced," Dennis delivered quizzically, as though he were trying to solve a particularly difficult puzzle.

"No kidding? Really? Well, he might have been confused. It happened gradually, so there was no real marker, no big separation for the kids," I offered.

"He claims he thinks it 'just sort of happened,' but he doesn't remember the day or the event. Gail, *every* kid remembers that day. Even if they remember nothing else about childhood, they remember that."

Dennis was baffled and it troubled him that Will evinced no anger, resentment, or confusion about the divorce. So what kind of imperceptible scar *did* it leave?

In a letter to his favorite cousin, Alice, in California, Will refers to the "bad news" he doesn't want to talk about—the divorce. He was eight and a half years old at the time. We had broken the news to him two weeks earlier.

July 2, 1992

Dear who ever gets this (and I know who it is.),

I can not wait to see you. I don't know your favoret color. So how are you? Im fine. My mom told me that we are going to see our Aunt and Uncle when we're there. They'll really spoil us. That is the good news. The bad news I don't want to talk about.

Let me think of some thing to say.

9:34 p.m. . . . 9:36 p.m. I've got it! Have you been whatching the U.S. basketball team? Thay're realy kicking some butt. A week from tomoro I get my kast off. I herd Ben broke his finger. That's to bad. We'll still have fun. Yes I am in a rush and I don't know why.

I am going into the third grade. I have to go to bed. I'll finish this in the morning. At 11:30 my Aunt Lee is comeing. I hope she

brings her card game Uno. Later we are going to see Sister Act. Yes it
is a long letter. Let me think for a second. Make that a minet. Oh!
Did you hear that we got Nintendo? I don't think we told you. We
have sixteen games. It just started raining. It stoped pretty quick. I
don't have any more to say. I'll see you in a few days.

Love,
Woo.

The summer prior to our separation, I had been diagnosed with major depression and was hospitalized at the Psychiatric Institute of Washington for five weeks in August 1991. The onset of my illness had a long lead-up. But once I was diagnosed, I realized I had been fighting clinical depression all of my adult life.

At first Bob and I didn't tell our family about my illness or the hospitalization. I wanted to protect them from worrying—perhaps protect myself too from their reaction. The boys were at the tail end of their extended visit with the relatives on the West Coast, but by my second week at PIW I missed them so badly that we asked their grandparents to put them on a plane and return them to Washington earlier than planned. My sister Suzy flew out from California to care for the boys. The boys adored her and she doted on them; if anyone could make the situation less difficult for the children, it was my sister.

Max was almost ten and Will was seven and a half. Bob and I explained what was happening as you would explain a physical ailment: "Mom's sick and in the hospital, but she's getting better."

At first the boys were confused; they couldn't interpret the mixed message. "Why is Mom in a hospital when she doesn't look sick?" "What do you mean it's in her head?" Bob and Suzy took pains to lessen the trauma and the kids came to visit three or four times a week. Max complained that the place "had a weird smell" and Will thought it amazing that the nurses allowed the television to remain on in the common room twenty-four hours a day. As days turned into weeks, I imagine that my children accepted what the adults told them about depression without really comprehending. Once they ascertained that I wasn't going to die or disappear on them, I think they adapted to the circumstances as best they could. It was the beginning of the new school year; Max began fourth grade and Will started second; school provided a bit of a distraction from the events at home.

After a few weeks, I was permitted a short, supervised visit outside the hospital, and we would go to dinner or for a weekend hike. I tried to be as momlike as possible during these peculiar outings, but after a few hours I was exhausted and longed to be back at PIW. One Sunday afternoon after a picnic in the park, Bob checked me back into the unit. He turned to go and remarked sympathetically, "Don't worry, kiddo. We'll have you out of here in no time."

I stunned both of us with my response:

"No, no, you don't get it. I'm safe here."

So many writers have covered the subject of their depression with excruciating detail and poignancy; sometimes I wonder if there is a writer on the planet who *hasn't* walked the public through the overindulged garden of his or her depression dementia. The body of literature on the subject—some of it worthwhile, some of it drivel—has become in recent years so voluminous it causes me to wonder: If depression is so common, why is it still so mysterious, so inaccessible, and so stigmatized?

I am not going to attempt to characterize the multiple permutations of the illness I experienced on and off from my nineteenth year forward. But I believe that William Styron, in *Darkness Visible: A Memory of Madness,* hits the mark when he begins his book with a quote from the Book of Job:

> For the thing which
> I greatly feared is come upon me,
> and that which I was afraid of
> Is come unto me.
> I was not in safety, neither
> had I rest, neither was I quiet;
> yet trouble came.[2]

Styron captures depression's essence when he equates the "feeling" of depression as akin to being trapped in an overheated room, with no prospect of escape. Depression is not unhappiness, grief, a bad mood, or disappointment. It is exquisitely more complex and harder to characterize. In fact depression is the *absence* of emotion, an existence in a lifeless void where there is no looking forward to a good meal, enjoying a favorite piece of music, or stirrings of affection for a beloved friend or family member. That's the "intellect" of depression.

As for depression's physical manifestation, imagine those few minutes when your skin becomes clammy, your mouth is dry, you feel flushed and desperate—and then you vomit and the moment is over. That brief moment that precedes regurgitation, *that's* what depression feels like to me. Only the sensation is unending and there is no relief. Trying to describe depression is a bit like trying to define pornography. Paraphrasing the late U.S. Supreme Court Justice Stuart Potter, I cannot adequately put words to it, but "I know it when I see it,"[3] or, more precisely, I know it when I feel it.

My battle with major depression began in earnest during my sophomore year of college in the fall of 1969. I remember lying on the built-in dorm room bed with its orange batik spread and a van Gogh sunflower print tacked up on the cinder-block wall, too ill to think, too ill to move, desperately trying to manage the bare bones of college-dorm interaction, all the while feeling abject misery.

It would be years before I could place a moniker on the ponderous mixture of pathos and anxiety I felt. Just as Will characterized the run-up to his suicide attempt as being "overcome by a black wave," I had the very real sensation of diminished physical presence. I felt as though I were losing parts of my body, myself. It did not occur to me that the losses were transpiring in my brain or that these sensations had a chemical genesis.

Clinical depression runs through college dormitories during sophomore year like frat boys on a panty raid. It is not hard to identify its victims—they start by skipping classes, withdrawing into their dorm rooms, turning sleep schedules upside down, increasing their intake of alcohol, or experimenting with drugs.

Colleges are full of these walking wounded young adults; a few get help, but most do not. In the year 2000, roughly 15 million students were enrolled in degree-granting institutions in the Unite States. Half were less than twenty-five years of age. In a number of recent surveys, ten percent of the students attending universities reported seriously considering suicide in a given year; two percent actually attempted it but only one in four young people sought help for their depression.[4]

According to Dr. Putnam Ebinger, a friend and colleague and former associate dean of Georgetown University's School of Foreign Service, college students with depression fall into three categories:

- freshmen who are homesick and having difficulty adjusting to life away from the family
- sophomores struggling to stay afloat
- seniors who start failing classes and become depressed out of fear and anxiety as they approach the end of their college lives

Dr. Ebinger adds, "Then you also have the sporadic cases of students confronting a more specific situation, from parental divorce, to date rape, to relationship breakup, to anorexia and other mental ailments."

Seldom do these students confide in friends or family. Sometimes they are unaware that they are suffering from depression; more often, however, embarrassment and fear of exposure and stigmatization keep them isolated and alone.

A spate of recent suicides on university campuses has sparked uproar. Increased efforts are underway by university professionals and health care providers to promote awareness about signs of depression and suicide risk on campuses across the country. But the debate has also raised questions that go to the heart of how we define the middle passage between adolescence and adulthood.

Sensible parenting suggests that you keep a child home from school when he or she falls victim to a demonstrable physical illness. No parent would send a child to college with tuberculosis or hepatitis or even the common adolescent virus mononucleosis. But many kids show up freshman year of college with steamer trunks full of depression, anxiety disorders, and addictions, desperately hoping the change of scene will work a miracle. (It rarely does.) And parents are often, understandably, anxious to see their off-balance teens move their passels of trouble into the campus dorm. I can sympathize. The angels of our better nature want to believe what we want to believe. And the inescapable truth is that we want to believe our children are growing up well and healthy; sure, there are rough patches, but in the end we reserve the right to airbrush out the obvious.

Unfortunately, by shifting the burden of oversight out of the house and beyond paternal control, we have made the problem more difficult by erecting legal impediments preventing parents from taking quick action to come to the aid of a child who is dangerously dysfunctional. Civil rights and liberties intended to protect our children's privacy allow that once a child turns eighteen, he or she becomes an adult in the eyes of the law and parents have a hell of a time trying to *impose* medical intervention—even if the school, medical personnel, or the authorities deem it appropriate.

Dr. Ebinger suggests that if parents know their child is depressed, they should get a support network started by visiting an academic dean, visiting the psychiatric counseling center at the school, and giving permission for the two to interact. Even though a student is over eighteen, he or she can give permission to school authorities to talk to parents and, perhaps even more important, to school authorities to talk to each other. Dr. Ebinger also recommends that school officials urge a student's friends and roommates to alert them when they suspect a classmate is suffering from depression—even at the expense of alienating the student. "Students often came to me worried about a friend and I would get moving on that knowledge," she offered.

Ultimately, whose responsibility is it to ensure a young person's health and well-being once he or she has left home? Society's institutions, including universities, are loath to get in the middle of the debate over how and when our children reach maturity. But once a student lands on school turf, it is presumed that colleges and universities offer certain guarantees regarding health and safety.

The debate over institutional responsibilities to students versus the family's responsibility for their child's health and well-being will doubtless continue over the next decade, and I surmise it will require that the two communities come together to hammer out precise guidelines weighing privacy against security and health. Meanwhile, if you suspect your college-age son or daughter is suffering from depression or another affective disorder, do not expect the campus environment to offer a salutary benefit; be prepared for the opposite.

I wrote my mother a letter fall semester of my sophomore year, in a struggle to describe my misery: "I feel so alone, so confused and hopeless," I confided.

I do not know if my confession alarmed her or not. I think she may have put it down to a spate of overly dramatic melancholy, because she wrote back, "Gail, we are *all* alone. We come in that way and we go out that way. It's how you *cope* with the aloneness that measures your personal worth."

Right. Good advice for an existentialist, but I thought, "Jeez, I'm out on a limb being eaten by snakes. Does it have to hurt so badly?" I didn't broach the subject with anyone again until much later.

Was I aware that major depression can usually be traced back to genetic makeup? No way. No one in my immediate family was ever diagnosed with a mental illness. I was only told about a great-aunt's suicide after my diagnosis at age forty. If I knew now . . . But three of my four grandparents were alcoholics, or "heavy drinkers"—the term "alcoholic" was verboten in our household; it never applied to us, just "others" who couldn't control their liquor. There was much too much alcohol consumed in my family, and even as a young kid, I was able to discern a certain "mood shift" after the adults were a couple of hours into "Cocktail Hour."

No one in the field of medicine now disputes the link between alcohol (or drug) abuse and depression. Clearly, some people "self-medicate" with pills or liquor as a means of coping with depression. Who succumbs to addiction and who does not, however, remains a great mystery, but one that I think we will unravel in the next decade as genetic research untangles the web of brain and behavior.

Reflecting back on it, I consider my childhood a happy one, although there were some major hurdles. I was hospitalized with polio when I was four and suffered paralysis on my left side, but, with physical therapy, I was lucky enough to regain complete mobility after a year or two. And then there were the constant moves required by my father's career as an engineering executive. I attended ten different schools over the course of twelve years; it was hard when I was young but was traumatic when I was a teenager. And we didn't do the kinds of things many families do—have sit-down meals together every evening (my father never arrived home early enough in the evening), attend church regularly (my parents eschewed organized religion), engage in sports or large family reunions. But my parents, my younger sister, and I traveled and lived in interesting, colorful places, and I believed that an exotic childhood was somehow more spectacular than a "normal" one.

In a 1992 profile in *USA Today*,[5] the hugely successful mystery writer Sue Grafton suggested that "no one with a happy childhood ever amounts to much in this world. They're so well-adjusted, they never are driven to achieve anything." She credits her upbringing by "alcoholic, genteel, college-educated" parents as a blessing. She explains, "I had this great freedom because there was all this benign neglect going on." At one time I would have endorsed Grafton's supposition. I don't anymore.

When I was growing up, I held the reputation in the family as "the difficult kid." In many ways, behaviors my mother ascribed to me as a young child carried the same vexing traits I saw in my son Max: fearfulness, anxiety, caution, an outsized temper, and a desire to please persons beyond the family.

As an infant I rocked my crib so violently during the night that the crib would scoot across the wooden floor; in the morning my mother would discover the crib and me clear across the room. When I was three years old, my parents shaved my head because I had pulled out tufts of my own hair by the fistful until my scalp looked like a Wiffle ball; at four, I habitually smacked my head against the concrete sidewalk in front of our house whenever I was in a fury and able to break free of my mother's grasp. I am sure the constant purple lump on my forehead must have looked suspicious to neighbors and family, but was no doubt explained away by the "difficult child" label.

Today, such behavior would be cause for a thorough work-up with a child psychiatrist; psychiatrists and pediatricians would probably posit a deficit in serotonin production—and rightly so—if a child showed up at a clinic nowadays with these same self-mutilating tendencies. But not back then; not in the 1950s.

Finally, my struggle with depression came to a head in the summer of my fortieth year. I was deeply confused by a marriage that no longer worked and trapped in a job that had spun out of control both personally and professionally. I confided in a colleague: "You know, I don't know what's wrong with me. I am no longer at home in my body."

As the summer of 1991 ground down, my mood continued its vertiginous slide. My boys were my sole anchor. In early August I escorted them to California to be with their cousins, aunts, and uncles in the north and their grandparents in the south for a month, a sojourn they relished and repeated every summer since infancy.

I flew back to the East Coast without the kids in mid-August and returned to a fragile marriage and a job that had taken an unpleasant downturn. I nosedived into a deep depression. I was lost without my children.

I had struggled with these "moods" before, but this one had no bottom. I had often fantasized about suicide. This time, however, I found myself contemplating not just how but when I would end my life. For the first time, I imagined both the method and manner and ran the details over and over again in my mind, sucking on a mental lozenge that offered the fantasy of relief.

Bob came home from work one evening to find me sitting, rocking and mute, in the dining room. I had not been to the office in two or three days; nor had I bathed or dressed or eaten or ventured out of the house. Bob had never suffered from depression, but mental illness ran in his immediate family: after a long and debilitating battle, his sister was diagnosed with bipolar illness when she was in her early thirties. As I sat curled up on the floor in the corner of the room, he, thankfully, discerned the seriousness of the situation and insisted that I call a suicide hotline.

I had never consulted a doctor or therapist before about depression. My only prior experience with the mental health profession was when Bob and I sought out marriage counseling as our marriage began to skid. The process threw us together with an incompetent, self-absorbed psychotherapist who at the end of our fourth session burst into tears and exclaimed, "You two are such a nice couple, I don't think I can handle this."

"Well, this is not really working for us either," I retorted sarcastically. I later learned that the therapist herself was in the throes of a marital crisis and instead of putting her practice on hold, she carried her personal baggage in her briefcase and brought it into her sessions with patients. I had little confidence in therapy's ability to help me. Death, on the other hand, sounded like just the ticket; it was seductive and as palpable as an elixir just out of reach.

I made the call to the suicide hotline.

"Yes, I am thinking of harming myself."

"Do you have a method in mind and can you talk about it?"

"Yes, I have a thought as to how to go about it and no I don't want to talk about it."

"Have you consulted a doctor?"

"No."

"Are you willing to talk to a doctor?"

"Perhaps."

"We'll have someone contact you to set up an appointment right away."

"Okay."

"Are you safe where you are for the moment?"

"Yes, I think so."

"Is there someone who can stay with you?"

"Yes, my husband."

"Okay, we'll have a therapist contact you right away."

A therapist saw me that evening and sized up the situation immediately. He dispatched me to a psychiatrist (no mean feat given it was mid-August in Washington, when most professionals have fled the city).

The morning of Friday, August 23, 1991, found me in Dr. Salerian's office for the first time. I refused his offer to sit down and instead began rearranging the books on his bookshelf. I was disheveled, agitated, and unable to control a steady drizzle of tears. He asked me, "Are you suicidal?"

"Isn't everybody?" I replied earnestly.

I was hospitalized at the Psychiatric Institute of Washington that same day. I was given a berth in a dormitory-style room, reminiscent of college lodging, which I shared with three other women. The view from our fourth-story window looked down onto Johnson's Nursery and Garden Center where symmetrical rows of flats pulsing with golden marigolds, bloodred salvia, and autumn-colored chrysanthemums blanketed the hot asphalt.

"Sharps," any personal item that could be used for self-harm—such as a compact with a mirror, a hair dryer, or a nail file—were stored upon arrival on the Mood Disorders Unit at the nurses' station. Personal effects such as clothes, books, and photos were put away in an assigned upright wooden bureau. The windows of the building didn't open. I perched myself on the ledge above the air-conditioning unit and stared out the window at the nursery below for hours.

Gradually, I fell in with the routine on the unit. "Community wake-up" was announced over the loudspeaker at 6:30 AM, reminding you of the day of the week, the month, and the day's agenda. Patients saw their doctors for half an hour each AM and lined up for meds before being escorted down to the cafeteria for breakfast.

I was a novice and not inclined to be participatory, but I was also too polite, too accustomed to wanting to please others to buck the routine. I did not want to leave my bed in the morning—or at any point in the day—those first few days, but I was coaxed matter-of-factly by Dr. Salerian himself, who appeared at my bedside at 7:00 AM like an apparition from an army training film.

"Gail, I want to see you in my office in ten minutes." My God, the principal had spoken. I reluctantly put some clothes on and lumbered down the hospital corridor to meet with him.

My first Monday morning on the unit, several of us (all patients of Dr. Salerian) sat in a circle for the 10:00 AM group session. Dr. Salerian introduced me and asked me to "share" with the group my reasons for being there. I recoiled in horror and stammered something about "being depressed" before I clammed up and stared at my lap. I secretly hoped a meteor would crash into the building and incinerate the lot of us, Salerian included.

A reluctance to "share," however, didn't stop Dr. Salerian from telling my cohorts why I was there, exposing all the ugly details: failing marriage, sinking career, disastrous entanglements . . . Oh, my God, why was he doing this? It was mortifying. I sought anonymity for my problems, not exposure. I had no intention of sharing anything at "Group"—or in any setting—with *these* people, people I didn't know and with whom I had nothing in common. What would it accomplish? Why had I submitted myself to this?

Conformity has its virtues. Eventually, I melded with the rest of the "patient population," swimming with a tide of therapeutic sessions: Group, Art Therapy, Psychodrama, Occupational Therapy, Movement Therapy, and, for the advanced members of our group, a once-a-week physical activity that entailed tightrope walking and "trusting others" called Challenge (the one therapeutic offering I managed to escape during my tenure at PIW). Who knew so much time could be devoted and so many methods employed to heal sick minds?

From time to time I felt as though I had wandered onto the set of a sitcom. One Friday afternoon we were treated to a session of "humor therapy," which consisted of back-to-back Three Stooges movies. (They were *not* funny.) During an hour devoted to "relaxation therapy," we were urged to imagine ourselves "in our own special peaceful space," to the background noise of pseudo–beat poet Rod McKuen's "Listen to the Warm." (Now, that *was* funny.) We modeled clay into hideous shapes (Art Therapy) and exchanged roles with one another, acting out "alternative solutions" to life's complex problems (Psychodrama). And every Saturday night, the community voted on a movie (nothing with an R rating) to watch over pizza and juice. Arnold Schwarzenegger's 1990 classic science-fiction thriller *Total Recall*, in which the bad guys insert fully developed memory chips into the minds of unsuspecting victims, somehow managed to evade our staff censor. It was a hands-down favorite.

I also learned that illness is The Great Equalizer, and came to a reckoning in the first few days and weeks as I began to appreciate the leveling effects of depression and institutionalization.

Members of the "community" were as diverse as vacationers at Disney World on an ordinary day. Every walk of life, ethnic group, and economic stratum was represented. The Mood Disorders Unit boasted a television reporter; a China scholar from the Library of Congress; a CIA analyst who specialized in strategic minerals; a drug-addicted contractor who tried to run his floundering house-painting business from the single pay phone in the common room; an elegant, older African-American doctor who, at one point, had been a successful psychotherapist; an abused young Hispanic mother; a sweet-natured drug dealer with a sixth-grade education; and a thirty-year-old telecommunications manager responsible for outfitting the federal government with its voice mail system—thirty or forty men and women all totaled.

When you are severely depressed, you land on the bottom and you grope in the dark for a while until you see a flicker of light somewhere above—a fast-acting drug, a sympathetic insight, a resolute guide to help you out of your trap. By then, you are stripped of all your tightly held precepts about who you are and your role in the cosmos; you are just a tiny broken thing and your pain and suffering is indistinguishable from the pain depression inflicts on the house painter, the abused mother, or the CIA analyst.

And pain is relative; my particulars may be "better" or "worse" than the patient next to me, but individually our biological framework limits our ability to tolerate suffering; *that* is what brings us to our knees, flips the switch of our depression, and forces us to retreat from the rest of the world. *That* is what we have in common.

Maybe it comes with the territory: shared experiences in groups organized around a common goal—or shared adversity—are often powerful and life-changing. You see this phenomenon in programs for addiction recovery and in gatherings of the fervently religious or fanatically political. My hospital stay with fellow depression sufferers was humbling and instructive. I was outraged to see so many people, good people, wounded people, laid low by this disease. No one "deserved" to be depressed; no one had "earned" it. The experience taught me never to judge too quickly or too harshly. Depression is an equal-opportunity illness.

Late one night three or four weeks into my stay, a small fire erupted two floors above my unit. I was roused out of drugged sleep well past midnight by the sound of an alarm that bored through a dream of zoo animals. Unhurriedly, resentfully, we pulled ourselves out of our beds as the nursing staff marched through the corridors, bellowing orders and taking head counts, trying, with mounting urgency, to herd the mass of us, in various stages of dress, down four flights of stairs to street level and the Exxon station parking lot adjacent to the hospital.

The hospital staff faced an uphill slog from the get-go.

"Let's move, everybody! No, leave that stuff behind, you don't have time." "Everybody out?" "Anyone seen so-and-so?"

It was dawning on the seriously suicidal patients among us that a fire in the building held unspeakable possibilities. ("With any luck, I'll succumb to smoke inhalation.") Some dragged their feet and held back, hoping to get lost in the patient shuffle: "No, no, that's okay, you just go along without me," or "You go on ahead, I'll be along in a minute." The staff stiff-armed the last of the holdouts, like a high school coach forcing his least able players onto the football field.

Taken individually, we were strange fruit; collectively, we were partners in suffering unleashed from confinement and eager for a little diversion, no matter that it entailed the possibility of being trapped in a burning building. We became as giddy as a kindergarten class on a trip to the insect museum, as our caretakers hustled us out into the soupy September night.

Once we hit the street and everyone was accounted for, we jostled and poked each other, making dark jokes about the staff's efforts to coax the Mood Disorders wing out of harm's way. Marooned in the parking lot—some of us still attired in sleepwear, some in street clothes—the gathering took on a carnival atmosphere. (Lights! Sirens! Action!)

Two or three fire engines roared to a stop in front of the building and began unfurling pythonlike hoses. We stood in chaotic, agitated clusters, like fireflies in a jar, and sucked on air as sticky as cotton candy. A couple of my fellow unit-mates body-slammed the vending machines fortifying the fence of the gas station. Lo and behold, the reluctant coolers gave up multiple cans of soda. Someone had even managed to tote a boom box, despite the admonition to drop everything and exit the building.

Under the yellow sodium vapor lights of the gas station, we cranked up the music. The smokers smoked and the rest of us swayed. Given the hour, there was next to no traffic on Wisconsin Avenue; we had the city to ourselves.

Out of the corner of my eye, I noticed Eleanor, the psychotherapist cum patient, standing by herself, smoking and smiling wistfully at the scene, as if she had seen something like this before but couldn't quite place it. Her platinum-blond wig was askew; I assumed that in the rush to leave her room, the towering hairpiece had failed to connect with her center of gravity.

"Eleanor, your wig's turned around—it's on backwards." Surely this proud, stately woman did not mean to appear in public so radically out of alignment.

She looked at me and winked. "I know." She smiled before taking another long drag on her cigarette. The wig stayed right where it was. Party hats all around!

Soon enough the "all clear" sounded. False alarm. We were never in any real danger. Cigarettes were grudgingly stubbed out and we dragged ourselves back into the building. But for me the minuscule slice of time we shared outside the walls of the Mood Disorders Unit that night was as precious as it was surreal.

I returned to my narrow bed, fell deeply asleep, and dreamed we were standing under the gas station's sodium vapor lights: everyone on the unit was mysteriously and gloriously encrusted in an outer casing of multicolored glitter. No one was tragic or sick.

I was discharged after five weeks—Dr. Salerian had pushed my insurance as far as it would go, but they were ready to cut off any further inpatient care. I was not yet feeling any relief from the medication—it would be two months before I noticed a lift—so I retreated to home, at odds with myself and with everything around me, adrift in a backwash of recovery.

In November I flew out to visit my sister Suzy in California for a couple of weeks by myself; the kids stayed home with Bob. Suzy's keen wit and empathy always soothed me, and she possesses an esthetic sensibility that makes all things shabby seem lovely and valuable. At some point during the two-week stay, I awoke one morning and sensed a subtle shift. I felt as though I had been relieved of a heavy physical load carried so long that I forgot it was attached until the tonnage lifted.

I experienced a cluster of physical sensations—colors grew brighter, noises and language connected with their origins—and an undeniable feeling of lightness. "Aha! So this is what it feels like to be well again." It was my first glimmer of recovery and I prayed it was the real thing.

Complete recovery was a long, hard slog, like climbing out of a slippery ravine. Wellness returned in pieces: first came a willingness to venture out of the house; next, a more natural cadence to my speech; finally, laughter and an appreciation for the small everyday things, the fun things. *And* the compulsive rocking ceased. I still had to confront some major problems: At home, Bob and I had to sort out whether or not we would remain together, and I had to face the fact that I was in an untenable and unpleasant work environment. Above all, I needed to try to restore a sense of normalcy to our household for the children's sake. But after a year, I had fully recovered from depression and the episode became a veiled memory.

It is easier to deal with a second episode of depression—easier to define the onset and easier to accept that it runs its course. When I was struck in 1996 with yet another episode of major depression, I complained bitterly to Dr. Salerian: "I am devastated that this keeps coming back. I can't believe I have this shitty recurring illness!" I wept with exasperation. Balls of sodden Kleenex made shapes in my lap, as I sat disconsolate and ragged in his downtown office.

"For Heaven's sake, Gail, you *don't* have a recurring illness!" he reprimanded me. "You have a *chronic* illness. But you *don't* have AIDS, you're *not* schizophrenic, you have depression. Now learn to deal with it!"

Over time, I learned the markers to watch for (the onset of confused speech and a struggle to find the correct word; a propensity for misplacing familiar objects; persistent and uncontrollable rocking) and the triggers (stress and anxiety; lack of sleep and exercise; too little sunlight or outdoor exposure). And I learned that absent a cure for clinical depression, the illness can be managed.

Most people can obtain relief by taking antidepressants and/or engaging in talk therapy. Some people achieve immediate relief from depression with antidepressants alone; others see little relief from medication but, over time, derive benefit from cognitive behavior therapy, or CBT, as it's known.

Cognitive behavior therapy trains patients to recognize negative thoughts and behaviors and helps them erect mental barriers to these thoughts and actions. Recent research suggests that both antidepressants and CBT can be effective, but that the two treatments work in very different ways.

A recent study reported in the *Archives of General Psychiatry*[6] suggests that CBT effects a change in the functioning of the cortex, the region of the brain charged with thinking and reasoning; drugs, on the other hand work on areas of the limbic system that govern emotion, sensation, and memory. The two regions of the brain play distinctly different roles in depression.

Some clinicians who treat depression believe that either talk therapy without medication or medication without talk therapy can provide relief from most depressions; but most psychiatrists recommend both medication and some form of psychotherapy taken together for their severely

depressed adult patients. Recent findings underscore that attacking the illness from two different angles, utilizing a combination of antidepressants
with therapy, is more effective than either treatment on its own.[7]

This approach has proven to benefit adolescents as well as adults.
The results of a study funded by the National Institute of Mental
Health and made public in August 2004 demonstrated significant
improvement in teen patients diagnosed with moderate to severe
depression, who were treated for twelve weeks with a regime that
included fluoxetine and cognitive behavioral therapy.[8]

I understand the impulse to shun the medication and rely solely
on psychotherapy; people often reject the notion that the brain, like
any other organ of the body, can be "fixed" by taking a pill, or that a
person needs to take medicine for a disease whose roots are in the
mind of the sufferer. But Dr. Robert Sapolsky, professor of biology and
neurology at Stanford University, speaking on the public radio broadcast *The Infinite Mind*, summed it up best: "Depression is as real a biological disorder as is diabetes, and you don't sit down a diabetic and
say, 'Oh, come on. What's with this insulin stuff? Stop babying yourself.'"[9] As long as you are willing to experiment until you get the
dosage and formula right, and put up with minor side effects, antidepressants can be a godsend.

It is important to bear in mind, however, that all drugs are toxic
and should be prescribed by competent physicians who closely monitor their patients. A leading authority on psychiatric drugs, Dr. Samuel
H. Barondes, a self-proclaimed fan of antidepressant medication,
admits that the drugs don't always achieve their intended results and
that "even the best of them are blunt instruments that have a large
number of effects on the brain, only some of which can be considered
therapeutic."[10] And, because of differences in the way our bodies
process the drugs, there is always the chance that a patient may experience an "idiosyncratic" response to the antidepressant.[11]

In more than a handful of instances, an idiosyncratic response has
resulted in tragedy: suicide, homicide, or inexplicably harmful behavior. The history of antidepressants is replete with cases demonstrating

the adverse effects of the drugs, and the controversy over their use has spilled out of the medical establishment and into the media, generating widespread anxiety. I will have more to say about the controversy regarding antidepressant medication and adolescents in a subsequent chapter. But it bears repeating: *these are powerful, potent drugs.* Anyone prescribed an antidepressant, be it an adult or a child, must be closely monitored for adverse reactions.

Antidepressant medication has been around since the middle of the last century. In the 1960s, tricyclic antidepressants (TCAs) were the first to be used to treat depression,[12] adjusting brain chemistry by addressing a deficit of chemicals called neurotransmitters, which act to relay messages in the brain. The three neurotransmitters known to be at play in depression are serotonin, norepinephrine, and dopamine. The more recent class of antidepressants, serotonin selective reuptake inhibitors (SSRIs), which came into widespread use in the 1990s, are more finely tuned to act upon the individual neurotransmitter—hence patients experience fewer side effects than before. But the scientific community's understanding of the precise way these drugs work is limited.[13]

It is impossible to predict which antidepressant will work for a given patient, or why some individuals require combination therapies— two or more drugs taken in tandem—before they see results. Nor is it clear why it takes several weeks of continuous use for the drugs to take effect. Dr. Barondes explains, "The influence of these drugs on neurotransmission is apparent within minutes . . ." [but the] "immediate changes in neurotransmission are just the first step in a multi-step process that relieves depression by gradually changing the brain."[14] Clearly, we are in an era akin to the pioneering days of aviation when it comes to deciphering how the brain works.

For half a dozen years after my diagnosis, I experimented with the medication, tapering off antidepressants to see if I could control the illness without psychotropic drugs. I even tried a yearlong course of St. John's wort, a popular herbal remedy widely used to treat depression in Europe, though its claims of efficacy have been disputed by recent trial data.

According to Dr. Salerian, in his experience it takes his patients who suffer from chronic depression approximately five years to come to terms with the notion that they may be better off taking a sustained low dosage of medication, rather than starting and stopping medication as their depression mushrooms and wanes. I was no exception to his rule; five or six years after my first suicidal depression, I finally came to accept that I needed a pharmacological regimen to sustain my mental health. And there may be lasting benefits.

In the past few years, startling evidence has emerged that proves patients with chronic depression suffer reduced brain function. For the one out of ten Americans who suffer from depression, *Listening to Prozac's* Dr. Peter Kramer says the evidence makes "diagnosis and treatment all the more urgent."[15]

Specifically, studies utilizing magnetic imaging scans show "statistically significant" reduction in the size of the hippocampus—the area of the brain responsible for learning and memory—when measured against the brains of nondepressed subjects.[16] In the neuroimaging study cited, patients with depression showed a nineteen percent reduction in hippocampal volume. Theorizing that depression was the root cause of the brain shrinkage, the study took pains to eliminate overall brain size, alcohol exposure, age, and education as variables, so what you see is a picture of a brain in distress as a result of the illness.

Further study by Dr. Yvette Sheline, a professor of psychiatry and radiology at Washington University, showed not only that there was a decrease in hippocampal volume, but that the effects of depression were cumulative over the lifetime of a person's illness. The research indicated that the length of time a patient had been depressed—the total number of days a person suffered from depression during his or her lifetime—predicted the size of the hippocampus. The longer the person suffered without treatment, the smaller the hippocampus. The study concluded, "Antidepressants may have a neuroprotective effect during depression."[17]

These findings, if they bear out in further clinical tests, will come as a shock to persons who suffer from chronic depression, but there is a silver lining: Recent studies suggest that neurons in the hippocampus, unlike neurons in other parts of the brain, have the ability to regenerate, suggesting that pharmacological intervention may be critical to the long-term health of the brain.

Looking at yet another critical part of the brain, evidence shows that "depressed patients suffer significant loss of cells in the prefrontal cortex, the part of the brain involved in 'discerning reward versus punishment,' altering moods and risk taking,"[18] which may help explain the anatomical and chemical differences scientists observe in brains of persons who committed suicide when compared to the brains of individuals who died from other causes.[19]

In the coming years, we will gain much more knowledge about the brain and behavior and how these very complex chemicals work. Meanwhile, I continue to take antidepressant medication prophylactically, and every few years, when I feel I no longer derive the same benefit or sense the onset of major depression, we rejigger the pharmaceuticals, adjusting for newer and more targeted medications as they come on the market. And if the pharmaceuticals were to fail me, there is always electroshock therapy (ECT).

Electroshock therapy is the ultimate boogeyman of therapeutic treatment, because of the perception that "the treatment actually alters the brain, changing a person's personality and character,"[20] a misperception founded in medical lore and surrounded in myth since its introduction sixty-five years ago. No one knows why or how ECT works precisely, but its efficacy is well founded as an "effective and safe treatment for those with severe mental illness,"[21] especially in cases of major depression where no pharmacological interventions proved effective.

There is ongoing research on "brain pacemakers," which in the future may obviate the need for pharmacological solutions to depression and other psychiatric illnesses, but thus far, the pioneering ventures have stumbled over FDA approval or been too costly to benefit the general patient population.

I am not happy to be a depression sufferer, but no one escapes life without a personal crucible. This one is mine.

My baby needs a pilot

She has no magic wand

To help her part the troubled waters

Of the Rubicon.

But in my soul I know she'll

Have to go this one alone.

After all that is the only way she's ever known

    But there is no lamp in all this dark

    That could chase away her shadow

    From the corners of my heart

I pray she rides a dolphin

 But she's swimming with the shark

Out where none can save her

Not even Noah and his ark.

      from "My Baby Needs a Shepherd"
      by Emmylou Harris

5

LETHAL SECRETS

If you don't have anything nice to say about your former spouse, don't say anything at all—at least, not in front of the children.

As I said, there can be no "good" divorce for children. But some are better than others. So why are so many divorces fought in the green zone that should provide a cordon sanitaire around the sanctity and safety of children? Most divorces make most people temporarily crazy. But the lengths to which you go to protect your children from the fallout of the divorce will help them heal faster and leave fewer scars.

In the immediate aftermath of our separation, during the summer of 1992, Bob and I worked out an accommodation: we kept the children in the house and shared responsibility for caring for them. I moved temporarily to live with a friend, who lived around the corner from the boys' school. After school I retrieved the kids, and Bob and I spent most evenings and weekends at the house together with them, eating dinner and sharing chores, attending soccer matches, and shuttling the kids to various outings.

Although it was awkward at first, the routine soothed us all over time, and a year into our separation, I moved back into the house and we shared the residence. Bob and I reached an easy accord in which we took turns—one week on, one week off—assuming responsibility for staying home evenings and weekends with the kids. Holidays remained the same, just as they had in the past, everyone on both sides of the family gathered; relatives graciously accepted that if Bob and I could handle the situation, then they could make accommodations, too. There was a surfeit of caring adults in the boys' lives, family and friends, who supported our children. It does indeed "take a village."

The logistics became more complicated when Bob relocated to California for a job in 1995. It was a challenge to keep the village intact once it traversed state lines. Bob was offered a dream job, one he had coveted for several months with a publishing offshoot of Time Warner. Unfortunately, the offer came shortly after I too had changed jobs—also a plum job, with a humanitarian organization that suited my skills and my interests, working to advance the campaign to ban land mines and address the needs of innocent victims of war and conflict.

Bob and I had often talked about wanting to move back to our roots—all of us together; our families were California natives and the kids were close to their cousins, aunts, uncles, and grandparents. But the timing was all wrong: I felt I was just reassembling my life and I did not want to be uprooted.

Will was still in elementary school and Max had two years to go before high school, so we decided that when Max was ready for high school, the boys would join Bob in California, where, we hoped, we could take advantage of better public schools than the District of Columbia offered. In the interim, I assumed the mantle of single mom. Bob spoke to the kids every evening by phone and commuted cross-country once a month for a long weekend with them.

The big move came as Will was about to enter seventh grade. By then Bob had met and was living with Melissa, an energetic, warm, and engaging woman my age, who was thrilled at the prospect of partnering in raising the boys. I wholeheartedly approved. It was apparent that Melissa was a good match for Bob and I was earnestly delighted to see him happy.

I am sure Melissa got more than she bargained for in those first few years: bringing surly teenage children into a nascent romance is fraught with challenges that only an expert animal trainer can appreciate.

I put the boys on the plane for California and their new home in Palo Alto in late August 1996. I dreaded their departure all summer and, although I tried not to show it, I was anguished over the move. Now it was my turn to make the cross-country commute to parent-teacher nights and special events. More than once I considered pulling up stakes in Washington and following the boys, but I had no confidence in finding a job to rival my current situation, and by then I was involved in a serious relationship with the boys' former soccer coach and longtime family friend, Jack Brady, whom I eventually married.

But now I would be the one to miss, as Bob had, the everyday, commonplace bits of raising our children. Distance magnified the mundane and I felt rotten every time one of them had a tooth extracted or a sore throat, or scored in a triumphant basketball game. I wanted to be there. I was heartsick whenever I heard about a homework assignment that went missing or a new friend whose jokes were a riot. I just wanted to be there. The backdrop to my day-to-day existence was gone. I was no longer the "custodial" parent, and at times my diminished role made me feel shame and embarrassment.

At ages twelve and fourteen respectively, Will and Max started the school year in a new state, in a new house, with a new adult in a parenting role: Melissa. She and Bob would marry three years hence, in 1999, but in September 1996, as happy as my children were to be living in California with their father, closer to cousins and grandparents, the move must have been a colossal adjustment for them.

From the get-go, Max seemed to thrive. He was a freshman at Palo Alto High School and found it liberating to be attending a public school for the first time after years of parochial schooling. Palo Alto High had a diverse student body and Max quickly befriended a number of teenage musicians who shared his fervor for the punk rock scene. He identified with "straight edge" punks and adhered to their code, abstaining from drugs and alcohol; he became a vegan, shunning the consumption of all animal products; he refused to wear leather. He discontinued playing sports and instead expended that same energy on his music. And true to the perfectionist he was, he always maintained top grades in school. In a nutshell, Max carved out a persona that anchored him through the remainder of his adolescence, even though others in his midst floundered.

On the other hand, Will's first year at Jordan Middle School in Palo Alto was a test for all of us. I would fly out to California to participate in the kids' school activities on a regular basis. On our first parent-teacher night, Bob, Melissa, and I trooped off, ready to introduce ourselves as the odd trio we were—a copasetic combo of ex-husband, partner, and ex-wife. We marveled at the offerings unveiled by an impressive teaching staff at the affluent Palo Alto public school.

Will said he liked it "okay" but for the first time in his life he was "the new kid"; he wasn't used to having to put an effort into making friends. His network of friendships in Washington had come automatically with the territory of Holy Trinity Elementary School and his soccer buddies. This was a radical adjustment for him.

Will appeared to be adjusting to the home life sufficiently well. He spent evenings playing board games with Bob and Melissa and he became a devoted companion to Melissa's dog, Buster. But for the first time in his young life, he had no interest in joining a sports team and spent many weekends hanging around with family or by himself, in lieu of friends.

In December 1996 Will had just turned thirteen, a particularly awkward and transitional time for any adolescent. Midway through the seventh grade, small signs of anxiety began to crop up. Will now said he hated his school in Palo Alto, his grades were erratic, and he hadn't made many solid friends. For Will, who'd grown up in the ethnically and economically diverse urban setting of Washington, D.C., Palo Alto, California, was, by contrast, rarefied air. After a rather smooth beginning, even Max, ever forthright, declared, "This town lacks compassion!" which we understood to mean that Palo Alto's showy affluence and stratified demographics were at odds with his notion of what city living should be like.

Bob and Melissa also missed life in a larger urban setting, and, with the boys' enthusiastic endorsement, they moved from Palo Alto to San Francisco before the beginning of the next school year, even though it meant relocating both kids to new schools yet again.

In San Francisco, both boys—now aged fourteen and sixteen—

enrolled in ethnically diverse, urban Catholic schools, which resembled more closely the environment they had grown up with in Washington. In the fall of 1997, Will started eighth grade at a small parochial middle school in San Francisco's Noe Valley neighborhood. But Will would have to make yet another school change after eighth grade, to the high school Max attended, Sacred Heart, a large coeducational Catholic school, with a heavy emphasis on academic achievement and a diverse student body, in the heart of downtown San Francisco.

By the time Will was in the ninth grade, his freshman year at Sacred Heart, we thought that he had made the transition to high school relatively well, although there were times when he appeared adrift and unhappy. Was it normal teenage angst or something much darker? He resumed his interest in playing sports and joined the junior varsity basketball team, where he picked up new friends quickly. But each semester was a crapshoot. One quarter he produced three A's and three F's—the F's in the easy stuff. Once again, we chided him for lack of organization and for failing to be forthcoming about the demands of his courses.

Both boys spent Christmas vacation, spring break, and summer vacations in Washington with me. At the end of his summer vacation in 1999, Will cautiously probed a "what if" one evening as we were on our way to a Chinese restaurant for a farewell dinner.

"Do you think, if I wanted to, I could get into Gonzaga? I mean, if I wanted to, do you think I could live here in Washington and finish high school here? I know not this year, but maybe next year?"

My heart stopped.

I missed my kids terribly. Nothing would have pleased me more, as a mother, than to have Will back in Washington. Jack welcomed the idea; Will's stepbrother, John, was overjoyed at the prospect. But revisiting the plan for the boys' residence wasn't the resolution Bob and I had struck. To reconsider our decision to move the boys in the first place would raise hackles and prompt a fissure in the pleasant and relatively easy accord between us.

"Why would you want to move back here, Will? I thought you

pretty much liked Sacred Heart and living in the city. And I know you're happy to be around your cousins."

"I don't know. Maybe I wouldn't move. Maybe I just want to think about it. Maybe I just need a change." I could see his mental wheels turning. We needed time to let this notion play out, to see where it would take us.

"Well, you bet, I would welcome you back if you wanted to transfer here, but we need to figure out if that's really a good idea—you've already changed schools a couple of times, and Dad would be really sorry to see you move. He wouldn't want you to move. And you don't really want to be apart from Max."

"Yeah, I know, but Max is going to be out of the house next year. He'll go to college and I'll be the only one at home and if I come here, John's at Gonzaga and all of my friends are there, too."

"Well, sweetie, we can keep talking about it, but let's go slow and see how you feel later in the year."

What did Will mean by, "I just need a change"?

With trepidation, I broached the subject with Bob in early fall. He was understandably upset and waited for Will to bring the subject up himself. He wanted to hear Will's reasons firsthand. Bob's objections to a move for Will were not groundless: Why change schools again? Wasn't Will finally settling into a routine, getting his academics together? Hadn't he connected with a good group of kids?

Will had been required to adjust on a number of fronts: to a new stepmother who held strong views about disciplining teenagers and about what constituted acceptable adolescent behavior (which, for the most part, I endorsed and supported); to my role as the "noncustodial parent"; to our homes at opposite ends of the country; and to leaving his childhood friends, though he had made new ones. And finally he seemed to have come to terms with the fact that his parents were irrevocably separated and reattached to new partners—with all that entailed—and he accepted it without demonstrable or obvious signs of discomfort or disapproval. By all counts, he looked to be a well-adjusted kid. At least that's what I wanted to believe.

I tried to hold back as the conversation about a possible move unfolded; to lobby for his relocation would have been unfair to Will—and to Bob—but I admit it was hard not to be biased. Selfishly, I wanted Will to spend the last two years of high school in Washington with me. It would be the last time I would have a child in the house, to love close at hand and to parent. Of course, Bob felt the same, only worse. I'm sure he felt that this development was, in some measure, a referendum on his new household. I don't believe it was. In hindsight, I think Will had already begun to slide into depression. "I just need a change." (Translation: "I need help.")

Will made out the application for admission to Gonzaga High School in Washington on his own, without the help of either parent. I thought it would be a test of his determination to move if he followed through with the application process, and we set admission to Gonzaga as a condition for changing households.

Will was accepted at Gonzaga as a junior transfer for the fall of 2000. I pressured Bob to approve of the move.

"Will's never asked us for anything in his life. He's always been a good sport and gone along with the plans we made for him. He didn't have a say in the previous moves, or our divorce or choice of new partners. I think we need to let him do this, Bob."

Bob was anguished, but he relented and Will closed out his sophomore year at Sacred Heart, bidding good-bye once more to school and friends.

In mid-August 2000, Bob and Will made a father-son cross-country drive, checking out national parks and giving Will, now sixteen years old and road legal, a chance at the wheel for miles on end. The two of them arrived at our Dupont Circle townhouse in downtown Washington, D.C., with a carload of valuable teen possessions and a bag full of dirty laundry. Jack and I had married the year before, so John and Will were now officially stepbrothers. John and Jack were thrilled to have Will back and I was over the moon. John was entering his senior year at Gonzaga, so he and Will would be attending school together. The house quickly filled up with boys, Will's friends from before and John's high school buddies. Ours was a funky testosterone-laden household, but, God, I couldn't have been happier.

A few days before Labor Day in August 2000, Gonzaga's semester began. Will met with his guidance counselor, Bill Wilson, and signed up for a strenuous curriculum, including two advanced placement classes.

Off the two boys went on the first day of classes, teasing and joshing like sixth graders. But Will came home with a boatload of books looking exhausted and discouraged.

"Oh dear, sweetie, what's the matter?" He collapsed, long limbs sprawled out on the couch, eyes closed.

"Nothing."

"You look really tired . . . or something." I was digging.

"No, I'm okay," was all he offered.

Something in his expression that afternoon—an element *beyond* sad—and a disconcerting heaviness about his movements seemed like a harbinger of things to come. I had a sinking feeling: this wasn't what I expected.

By September, Will's school year got underway. But as summer turned to fall, I became increasingly anxious about his mood. Was his decision to move back to the East Coast really based on simply "needing a change" or was it something darker, more urgent? Mother's intuition: I couldn't shake the feeling that something terrible was about to happen. My instincts told me that Will was battling a secret demon.

I decided to confess my fears to Dr. Salerian. I told him that I was wracked by visions of improbable accidents involving Will: I worried that he might be crushed by a structural beam at the construction site at Gonzaga or that he might be shot in a road rage accident.

Dr. Salerian reassured me, "It is normal to feel anxious about a child in the middle of a transition. What you're feeling isn't out of the ordinary. You just have to get used to having him back with you full-time." I wanted to believe him.

By the time the first quarter was over in early October, Will was excelling in school and had organized a CYO (Catholic Youth Organization) basketball team with his friends. He received high honors for his first semester's grades and he was flirting with a girl, Megan Mathews, a sophomore at a public school in Silver Spring, whom he had met through his cousin Stephanie. By Halloween, he and Megan were a regular item.

Will was two years older than Megan, and since he was able to drive, he held the allure of "the cool older guy from Gonzaga with a driver's license." On the surface, Megan seemed outgoing and bright. She had been elected to participate in an intense communication arts program offered by her public high school. Will's understated charm and reserve most likely drew her to him and challenged her to draw him out. I think he was looking for someone he could confide in. There began a relationship of late-night phone calls, visits between her house and ours, huddling together on the living room couch watching videos, and weekend nights out for bowling or movies. Pretty routine stuff.

But around Thanksgiving Will complained that he was tired all of the time. He had difficulty getting out of bed in the morning and an even harder time falling asleep at night. I often found him talking on the phone, presumably to Megan, as late as 1:00 AM; I insisted that he get off the phone and get some sleep. Sometimes we heard him wandering around the house at 4:00 AM. He was losing weight and claimed he had little appetite. He was increasingly withdrawn and his humor had a bitter, fatalistic edge to it. What was going on? Was he just "transitioning"?

By the time his fall semester was winding down, Will was falling off the edge. On a Sunday evening in early December 2000, I found him lying facedown on his bed, schoolbooks and papers in messy piles all around him. He had been crying.

"What on earth's wrong, Will?"

"I just can't do this anymore," he said, in a tone anguished and deadened. He sounded like an ancient tormented soul. "It's just hopeless." He began to sob.

How could I have allowed this to go on for so long without recognizing it for what it was? All the warning signs were there. ("How could this happen? Not Will. Not the easygoing, cheerful kid.") He had been knocked flat by clinical depression. I, of all people, should have known. Like a recurring nightmare, this was my illness, my depression, making its unholy imprint on my precious child.

"Will, we're going to get you some help, buddy. I think you're depressed. We're going to fix this. Right away. I promise." I lay down next to him and cried with him. I was wracked with fear and guilt, but I knew with steadfast clarity what needed to be done.

First thing Monday morning, I took him to see Dr. Salerian, to assess Will's situation. Will was diagnosed with major depressive disorder on December 11, 2000, four days after his seventeenth birthday.

And so it began: medication, therapy, and what we believed to be an aggressive effort to root out the disease. Will went to the West Coast to visit family during the break and we hoped to see signs of improvement when he returned. Soon after New Year's 2001, he started his second semester at Gonzaga, but by mid-January it was evident that he was fading further from our grasp.

By this time, Will's relationship with Megan was intense and secretive. They spent hours in deep, brooding telephone conversations; I suspect they were trying to console each other, and Will confided to me that "Megan's got some issues with depression herself. She's taking meds and stuff."

It is hardly surprising that the two of them were attracted to each other. Educators and clinicians alike can attest that teens with vulnerabilities, illness, and dysfunction are drawn to each other with uncanny magnetism. Maybe they offer each other a safe haven of sorts, consumed as they are with the other's pain.

Late one night in mid-January, Will, anguished and in obvious pain, confided to me he wanted to "end it all." The next day I called Dr. Salerian. He recommended immediate hospitalization, and Will, too ragged and broken to fight, gave in.

January 2001: Salerian practiced out of the Psychiatric Institute of Washington, where he also served as medical director. Although the hospital had an adolescent wing, Dr. Salerian declined to place Will there, describing it as "too dangerous, too dysfunctional." The adolescent unit housed kids whose issues were, for the most part, the result of behavioral problems, substance abuse, physical abuse, or neglect; about half were wards of the court—abandoned by a miserably inadequate health care system or families without resources to care for them. Dr. Salerian convinced me that Will belonged instead on the Mood Disorders Unit.

"Look, Gail"—Salerian tried to comfort me the day of Will's admission—"I want him here on my unit, where I can keep close watch on him. I will care for him as though he were my own son." A consolation of sorts.

I drove Will to the hospital midmorning on Tuesday, January 16. It was a crystalline winter's day. We were winding our way through Rock Creek Park, patches of old snow snaked between tree trunks.

Will, lightly, with a brief flash of humor, said, "Mom, I hope you aren't thinking of buying me a puppy because of this?" The two of us knew full well that a puppy wasn't going to solve this problem.

"No, sweetie, but I *am* thinking of getting you a pony," I joked.

He chuckled and then remarked offhandedly, "I feel like I'm in someone else's body."

Wow! His admission caught me off guard: it was hauntingly reminiscent of my first major bout of depression, when I confessed to a colleague that I felt as though I were no longer at home in *my* body.

"So, whose body do you think you're in?" I teased. I hoped to stretch the levity of the moment a little further.

"Ummmm, Christina Aguilera's." We both giggled.

Like a condemned man who has run out of reprieves on his way to the gallows, he offered up a humorous parting shot. God bless him for his humor. He was going to need it.

Will was housed on the same floor, same corridor, in the same room I stayed in during my hospitalization at PIW ten years earlier. At seventeen, Will was the youngest person on the unit by several years. My heart tore open seeing him there, but I trusted Salerian's judgment.

At least he was safe in the hospital while we tried to sort out why the medication wasn't working.

While he was there, doctors conducted a complete physical and a battery of psychological tests. Bob flew out from San Francisco and everyone in the family spent some part of visiting hours every day with Will at PIW. Will spent most of his time writing descriptions of the other patients on the unit in his journal and putting in all the time he could on the pay phone in the corridor outside of his room, talking to Megan.

At the end of seven days he was released. There were no surprise findings, no breakthrough. We already knew the diagnosis: major depressive disorder.

> This is the first PIW admission for this 17 y/o WM. He has been treated for depression for the past 2 months. No prior history of psychiatric problems. No specific precipitating events. No physical complaints at this time. Patient confided in mother and g.friend of suicidal intent.

On January 23, when Will was released, I asked Dr. Salerian, "Do you think Will's suicidal?"

"I think he engages in suicidal thinking, but I don't think he will act on it." Hardly reassuring. Dr. Salerian's words carried far less confidence than I wanted to hear.

Back at home, it didn't seem to me that Will was getting better—the new drug regimen was not providing him any relief yet. I think he felt trapped. I doubt if he believed we would find a remedy for him. Furthermore, I am convinced that his first hospitalization gave him a window to the garish landscape of mental illness, which both terrified and embittered him.

In his journal from that first hospitalization, he captures an encounter he had with an elderly female patient named Gene. The uniqueness of their exchange seemed to have haunted him for months to come.

Gene was at the hospital. The Psychiatric Institute of Washington. She was at the age where her age could no longer be determined. She could be 60, 70, 80 . . . I really have no clue. She was old. She walked quickly, but with a slight limp and dressed in blue paper-fabric hospital pants, rolled up to the ankles, a large bright blue sweater, and white tennis shoes. She was a small woman, accentuated by the size of her sweater. Her hair was black and hung to her shoulders, wide eyes, small black whiskers above her upper lip and under her wrinkled chin. Her eyes, so wide, almost sad. I had noticed her before but hadn't paid attention. But now she sat across from me in the lounge and talked to herself, mumbled words I couldn't begin to understand, as was her custom. I was used to this and paid no particular attention to it, but then something strange happened. She started to cry. She wasn't bawling, rather crying as she spoke. I sat uncomfortably for at least a half-minute. I felt so terrible because for the first time . . . I looked at her, a woman so beautiful, so precious in her own way or maybe in my eyes, I looked at her and she was crying. Until now she had remained another homeless, faceless elderly schizophrenic woman, who I occasionally smiled at and tried not to stare at obtrusively as she talked to unheard voices. But now, for the first time, I opened my eyes to give her a name and a face and she was crying. I didn't know what to do. I wanted to sit, but I couldn't just sit, could I? I wanted to leave, but I couldn't just leave her to cry, leave with only her overpoweringly sad face in my mind. Could I close my eyes? I stood up and walked across the room. I pulled a small coffee table towards her chair and sat down, took her wrinkled hand, gave it a squeeze and told her in the most comforting voice I could find, not to cry, everything is going to be all right.

What happened next surprised me. She took my hand and held it to her cheek and continued to cry. I tried to console her as best I could, not knowing what to say. But then she stopped. She stopped and looked up, taking my hand in hers and shaking it.

She smiled at me and nodded, holding onto my hand. I've never been so happy in my life.

Sitting in a neighborhood café on a winter's night in 2004, I was finally able to pose the question that confounded me most in the three years since Will's suicide attempt. I arranged to meet Dr. Salerian to talk about this book and a writing project he himself was engaged in about the effect of major depression on the decisions made by President Franklin D. Roosevelt shortly prior to his death.

Alen Salerian had become, over a dozen years, a reliable friend. Not socially, but professionally. I remained his patient after my initial diagnosis in 1991. I have since learned that not everyone is adept at the practice of psychiatry. Dr. Salerian exudes compassion for his patients. I trust his judgment, and over the years he has helped me interpret the pharmacological conundrum surrounding antidepressants.

But a particular question haunted me ever since our conversation upon Will's release from PIW after his first hospitalization. "I think he engages in suicidal thinking, but I don't think he will act on it." I played Dr. Salerian's statement over and over again in my mind and I wanted to ask him candidly if he thought he had erred in his judgment about Will—or, worse still, did he assume all along that I would know better than to let Will handle his own medication? Had he failed to instruct me to do so? Had I missed something? Had he? As uncomfortable as it was to raise the issue without appearing to cast blame or seek an excuse for my own failure, I needed to know what Salerian thought had happened.

"Alen, I finally got all of the records from Will's file at PIW and I went through them with a fine-tooth comb. There's one thing there that really bothers me; it's awkward and I'm uncomfortable asking, but I need to know."

He put down his coffee cup; I had his focused attention. "There's a note in your handwriting on the initial admission assessment which says something like 'preoccupation with suicidal thoughts including OD.'"

Dr. Salerian did not appear startled *or* uncomfortable. I sensed I was touching on a puzzle he had already thought through.

"What should we have done differently?" I continued. "What should *I* have done? Should I have known better than to let him take his own meds? Did you warn me? If he mentioned an overdose to you, then he certainly had the means available. God, I hope I'm not putting you on the spot here—"

"No, no, Gail," he interrupted. "All these are the right questions. And, no, you've touched on some very critical ways in which I look at patients—especially teenage patients. No, it was *my* fault. Let me explain. First, there are two things going on, really. I usually assume, because you are trying to build trust, trust and responsibility with your patient, I have them assume responsibility for taking the meds. It's an important part of what they need to do.

"Second, these newer drugs, the SSRIs, have a greater degree of safety—they're much less lethal, so you don't think about a patient being able to kill himself with an SSRI. But I realize now, it was a mistake. I don't ever let a young person handle his own meds anymore. I give them to the parents to give out. Will surprised me. It was a wake-up call. I had to rethink the risks."

Salerian sat back in his chair. I nodded and neither of us said anything for several seconds.

"So, how's your Roosevelt project coming along?" I asked after a decent interval. I took a sip of coffee. I wanted to get the conversation back on a lighter track.

I was grateful for his candor and his honesty. Was Will's depression so severe by early 2001 that he posed a suicide risk? Yes, indeed. Were we all, his family, his doctor, his therapist, doing everything in our power to see that he got better, that the risk dissipated over time? Yes, I believe we were. I, like Alen Salerian, never imagined Will would "act" on a suicidal impulse. He fooled us.

By definition, adolescents are perturbing. They do things to disturb us. They are illogical and erratic and engage in risky behaviors that should be left to professional acrobats and NASCAR racers.

Will had always had a girlfriend. Girls were drawn to him like ants to a glazed donut. So when he and Megan began dating in the fall of 2000, I didn't think there was much going on that was out of the ordinary. The relationship passed for your garden-variety teen romance—at least on the surface.

But what I didn't know was that Megan was a cutter.

Dubbed by high school counselors and therapists "The New Anorexia Nervosa," self-mutilation by cutting has reached epidemic proportions. According to a number of sources, as many as ten percent of American teenage girls cut themselves. Why? Again, there is no one answer. You have to assume our current culture, where kids, overwhelmed with adult issues, growing up too fast, is the petri dish in which these aberrant behaviors flourish and mutate. The culture of violence, the media, disintegrating families, abuse, neglect, and so on. It is a litany all too familiar.

But cutting? I have to admit, wanting to die is something I understand, something, in my most dastardly depressions, I have found alluring. But I do not understand cutting.

"A cry for help," is the way most clinicians characterize cutting. A symptom of an underlying psychological problem. And since physical pain is easier to tolerate than emotional pain, cutting becomes a way of coping, of flirting with a public declaration: "Look at me! I'm in pain!"

Cutting is the method of choice by which adolescent girls express self-loathing. And it's contagious. Most girls begin cutting after seeing a friend do it or through popular culture, and they harbor the illusion that they can control their habit.

Few adolescent boys routinely cut themselves. Psychologists theorize that women internalize anger, men act out. Hence girls are more likely to cut themselves than engage in strenuously edgy behavior such as excessive drinking, driving too fast, or fighting. But cutting should not be dismissed as a gender-lite pathology. *All* cutting needs to be treated seriously. According to the Web site informedparent.com, studies show that thirty percent of girls who cut themselves eventually develop a psychiatric disorder—depression, bipolar disorder, or borderline personality disorder. And the longer the cutting goes untreated, like with any addiction, the harder it is to stop.

Megan and Will, Will and Megan—caught in a downdraft of teen depression. They supported, fed, and reinforced each other's illness. And in certain respects, they were each other's salvation in time of need.

Megan writes:

The cutting started with the beginning of high school. Cliques began to form against the backdrop of harsh fluorescent lights glaring off linoleum. Several other middle schools fed into my high school, creating a population of about three thousand. I had been popular in my middle school, part of the group of girls to be feared. In high school, however, I met the classic and tragic fate of slipping from favor. My old friends quickly began forming groups with the new kids and I was left behind.

One day I realized that I was unconsciously dragging a short, jagged fingernail across the vulnerable flesh of the underside of my forearm. The resulting pain was so raw and refreshing and a few hours later my work resulted in a neat line of bright red welts. Part of me hoped someone would see it—preferably one of my old friends. The appealing fantasy had them all rushing back to my side with worry and concern.

No one ever saw the marks, and eventually I made my way back up the social ranks. I found a boyfriend who was acceptable and everything looked great in pictures: I was pretty, well-liked, got good grades and felt powerful again.

But even though I was outwardly happy, the cutting had become a habit. It wasn't too physically destructive yet, mostly scratches with thumbtacks and shards of metal. I didn't really focus much on it; it had just become something that I did sometimes. The marks would usually fade within a few hours. On the surface, everything was fairly stable, so I felt no reason to acknowledge my underlying unhappiness. It just hung there, a dull, familiar sort of pain that had been with me as long as I could remember.

High school was certainly not the beginning of my depression. At eight or nine I distinctly remember throwing myself on the ground and banging my head against the hardwood floor when I got in trouble. I would scream things like "I hate myself," or "I want to die." Once I even took the corner of a marble soccer trophy and slammed it against my temple.

In middle school I would make detailed suicide plans in my journal, scratching out diagrams of jumping off the roof. Normally this was in response to punishments that I couldn't talk my way out of. Losing control triggered the impulse and provided the reason for my self-destructive fantasies. Cutting gave me momentary release from my misery and a sense of control.

At the end of ninth grade I cheated on my boyfriend and when I came home from an idyllic time away at summer camp, I discovered that my ex-boyfriend had found out what happened and sought revenge. He called my house in the middle of the night with some friends, and when my parents angrily answered the phone the boys unloaded the details. Upon hearing such crude language in the middle of the night about their teenage daughter, my parents called the police. I had to talk to a police officer, have repeated conversations with my parents about appropriate sexual behavior for a tenth grader and accept a forced apology from the ex-boyfriend all in the week leading up to the start of my sophomore year of high school.

Now I had an excuse, I had permission to be unhappy, and this tore the floodgates open. I spent hours in a heap on the floor, my body wracked with spasms of sobs. The only thing to relieve the desolation was cutting, and I did it constantly.

At summer camp I had begun using pushpins, which excited me because it drew a thin string of ruby drops of blood behind a slight line of shining metal. My arms were covered in neat rows of red and brown scabs. They were perfection to me—my new pastime and saving grace.

School started and I was completely alone. A few of my closest friends still put in the time for short courtesy calls and rushed hallway hugs. The unrecognized depression that punctuated my late childhood was taking over though, and I spent all my free time dragging the pushpins across my arms and crying.

In public, however, it was not sadness, but cynicism that defined my personality. I was a constant tirade of biting remarks and eye rolls. No one was allowed to see the new truth of my existence and my arms were covered in public and eye make-up took care of the constant puffiness around my tired and tear-flooded eyes. All this cover-up managed to alienate the few friends I had left. People did not know what to do and grew more jaded and more bitter; most were so perplexed or weary of me that they gave up.

I made the field hockey team that fall and was required to wear short sleeves. I upgraded from a pushpin to a miniature Swiss army knife and confined the cuts to the thin section of my left arm covered by my watch. The knife was new and sharp and yielded far more satisfying results. Since I was cutting around the curve of my wrist and against the bone, it required much less effort. I barely had to push down and my blood would spill out of the opened skin in amounts that, at first, even I found shocking.

I would hold my arm up and watch the steady stream of drops cascade down the smoothness of myself, falling to my lap with a mixture of tears. When I was finished I would soak the blood up with a pair of white tube socks, monitoring the patterns created as the redness seeped into fibers of the cotton. I stowed the socks in the back of my closet behind old sweaters and would occasionally take them out and finger the crispness of the browned blood. Their metallic smell was calming. It was satisfying to know that many of the cuts were probably deep enough to warrant stitches, or at the very least, a butterfly bandage. The scars would be beautiful, I thought.

Everything made sense when I could localize the pain to my arms. I was quiet and calm when I did my routine afternoon cutting, feeling wonderfully dramatic and free, as the misery balled up in the pit of my stomach. Tears fell down my cheeks as I stared up at the spinning ceiling fan and then back at the redness. The deeper I went the more control I possessed. Shutting my eyes, the gleaming blade replaced the images of the day and my emotional pain with pure and ephemeral serenity.

I took myself seriously, but at the same time I never really believed I was hurting myself. I never thought that I *had* to cut myself. It was more like I was emulating the stick figures of teenage angst on television who locked themselves away and tore at their skin in this new self-destructive fad. Cutting was becoming the new breakout trend, edging up to the status of anorexia and bulimia. "You are completely full of shit," I would tell myself. "You can stop this when something more interesting comes along. There is really nothing wrong with you."

My parents began to notice the cuts. The wounds were not well hidden by the watch anymore because cutting everyday only allows you to go over the same wound a few times. They took me to my room and told me I would start seeing a therapist. I wouldn't let them see my arms. I didn't have the energy to deal with people who were scared of what I was doing. The thought of my mom crying or feeling sick to her stomach was just too much for me.

So when I went to see the therapist for the first time, I was sort of excited. I was proud of my cuts and forming scars, and I looked forward to a venue that would allow me to show them off safely. I was interested to see how the doctor would judge the severity of my cuts in comparison with others she had seen.

I had my first appointment a few days later. The therapist immediately asked me to pull up my sleeves. I displayed my forearms proudly and fed her all the information I thought she might want to hear about why I was doing this. In reality I had absolutely no idea. I spouted off things about my parents' divorce and the hardships of high school. She nodded and eagerly scribbled notes. Although I had cut myself pretty badly, I was startlingly articulate and so full of shit that it passed for self-awareness. I knew what to say and how to say it to make therapists, doctors, and even my parents think I was on the up and up. No one, not even I, came close to realizing the extent to which I was affected by this illness.

At our second session I agreed to stop cutting and the therapist instilled in me a passionate new identity. Making people happy was very appealing, so I dropped the personae of self-destructive teen and took on that of a young person in recovery. I decided never to cut again, and I was proud of my reformation. My parents breathed a huge sigh of relief, and I became the perfect daughter, who went through a little rough spot, but overcame the experience completely.

I celebrated six weeks of not cutting with my therapist who even bought me a cake. We each ate a slice as we talked about potential boyfriends in my life. My "normal and happy" act was thick, but I was beginning to unravel underneath it all.

One day my parents and I fought. Instinctively, I dug through the bathroom drawer for a razor. I tried to pull an individual blade out of the four blade series. In my fury I quickly gave up and used the entire thing, dragging it sideways across my arm. I screamed as I cut, and, as if I couldn't see through the curtain of my fear and rage, everything was blurry. The resulting cuts covered a lot of surface area, and even though they were not very deep, they were visually satisfying. Each cut from each individual razor left a visible wound and they really hurt. I put on a dark long-sleeved shirt and let the blood soak through.

My mom ran upstairs to quiet my screaming. There was no lock on the door, so I used the bulk of my body to keep the door closed. I was terrified but knew that I had to do everything in my power to keep her from entering. The bathroom looked like a murder scene. There was blood splattered across the white counter and the tiled floor. My mother sensed this was not a typical tantrum; her motherhood adrenaline won out and she pushed the door open. She made me pull up my sleeves and she washed and dressed the wounds, all the while threatening to take me to the hospital.

We both knew full-well I was not going to the hospital; self-inflicted wounds of this magnitude would have had me institution-alized. There was a new terror in her eyes and we both knew things were escalating, although neither of us admitted it.

A few weekends later, in late September, my best friend Stephanie and I went to a concert at a club in Washington with her cousin, Will. It was a weekend, but because the concert would end late, we were going to spend the night at Will's house, with our parents' permission, since he lived in the city, just a few blocks from the club.

Will picked us up at Stephanie's house in Silver Spring, and because I was in tenth grade and had never ridden in a car driven by a peer before, I was thrilled. Will was a year older and recently moved to Washington from San Francisco, which only added to his allure. About ten minutes into the ride I decided that this shy boy with hunched shoulders and blue eyes had to be my boyfriend.

We drank beers in the parking lot with Will's stepbrother John before the concert started. I never felt so cool. These were the people I wanted to be friends with; I felt older than my fifteen years. A new group of friends would rectify my suffering social status at school by removing me altogether from that social scene.

Once in the club my friends and I danced to beats that res-onated deep inside our chests. Tendrils of smoke curled off the sea of lit cigarettes and made it almost impossible to breathe. Will stood behind me the entire time, occasionally swaying awkwardly to the music. Aware of his presence, I was self-conscious of every move I made. I felt a rush of excitement every time I summoned the courage to turn and ask him some mundane question. When he finally asked me if I wanted to go for a smoke with him I felt like I had made some headway.

After the show was over we went back to his house and drank bad sangria out of the bottle. His parents had gone to bed. We watched a movie and I went through the prescribed teenage flirting protocol, looking through his wallet, snuggling up next to him, holding his hand.

Stephanie and John had fallen asleep, so Will and I went upstairs to his room. We kissed for a while, and I thought I had finally broken through his friendly reserve. I was so drawn to him and his quiet mystery. Unlike other boys I had dated he wasn't purposeful in anything he did. There seemed to be complexity lying behind the flatness of his eyes. His obvious discomfort with the outside world didn't bother me; he was still older and therefore cooler. I was desperate to make it official.

With some slight urging on my part, Will and I were officially "a couple" a few weeks later. I battled his indifference with my insistence. We spent all of our weekends together and I found comfort just driving along in his mother's black Volkswagen with the heat blasting on my face.

I didn't tell him about the cutting, and if he saw the cuts he never asked, but there was a certain despondency in all of our interactions. Our morose phone conversations began as what seemed like simple teen angst. Gradually our talks went on for hours. When we were together, we physically clung to one another with unspoken need. Because of the depression, neither one of us slept much anymore, which allowed for late night calls. I would sit, curled up in the dark and whisper, hoping that my mom wouldn't hear. By Thanksgiving we were saying "I love you," another stage of our relationship brought about for the most part by my perseverance. The relationship was the only facet of my life in which I found stability and control.

Even with Will there to hang on to, I was slipping. My grades dropped and my depression overwhelmed me. My arms were entirely covered with crusty scabs and I was grateful for the cold weather so I could wear long sleeved shirts all the time. My therapist, who asked to see my arms at every session, also seemed overwhelmed by the damage I was inflicting upon myself.

Everything was just sort of numb; my smiles were cold and

forced, the falseness of my own laugh made me cringe. Getting
out of bed every morning was an excruciating process. If I made it
to the shower I would often sit under the water with my knees
hugged to my chest and cry.

My absences at school were accumulating, every day it
seemed that I came up with a new ailment allowing me to spend
the day under the safety of my covers. I developed an aversion to
the mere sight of my high school. Getting off the bus in the morning, eyes burning with exhaustion, my stomach would pitch with
dread. I was listless in class, and thought only of cutting as I picked
at the scabs.

I never thought of doing it at school, my cutting routine was
too ingrained and too perfect. The bathroom, with its mysteriously
sticky floors, was permeated with the smell of heavy floral perfume
and stale urine—an unacceptable environment for such a sacred
ritual. I saved my need to cut, packed it down for later, and congratulated myself for my endurance.

It was a Friday and Stephanie and I had decided to go to
Will's house after school. My mom had begun to sense something
unsettling in my interactions with Will, and when I told her my
plans she refused to allow me to go. I felt too much contempt to
even fight the decision and made plans to go anyway, against her
wishes.

Will and a classmate came to pick us up at the end of eighth
period. Will was driving the Volkswagen, the interior smelled like
beer. We all piled inside and sped off to his house. About half an
hour later my mom called. She tracked me down through
Stephanie's mother and Will's mom confirmed I was there. My
mom's voice on the phone was rife with anger and fear, demanding that I come home and citing the many consequences for my
insubordination. I refused, my voice rising with rage.

After cutting, fighting was the only other time I felt alive anymore. It filled me with anger and even dread, but it brought color
back to the seemingly permanent sallow of my existence. My mom

gave me half an hour to get home; otherwise, she said, "I'm calling the police."

Going home seemed the best option. I didn't want to involve anyone else in my family fight and I felt the familiar, desperate longing to lose myself in the situation. I longed to get to the point after the fight when my throat was sore, but everything was resolved.

Inside my brother met me with the "you're in so much trouble" smirk. My mom, in a livid whisper, told me to go to my room. I ran up the stairs, pounding the walls and banisters with flushed hands. My eyes flooded with tears and my heart raced. I felt a wave of panic as I watched from my bathroom window as Will drove off.

I found my razor and dug into my skin and dragged. Chunks of scabs were scraped away first and I piled them in the sink. The lines weren't so neat anymore; I went for whatever clean skin I could find. With the razor it always hurt more, and tonight that was exactly what I wanted. I had learned not to scream, even in my blinding rage, because I certainly didn't want to be interrupted before I was finished.

Cutting was a time warp, and I had been at it for almost an hour. The time on the clock shocked me when I finally emerged, but I was elated. I put on the ceremonial dark, long-sleeved shirt that was still stiff from last time.

A few minutes later, reality set in and I wanted to get out of the house. I walked downstairs, my face no doubt swollen and tear stained, and went for the front door. My mother noticed and came toward me, blocking my path. I pushed past her, told her I needed to take a walk, and she eventually gave up. We aimed at some degree of normalcy as my brother and sister looked on.

Outside the sun had set and the chill was bitter. I had refused a jacket and so I ran down the steep incline of our street to warm up. At the bottom there was a creek, protected on the roadside by thin, vine-tangled bushes. I pushed through them, feeling thorns through my clothes and made my way down the sandy bank. The moon was bright and I crouched down about a foot from the tiny creek. I could no longer be seen from the road, but I could watch the occasional car drive down the quiet suburban street.

The tears started again and I spoke to myself. My own voice was startling, hoarse and rough. I asked to die. Even though I was far from religious, I was pleading with God to stop my pain. The request was terrifying. It was the first time I had ever admitted the depths of my anguish. It took on its own momentum the more I said it and I felt more sure with each repetition. I thought about staying out and freezing to death in the cold, but then I saw the brake lights of my family's Honda round the corner twice. The sight brought me back to the surface of things, and all I felt was normal teenage anger. I waited for twenty minutes or so and then made my way back to the house.

I walked back in the door and saw that my parents were absolutely exhausted. My stepfather told me how they had looked for me, how scared they were. Then my mom had her turn. Somewhere in the middle of her speech I broke down. I told them how utterly unhappy I was and how hopeless everything seemed. Just the telling brought instant relief. I finally felt like things would change. They promised we would beat this together, and we pledged to get along. My parents hugged me and I even begrudgingly hugged back.

Will called later that night. He kept saying how worried he was about me. I finally confessed to him about the cutting and the depression. I asked him if he had ever been depressed and he told me he had been. He also told me he wasn't doing so well, and we promised each other we'd get help. I made him promise to get some medication and he made me promise to stop cutting. The fact was that he understood and I felt hopeful for the first time in a long while.

Will had told his mother he needed help. He started seeing a doctor and went on the Prozac. Will wasn't the most willing candidate for therapy, but he continued going, he said, for medication management.

At my next session I told my therapist that I needed more help. She agreed and said she had been thinking I was suffering from moderate depression for a while. She gave me the name of a psychiatrist and suggested I look into medication. On my sixteenth birthday I started taking Zoloft. I swallowed the first tiny pill in the psychiatrist's office before going to school. Taking a pill to make me happy made me nervous, but I was in such a hopeless place it seemed my only option.

I felt the results within a week. My mood was completely different and I had motivation again. I wanted to go out and do things and I checked back into school and friends. By Christmas I was feeling like everything was going to be fine.

But the therapeutic benefits of the medication didn't last long. Sometime after Christmas I came crashing down again. I started cutting again, and with it, the indiscriminate crying that could last for hours. The doctor increased my dosage, but I was troubled by side effects. My mouth was dry and my center of balance was gone—and I was still depressed. But this time it was worse than before. After a brief run at being happy I knew depression wasn't a way of life, and the disappointment of the temporary lift was crushing.

Cutting had become a drug, and I needed to increase the dosage. My younger brother had gone through a phase playing at becoming a Navy Seal and props for his fantasies included an extensive collection of knives. By now he had moved on to video games, but the knives were stowed in an old cigar box on his shelf. No one had thought to hide knives; no one would think that my desperation would ever reach that far.

I went into his room and selected one. It was a single switchblade fashioned from sturdy, matte steel. The blade was serrated and slightly tarnished, with bits of sap and flecks of rust adulterating the metal. I chose it because of the power it seemed to wield, and because the tip had been broken off and I thought my brother might not miss it if he ever went through his collection again. This knife, I decided, was only for use in special situations. I couldn't have too many cuts on my arms that needed stitching at one time. Infection, I had read, was something to worry about with that many open wounds.

In the New Year, Will and I fell back onto each other. I would physically enclose myself in him when we were together, crawling onto his lap with my face buried in his shoulder. Inhaling him, the scent of second hand smoke and manly deodorant, seemed to lull me to a brief place of peace. The two of us huddled desperately on the cheetah print futon in his basement, pointedly ignoring each other's instability. We were afraid to let go, even for a second. In the car he gripped my hand with his sweaty palm in between shifting gears.

I confided in Will. I would tell him when I cut, when I wanted to give up completely. He would hold me and often talk me out of it. Sometimes he even managed to persuade me that things would be okay. But Will hid his own unhappiness. I knew when he wasn't doing well because he would phone me in the middle of the night. I had my own line and I would keep the phone by my head in case he called, and when he did I would jump from my slumber.

The conversations weren't deep; it involved a lot of probing on my part to get the most basic information about how he was feeling out of him. His voice, normally subdued and halting, would be small those nights, and had a frightening edge of desperation. He begged me to take care of him, make me promise to never leave him. I promised, knowing I didn't have any resources to help him. For me the relationship was the picture of perfect intimacy, and it seemed miraculous that in the midst of our pain we had found one another.

On one of Will's bad nights, he tried but couldn't get a hold of me. He bit a chunk out of his forearm. When I saw the bandage he matter-of-factly explained that he had taken a deep bite of flesh from his arm and then spat it out. He lifted the bandage to reveal a bloody indentation. Maybe he was falling faster than I was, and although I was terrified, I was at the same time relieved. I wasn't the sickest person in our union, and somehow the thought was reassuring.

One afternoon in mid-January Will called. There was unusual background noise, clattering, unfamiliar voices, something that sounded like an intercom. He explained he was in a mental institution. He sounded fine, and was quick to make light of his situation. I burst into tears. He told me that his hospitalization wouldn't impinge on our relationship, he'd still call. He'd be out soon.

I ran downstairs and told my mom, who hugged me and told me "That's where Will needs to be." I could feel her body soften with relief to know that Will was out of reach. Her daughter could now shed her dead weight of melancholia, and she probably figured I would improve with Will out of the picture.

I wish I had known then what I know now about the depths of Megan and Will's bond, how intertwined the two had become and that the relationship hung on the symbiosis of their deep depression.

Jack and I had met Megan's mother and stepfather on a few occasions, just to "get acquainted." They were pleasant and easy to talk to, and honest about their concerns about Will's depression and its potential impact on Megan. They had every right to be concerned. I don't believe, however, they understood how deeply troubled their daughter was also. But we would find out soon enough as the two children continued their downward spirals.

Something as simple as boys

. . . And girls

Gets tossed all around and lost

In the world.

from "Mother of God"
by Patty Griffin

6

BROKEN HEARTS, DEEP WOUNDS

Memo
Date: January 24, 2001
From: Gail Griffith
To: C. Adkins; R. Chase; Fr. Meehan; S. Place, D. Smith; C. Warren.
    Gonzaga College High School
Subject: Will D.

*I want to report to you all that my son, Will D., was discharged
yesterday afternoon from the Psychiatric Institute of Washington,
where he had been hospitalized for the treatment of clinical
depression.*

   *He seems markedly better than he was ten days ago and we are
confident that he will continue to improve in the coming days—
although we are mindful that there are no "quick fixes." As you
know, medication for the treatment of depression takes time to work
its way through the system, and his physician is experimenting with
what works best for Will. He will continue treatment on an
outpatient basis.*

   *All of us—Will, his doctor and family—agree that he needs to
resume a normal schedule as quickly as possible. His doctor
recommends that he return to school this Friday, get re-oriented, and
meet with all of you to determine how best to make up the work he
has missed.*

Meanwhile, his father, his stepfather and I want to thank you for your expressions of compassion and concern. We look forward to working with you to get Will back on track academically.

Please do not hesitate to contact me, if a need arises.

Sincerely,
Gail Griffith

Throughout the fall and winter, the teachers at Will's school were flexible and understanding. Bill Wilson, Will's guidance counselor, confided that he too had battled clinical depression as a young adult. He understood what Will was going through and intervened with Will's teachers, asking them to permit Will to complete his coursework by whatever means he could muster. Bill Wilson and I continued to correspond long after Will left Gonzaga. A few years after Will's illness, when I was deep into "researching" the variables in Will's situation, I asked him to recount what he remembered of Will's time at Gonzaga. In November 2003, Bill Wilson wrote:

I remember meeting [Will] early in the school year because I make a point to see transfer students within the first week of school. He seemed very happy to be back in the DC area. I do remember talking with Will about Holy Trinity School and the fact that he knew some of our Gonzaga students because they had gone to Trinity together. I think this provided a bit of comfort to him as he moved into a new school in the junior year. I remember Will as soft spoken, intelligent, articulate, and maybe a little shy. I got the sense that he was confident that he would make the academic transition here smoothly and, in fact, he did. He was an honor roll student after his first quarter here and "things" seemed to be going very well.

I have to admit that I was surprised when we met during the fall semester and you and Will told me about his depression and his efforts to get help and how it was affecting his life in and out of school. When you later communicated that Will would go into

Gonzaga High School counselor Bill Wilson's reflections, November 2003:

I was saddened by the news that in mid-February Will had withdrawn from Gonzaga. I think it began to really sink in how tenacious Will's depression really was. It was sometime later that Will visited me after he left Gonzaga and filled me in about his job, his educational plans and about how he was doing. I was delighted that he took time to come by for a visit and was encouraged by the progress he seemed to be making. It came as a real shock when I heard that not too long after his visit he tried to take his own life.

Meanwhile, Megan's depression steadily worsened. I am convinced that Will's first hospitalization in mid-January 2001 threw her into a panic, exacerbating her illness. During the week that Will spent at the Psychiatric Institute of Washington, the two of them communicated furtively, via the unit's public pay phone. Were they feeding each other's pathological torment—or were they too far gone for it to matter?

By eerie coincidence, the two of them accidentally came face-to-face after Megan cut herself so horrifically that she was admitted to the adolescent unit of PIW overnight, while Will was housed just a floor below on the Mood Disorders Unit. This time her habitual cutting had careened out of control and both she and her family were forced to recognize the seriousness of her illness.

Megan writes:

Once Will was hospitalized I suddenly realized the severity of my own situation. Suicidal ideations, severe depression and a general need for more help were what made Will's hospitalization necessary. But those same things haunted me. Hospitalization was never considered in my case, in part because the hidden cutting offered no trace to the hopeless undercurrent of my daily existence.

treatment I understood that he was probably very frustrated and scared but was glad that he was going to get the attention and care he needed with the challenges he faced.

In my experience as a counselor I have had other students who have gone for inpatient treatment and have successfully made the transition back to school. When Will came back to school, we touched base and again I believed that he was feeling surer that he had begun to get a handle on his depression.

In February, following his first hospitalization, Will attempted to pick up where he left off, but with little success. It just wasn't working. He couldn't concentrate on schoolwork and he began disengaging altogether from his studies, school activities, and friends. The one passion I thought he would hold on to was basketball.

He had a hand in organizing his friends into a CYO team in the fall. It was a motley bunch of players, whose only real strength was that they loved the game. Will started the season strong and became one of the lead scorers in the first couple of games. But after Christmas break, his game was shaken. He showed up for practice and played the games, but two or three times each half, he excused himself from the sidelines, made his way to the gymnasium boys' room, and vomited. He returned to the court pallid and trembling. This was really upsetting to him—and to us.

Something to do with the medication, we concluded. When he wasn't playing basketball he was lethargic and exhausted; on the court he complained of feeling dizzy and nauseous. His basketball game faltered. Will's coach wondered what had come over him and one time let loose an exasperated "Hey, Will, what do you think you're doing walking off the court like that?"

"I'm sorry . . . I've got to barf." Will ran out of the gym, hand over his mouth.

Bob came to town for Presidents' Day weekend. He wanted to get a reading on Will's health and state of mind, but Bob returned to California only somewhat reassured. And Monday evening, before Will was to return to school after the long holiday weekend, we were thrown for a loop.

Around eight o'clock, I went upstairs to see how Will was coming along with his school assignments. A short English paper was due on Tuesday; a chemistry test was scheduled for Wednesday. Will was at the computer, but he heard my footsteps and swiveled in his chair to face me.

"So how's the paper goin', Woo?"

Will absentmindedly ran his hand back and forth, back and forth, messing up his hair. After a slight hesitation, borne no doubt out of reticence, he smiled up at me and said matter-of-factly, "I'm not going back to school, Mom."

I froze. "What?!"

"I can't. I'm not going back."

I slumped onto the hardwood floor and sat cross-legged with my head in my hands. "You can't do that, Will."

"I'm not going back."

I started to cry.

"It's okay, Mom. I've got a plan. It's gonna be okay. You'll see."

"Come on downstairs. We'll talk about this with Jack."

Legally, I couldn't prevent him from dropping out of school; he was over sixteen. We argued for hours. He was calm, dispassionate even. I sat in the kitchen, stunned, defeated as a dog kicked one too many times. Will unveiled his argument for both of us. I was too weary to focus. Weary of each new shift his life was taking. Each course correction registered seismically and this one was an eight on my Richter scale.

He had a plan: he would work full-time, earn his GED, and look into an apprenticeship with the electrical workers union. He was "at peace" with this decision—there was no talking him out of it— although over the next couple of days Bob, Dr. Salerian, and Will's therapist, Dr. Ainsworth, weighed in, all arguing against his decision to quit school.

But Will remained adamant and the finality of his decision gradually began to sink in. He was going a different route than any of us

envisioned for him. I tried to put a positive spin on it: Will wanted to take charge of his life; maybe the drastic change would rescue him from his depression. My mother reassured me:

"He's a great kid, Gail. They all get there by different means. Let him work it out." Maybe. Maybe she was right. But I didn't think so then; and now I know for certain. Findings in the 2004 President's New Freedom Commission on Mental Health suggest that fifty percent of teenagers who drop out of high school are suffering from a psychiatric condition when they leave school. I don't doubt it. But I was blinded by the living, breathing child in front of me and he certainly didn't seem like a sick kid anymore, not to me; not to anyone.

February 27, 2001
Mr. Michael S. Pakenham
Headmaster
Gonzaga College High School

Dear Mr. Pakenham:
I am writing to inform you that my son, William XXXX, a ju[...]
will be withdrawing from Gonzaga College High School. He [...]
missed a good portion of this second semester due to illness [...]
recently has found school to be more than he can handle, gi[...]
state of health.

We are grateful to Gonzaga for the compassion and g[...]
shown as we have struggled to come to terms with Will's [...]
over the past few months. We would like to thank all of [...]
and staff who have been of invaluable assistance. In pa[...]
thank Will's counselor, Bill Wilson, who has proven to [...]
most caring individuals we have met throughout Wi[...]

Although we are terribly disappointed that Wil[...]
this course, we have confidence that in time he wil[...]
strength and peace of mind.

With Will in the hospital I continued my downward spiral. He was no longer available to offer the brief periods of relief that had broken my fall. I became completely solitary, not knowing how to reach out to people without screaming for help. In therapy I was sullen, slouching down in my chair, my knees clasped to my chest. I didn't bother trying to explain my feelings anymore; it took too much energy to talk it out. And besides, my efforts elicited nothing more than the therapist's head nods and constant scribblings. One day I said nothing except "I feel like shit"; I think she started to get it. She offered another session later that week, but I refused. I couldn't deal with any more therapeutic disappointments.

A few days later I sat in school the entire day frantically thinking of ways to get out of my cage of melancholy. In Algebra II hopeless tears started pouring down my face, I felt completely trapped by my illness, with no hope of relief. Something had to change. I decided that suicide was my only option.

When I got home my mom was on her way out. I told her that I wasn't feeling well, mentally. She suggested that I take a bath and rushed out the door. My efforts at signaling for help were too little too late, and did not provide the warning signs I hoped for.

I retreated to my room and dug out my prized knife. I knew that in order to effectively kill yourself the cuts had to open the vein vertically, so I started carefully tracing the blue lines of my vein with the blade. The first cuts weren't very deep, only just enough to draw blood. I was flirting with my own mortality rather than diving right in. I moved to the top of my left forearm and brought the blade down hard, once, twice, three times. On the fourth go the impact resulted in a thick gash with the skin parted to reveal red gelatinous blood underneath. Blood started pouring out in such amounts that it soaked through my clean-up sock. I was a little scared now, there was so much blood.

Just then Will called from the hospital. I must have been very cryptic. I played with the streams of blood that rolled down my arms while I cradled the phone with my shoulder. I wouldn't tell him exactly what I was doing, but he knew immediately that something was very wrong. There wasn't much he could do from where he was, but he told me I had ten minutes to call my therapist or else he would call my parents.

I called the therapist; what follows became a blur, but the therapist called my parents and my prescribing psychiatrist. My mother and stepfather were slow to believe what was happening. At first they proposed placing me on twenty-four-hour suicide watch at home. But the vacant look in my eyes and the vast amounts of blood soaking through my shirt convinced my parents they needed to act urgently. At the recommendation of my psychiatrist, I was loaded into the car, headed for Children's Hospital. I remember feeling some apprehension, but I was so exhausted and in need of change that I didn't care anymore.

We drove to Children's Hospital, a good twenty-minute drive into the heart of town. My dad met us in the emergency room waiting room. It was surprisingly quiet. At triage the nurse calmly looked at my wounds and classified me as a suicide attempt. I was embarrassed, because aside from the gashes on the upper side of my forearm, the cuts weren't impressively life-threatening. I thought, "I could have done better."

The hospital staff took us to a little room with a round table and chairs to wait for a psychiatric evaluation. The light was fluorescent and irritating. All of my movements seemed mechanical and surreal. With so much charged emotion, a room that small was a disastrous place for all the pieces of my disjointed family. My dad pointedly suggested that my depression might be a result of fetal alcohol syndrome. My mother, horrified by the ridiculous charge, heatedly fought back.

The subject of Will and our relationship came up. The three parents decided I was not to see him as much anymore. This pronouncement quickly brought me out of my sedated state and I started screaming. The scene escalated to the point where someone removed me from the room and seated me in front of the tele-

vision. We waited some more. I was offered a Cinnamon Poptart—
an odd coincidence because Poptarts were one of Will's favorite
foods. These connections came back like disjointed sections of a
fever dream.

The psychiatrist, a small Indian man with silver, wire-framed
glasses, finally came in. He talked to me for a few minutes, asking
me why I did what I did and whether I wanted to continue this type
of behavior. I hated his questions and thought he seemed fairly
incompetent. Question after question. I appeared articulate and
responsive and he seemed frustrated with the contradiction
between my ridiculously maladaptive self-destruction and my
rational and calm explanations.

When the doctor suggested hospitalization, I panicked. The
psychiatrist assumed I understood that was where I was headed,
and after a few minutes I agreed. But when the subject eventually
came around to Will, the doctor demanded to know if my cutting
was an effort get into the hospital to see my boyfriend. I wanted to
laugh in his face, but instead I calmly explained that it was never
my intention.

Children's Hospital's psychiatric ward was full and I could not
be admitted. My parents decided to place me at the Psychiatric
Institution of Washington, which happened to be where Will was,
although he was in the adult unit while I was to be admitted to the
adolescent unit.

Hospital policy required that patients transferring to PIW from
hospitals had to arrive by ambulance. While waiting to be transported, it was as if someone finally remembered why I needed to
be taken to the hospital in the first place, and I was moved to a cur-
tained off room to have my wounds treated.

Again, an extended period of waiting before a nurse arrived.
He hovered over me, his dark skin held a golden cross around his
neck. He examined my wounds and asked what happened. Any
number of medical doctors had overlooked the scars and markings
for almost a year as they gave me shots or took my blood pressure;

most would just sigh and carry on. The nurse caught me off-guard by showing interest and I answered with some confident, smart-ass response about how they were self-inflicted.

As he cleaned the wounds he asked, "How could you do that to yourself?" and he told me I was a wonderful person. My mom stood off to the side and cried quietly while I cringed from the pain of the cleaning solutions in the wide, gelatinous gash. I bit my tongue so as to keep from telling him that he actually didn't have a fucking clue what I was like. Instead, I promised him I wouldn't do it anymore. The nurse seemed so genuinely disturbed by what he saw I almost felt bad.

He followed me out to the ambulance and told me, "Remember what I said." I really did appreciate the touch of humanism in this sterile and frightening environment. I refused a stretcher and instead sat on one of the benches in the back of the ambulance. My mom sat up front with the driver and the other emergency medical technician sat in the back with me. I was afraid I would get carsick, so I kept my eyes glued to the road by watching the windshield at the front of the cab. My mother carried on a cordial conversation with the driver. No one asked questions about my condition, but the EMT watching me offered me food. I declined; I wasn't hungry. She told me she had a couple of kids and was going to community college, which surprised me, considering she was at work in the middle of the night. I suggested that she go to sparknotes.com, the book summaries would really save her a lot of time. She wrote the info about the website on her hand.

We pulled up to PIW and the EMTs wished me luck as they helped me out of the back of the ambulance. An attendant met us at the door and we began another lengthy admissions process. I answered a lot of questions, none of which I remember and an admissions person took my picture. I was relatively calm, and utterly exhausted. It had been almost 24 hours since I had slept.

At long last, I was taken upstairs to the adolescent unit—and another check-in procedure, which mostly entailed going over rules of the floor. My eyes were totally glassy as I looked around at my new surroundings. The place was an awkward mix of orphanage and hospital. There were pictures everywhere and kids asleep on the floor. In the middle of the floor was a desk with a large white board and a nurse manning the desk. The whole scene looked to be straight out of *ER*.

As the door locked behind me I started to lose it. I broke into sobs and begged my parents not to leave me there. Something wasn't right. They insisted they had to go and left, looking very unsure themselves, and they promised to come back in twenty-four hours.

I didn't stop crying after they left. I sat in a chair feeling like I was going to stop breathing at any second. The man who had checked me in sat with me briefly, half-heartedly comforting me. I remembered that somewhere here Will was in the same building and I asked if I could call him. The attendant said no and left me to begin waking up the residents.

Slowly people began to emerge from their rooms, and those who were sleeping on the floor were harshly instructed to put their beds away. According to hospital policy, when you first arrived you had to sleep within sight of the desk, until the staff determined that you were not a threat to yourself or anyone else.

I was moved to a living-room type area. I sat on a couch and continued to cry for the next few hours, although I barely remember what happened, I just remember crying. Most of the other kids operated as if I wasn't there, but a few stopped and introduced themselves. One kid told me cheerfully that there was "another girl like you here," and when I asked what she meant she pointed to the only other white person on the unit.

I started to doze off and as the kids watched television I laid down on the couch and fell asleep. One of the nurses came over and told me to sit up. I hadn't been assigned a bed, introduced to any of the staff, or even shown where the bathroom was. I felt like no one knew I was there.

It was already lunchtime. I was still crying. The food looked awful and I refused to eat any of it. People started asking why I was there, and I pulled up my sleeves. Immediately I became the center of attention. Even nurses told me they had never seen anything that bad before. I began to feel better, my pride in my work brightened my mood. A girl who had befriended me in the morning told me she was there because her dad used to rape her. When she finally stood up to him, he beat her. She pulled up her shirt and showed me where he had whipped her with a chain—every individual link was visible. She said also that she was pregnant but fairly certain it was her boyfriend's baby and not her father's. The majority of the other girls added that they, too, were pregnant.

In the afternoon, some of us were selected for art. I sat quietly, hung back and watched the group leave. One of the nurses noticed me and took me with him in the elevator to the class. I asked him, "When am I going to be able to go home?" He motioned to my arms and told me I had a lot of work to do.

All of a sudden some weird survival instinct kicked in, and I decided to do whatever I needed to do to get the fuck out of there. I would bring back the old bullshit, and I ticked off for him some basic and easily "attainable therapeutic goals." He cocked his head as we got off the elevator, as if I had said something startling and during the art class I was participatory, upbeat, and desperate to convince everyone I was fine. Going back to the misery of my life at home was better than being here.

An hour later another nurse came downstairs and said my parents were upstairs waiting for me. I was relieved, but also worried since this was a surprise visit. Perhaps they weren't planning on taking me anywhere. I had learned not to place too much hope in quick fixes.

The nurse stood too close to me as we walked towards the elevator, which was directly across from the entrance to the adult unit, the "Mood Disorders" floor, where Will was confined. Suddenly, through the glass behind the ward's locked door, I spotted Will sitting in a chair reading a book. It was like a scene out of a movie or a play. Everything had come full-circle.

I stared at the boy I had considered my salvation, who was now locked and monitored behind a door that required a code to open. I realized then that I hadn't really had anything—or anyone—to fall back on. Not only could we—Will and I—not help one another, we couldn't even live safely on our own. Even so, I felt a rush of false comfort, and wished I could enter and curl up on his chest.

Will glanced up from his book and was stunned to see me watching him. He looked shocked, then gave me a half smile and a little wave. After the darkness of our conversation the night before, he was probably thankful to see me safe. I was an alarming sight though, my face swollen with tears and fatigue, un-showered and wearing dirty, rumpled clothes. The nurse shook her head as she glanced from me to Will and back at me and loaded me onto the elevator.

Upstairs my parents looked ragged. They said, "We're leaving," mysteriously, but we moved fast. Just before we exited the building, we walked back past Will's floor and I got one last backward glace at Will. My mom let out an exasperated sigh and we quickly shuffled past.

When I got in the car my mom explained that I would be going to another hospital, Dominion, in northern Virginia, near my dad's house. He was planning on meeting us there. My mom said, "There's no way I could leave you at a place like PIW," and she had been trying to find some place else from the moment they dropped me off the night before. I didn't really care, as long as I wasn't going back to PIW.

We reached Dominion. My parents and I said goodbye and I was led upstairs to the adolescent ward. The head nurse, a blonde, severe woman sat me down behind the desk and explained the rules of the floor. There was a basic hierarchy of privileges based on good behavior. When you got into the upper levels you could get as much as fifteen minutes of phone time a night.

I was assigned to a room and my name went up on the whiteboard next to my roommate's. I couldn't help it; I began to cry again. This place with all these locking doors, medications, and rules would be my home until someone deemed me healthy enough to leave. A girl in the common living room who had sat and watched me during the whole check-in process smiled at me and waved.

By the end of February 2001, one month after his first hospitalization at PIW, Will had dropped out of high school and was working full-time at my office doing data entry; he was a favorite of the twenty-something women who supervised him and it pleased him to be earning his own money. He dreamed of buying a Ford Mustang convertible and he downloaded print versions of various models, which carpeted his bedroom. We wanted him to gain a realistic sense of what it would cost to make his way in the world, so we stipulated that he pay a small amount of rent and contribute to the food budget.

He followed through on his pledge to sign up to take the GED test and made inquiries about apprenticeships with trade unions. He always made it to his therapist's appointments with Drs. Salerian and Ainsworth, and I thought I detected a subtle uptick in his mood. And, for better or for worse, he and Megan were still seeing each other.

Megan spent two weeks at Dominion Hospital, in northern Virginia, in an in-patient program for adolescents. Not long after her release, she returned to school and talked about having "gotten a handle" on her depression. She had a new psychiatrist and was taking medicine, but that was as much as I knew.

Will was circumspect about their relationship. I had spoken to Megan's mother and stepfather more than a few times. Clearly, they regarded Will as a threat and a hindrance to Megan's recovery. Who could blame them? I would feel the same if I thought my child was being infected by a kid with toxic issues.

One afternoon I got a call at my office from Dr. Ainsworth: "Gail, I don't want to alarm you—and I have an agreement with Will that I will not disclose anything he tells me in our sessions, unless I think it potentially harmful . . ."

"Oh, man, what next?" I thought to myself.

"What is it, Vaune?" I could feel the roots of my hair start to tingle.

"Has Will talked to you about wanting a baby?"

"Oh, Jesus. No. Definitely no. What on earth . . . ?"

"I think it's a fantasy, you know, a way of soothing himself, or to give himself a purpose, a project, a chance to get it right."

"Oh, God. Does he talk about wanting to have a baby with anyone in particular?" I hoped this was just conjecture. I knew Will was sexually active; by seventeen, he had had more than one physical relationship before Megan. Mercifully, he and I were able to talk candidly about sex and the responsibilities that go with physical intimacy. But conceiving a child was not on the agenda—fantasy or otherwise—as far as I was concerned.

"Vaune, I'd like to talk to him about this, if you don't mind. I'm afraid he's over the edge."

"I think that's a good idea. I will tell him I told you myself when I next see him and I'll tell him why I broke the confidence."

I confronted Will that evening.

"No, Mom." He reddened with embarrassment. "I told her I wanted a kid to love and she took it too seriously and got all worried. I was just kidding."

"You know, Will, if you *were* thinking about having a baby, it would be a huge burden, not just on yourself, but think of what it would do to the mother. You have no skills, no resources, no way of supporting a baby."

"I know, I know," he replied with mild indignation, as though I had offended him by pointing out the obvious.

* * *

From Will's journal, midwinter 2001:

> I don't know what I want. I think I want a kid. Maybe just a mini-me. Someone who looks like me and acts like me. I guess I just really want someone who thinks like me. Someone who makes jokes that I think are funny because it's the joke I would have made if I had thought of it first. I think I want my little cousin Kate. I'll file for custody as soon as I can.
>
> I also want a truck that drives in front of me wherever I go and digs a canal, followed by a truck that fills it with water. Then I could go wherever I wanted in a motorboat. And don't tell me to move to Venice, because I don't want to hear that shit. Don't be retarded.
>
> I think when I'm old I'm going to sing for money. I'll wear a hat—an old person's hat, and a suit (probably an old person's suit as well). One of those suits that you can't tell if it's brown or gray. And a tie. A tie that would look ugly on anybody but an old man. And I'll stand on the sidewalk, rain dripping from the brim of my hat, slowly seeping through the thick wool of my suit, and sing as businessmen hobble by, hunched under umbrellas and folded newspapers.
>
> That's when I'll be laughing. Laughing because . . . I don't even know why. Laughing because I can sing while CEOs, industrial and commercial tycoons mumble about stocks, mergers, cards, girls, anything into cell phones and walk carefully, trying not to wet their shoes, phones or raincoats. Laughing because I can't help but notice their irritated faces as my singing temporarily drowns out whatever they find so important on the other end of their phones. Laughing because . . . Laughing because I can.

It's 3:00 AM. Do you know where your depressed teen is?

In Dr. J. Raymond DePaulo's authoritative *Understanding Depression,*[1] he claims that more suicides happen between 4:00 AM and 7:00 AM, when, he says, "depression is often at its worst." I am amazed that parents aren't informed of this, but perhaps not many clinicians are aware of the statistic either. Too bad. If more parents knew, safeguards could be enacted to monitor depressed teens more closely in the early morning hours.

Practitioners who treat suicidal teens suggest that there's much anecdotal evidence to support the conclusion that nearly half of teenage suicide attempters aren't thinking of killing themselves even fifteen minutes prior to the attempt; it's unplanned. It may be an impetuous, irrational, and impulsive snap decision that propels a teen over the edge. Clearly, if we could get at that trigger, if we could keep them from the tipping point *by any means necessary,* it could be the magical lifesaver.

Dr. David Fassler, an expert on child depression, suggests that two elements need to be present for a child to act on a suicidal impulse: "*an available method*—for example, access to a gun, poisons, pills, or sharp objects such as razor blades—and *opportunity,* that is, the privacy to attempt suicide."[2]

On the surface, efforts to counter "available method" and "opportunity" seem easy to put into practice; these measures are no-brainers. But in actuality, parents of a depressed child may be embattled, just struggling to keep their son or daughter close to home. Too often, families in crisis do not know with any certainty where their children are, not out of lack of concern but because the family dynamic and structures have disintegrated. The child may have fled to a friend's house, or, worse still, be living on the street. Nor do parents learn, often, until after the fact that their child had easy access to all of the tools necessary—drugs, guns, poison, even an automobile driven at dangerous speed—to carry out a suicide attempt.

Beginning in December, at the onset of Will's depression, we imposed an early curfew of 10:00 PM weeknights, 11:00 PM on weekends, as a precaution to ensure that he kept regular hours and got enough sleep. And *absolutely* no drugs or alcohol. I knew Will occasionally smoked marijuana; he owned up to it when asked but offered that he smoked with friends no more than once or twice a month. I believed him. With less frequency, he drank an occasional beer; he claimed he did not like the way alcohol made him feel.

To state the obvious, marijuana is an illegal substance, and at seventeen, Will and his friends were too young to legally purchase or consume alcohol. I talked to Will's buddies. I urged them to help me out on this: Will was on a lot of medication for depression. Drugs and/or alcohol would only "mess him up" further. If he either drank or smoked marijuana he risked worsening his depression. And a kid with depression, one who may be suicidal, becomes, under the influence, even more likely to engage in risky behavior, to say "fuck it all" and give up. We repeated the prohibition each time Will left the house and hoped it stuck.

Who knows what Will's last thoughts were before he downed the contents of a month's worth of sedative antidepressant drugs late at night on Saturday, March 10. Perhaps *he* didn't know what prompted him to do it.

Suicide is inexplicable, "intensely unknowable and terrible," as Dr. Kay Redfield Jamison underscores in *Night Falls Fast*. To the perpetrator it seems like "the last and best of bad possibilities and any attempt by the living to chart this final terrain of a life can only be a sketch, maddeningly incomplete."[3]

Gonzaga High School counselor Bill Wilson's reflections, November 2003:

> As I look back I realized now that Will was carrying around more pain and discouragement than he was willing to or could communicate. I think he had great courage, but I also think that he did not want to burden others with the complete picture of what he was facing or feeling. I think he was genuinely grateful to the people in his life who really cared for him and who supported him and perhaps, did not want to let people down. I wonder if Will had a bit too much of a tendency to want to please people. I also realize that sometimes when depression is relentless and keeps pounding you that sometimes you can reach a point where hope is lost and you just want the pain to go away.

After Will's suicide attempt I had to get to the bottom—to the "unknowable," as Dr. Kay Redfield Jamison describes it, of his devastating act. Moreover, I was determined to divine a way to preclude it from ever happening again. Finding our way back proved to be a Sisyphean endeavor.

"Consultation record: Dr. James Griffith, Chief of Psychiatry, George Washington University Hospital." Discharge report:

[Patient] has a number of risk factors for lethality: male gender; adolescent; some substance abuse; organized plan with suicide note. He is at risk for a recurrent suicide attempt and needs psychiatric hospitalization."

Letter from Will's grandfather, Clayton Griffith:

San Diego
March 19, 2001

Dear Will,
Maga and I are so happy that you are now out of danger. I want to tell you about a near death experience I had about five years ago because I learned from the experience and you should also.

I had a cerebral hemorrhage and was in intensive care for several days. After I knew I was going to survive and had a "new lease on life," I felt I had been given a huge gift and I thought long and hard about what I might do to make the most of that gift.

I urge you to take advantage of your new lease on life and to think about the many opportunities and goals that lie before you. You are now possessed of a unique opportunity. Please seize it.

We love you so much.

Pop

Will spent three weeks from March 13 to April 2, 2001, at the Psychiatric Institute of Washington, miserable and confused, while we scrambled to piece together a long-term plan for his recovery.

Everyone was aware that Will was at extreme risk of making another run at suicide. Given the risk factors, it would not be unusual: the most likely candidate to succeed at suicide is a young male in the aftermath of a prior attempt.

I was scared and exhausted, running on fumes of anxiety. What more could we have done to prevent Will's suicide attempt and how could we prevent him from doing it again? We looked to everyone for advice about next steps: to Dr. Salerian, Dr. Ainsworth, and the psychiatric social worker assigned to his case; they all offered different strategies. It was not their intention to confuse. Rather, we were about to plunge headlong into the institutional chaos and lack of treatment options inherent in our mental health care system.

"Alen, what should we be looking for? Where do we go next?" Dr. Salerian and I spoke a few days after Will was back at PIW.

Ten years ago, standard treatment for an adolescent after a suicide attempt would automatically entail a six-month stay in an inpatient facility, as a matter of course. Anything less was not considered sound medical practice. As it was, Dr. Salerian battled our insurance companies every single day to recertify Will's need for continuing hospitalization.

"I don't know, Gail," Dr. Salerian offered. "There's not much here in this area. There used to be a residential facility, Chestnut Lodge in Maryland, but they're shutting down. You could try McLean in New England or perhaps Menninger in Kansas. I hear good things about them but they might be merging with Baylor University, I'm not sure. But I'll be interested to find out what you learn. There's not much out there that's appropriate for teens."

"What are you saying, Alen? You're making this sound hopeless. What do you mean 'there's not much out there'? How do we know what's supposed to work?"

"Well, unfortunately, for many families and kids it's trial and error. The insurance companies have made this nearly impossible. But be

sure that you find a place with an emphasis on therapy, on CBT [cog-
nitive behavioral therapy]. And make sure there's a good pharmacolo-
gist on staff who knows what he or she's doing."

I felt my fragile lifeboat leaking. Alen Salerian, the one person I
trusted to guide me through this horrific morass, had exhausted all of his
remedies. We were in the midst of a high-wire act working without a net.

Our nation's mental health care system is obstinate, capricious,
and obscenely inhumane. Managed care fought to limit Will's hospital
stay to ten days. We did not want him released without a residential
treatment program in place.

And Will was a mess by then, deeply depressed and suspicious of
our intentions. He argued fiercely against going to a residential treatment program. He wanted to come home and insisted we give him a
chance to recover with family and friends. Bob was spending as much
time as he could manage away from his job on the West Coast to be
with Will and help us find a solution. At PIW, Bob and I argued the
same ground over and over with Will: "You need to be with other
depressed kids; you need to be in a safe place; you need long-term
help." The conversations went nowhere. To me, Will looked like a
caged animal waiting to be released so he could throw himself under a
car.

April 1, 2001, the start of Will's third week in the hospital: Bob was
heading back to California Sunday evening. Will, Jack, Bob, and I sat at
a dilapidated card table in the common room on Will's unit. The TV
blared basketball in one corner and a handful of patients, unlucky
enough to be inside and not out "on pass," slumped on couches watching the game.

We had been at it for over an hour. Bob was distraught and torn.
He didn't want to leave town without the "next step" in play. I was in
tears. Will only reluctantly met my gaze.

"I can't have you living at home, Will. I can't do that until you get
serious help." Will looked away, his jaw set, signaling quiet rage.

Bob reiterated, "For us, Will, 'help' has got to be a residential
program."

All of the adults in Will's life agreed—nothing short of a therapeutic inpatient program would do.

"If you were home now, Will, do you realize what that would do to us—and to you? We would be so terrified for you, you'd have no freedom, no life—and neither would we."

I flooded the plastic tabletop with tears and continued, "I love you—we love you—more than you can imagine, but we won't take a risk with your life."

Will's expression had hardened into something made of wood. He stared intently at his father and me for several minutes. He didn't say a word. I began to wonder if he was in there—had his mind vaporized? Anger? Exhaustion? Hatred? What? No response.

Bob caught his flight back to California at 5:00 PM.

The phone rang at 8:30 PM. It was Will calling from the hospital: he wanted to strike a bargain.

"If I agree to go to a program, will you get me out of here tomorrow?"

"Absolutely," I assured him.

Discharge Summary
Patient Name: Xxxxx, William
Hospital Number: 000000
Date of Admission: 03/13/01
Date of Discharge: 04/02/01

I. INITIAL ASSESSMENT:

The patient is a 17 year old Caucasian male, who on 03/11/01, took a massive overdose of Remeron after writing a suicidal letter thanking his parents for their love, and asking for their forgiveness. The patient remained in a coma at George Washington University ICU for 48 hours, was medically stabilized, and transferred to PIW. This was the patient's first suicide attempt.

Past Psychiatric History: PIW in 02/01 for depression. Outpatient, Dr. Salerian in 12/00 to present.

Current Medications: Remeron 45 mg q.d., Prozac 80 mg q.d., Concerta 36 mg q.d.

Psychosocial/Family: Paternal aunt, depression; mother, depression.

Suicidal/Homicidal Ideation: Massive overdose with a suicidal letter on 03/11/01. Denies homicidal ideation.

Mental Status on Admission: A mental status examination was performed on admission. Mental status was normal other than depressed mood with blunted affect. No psychosis was noted. Due to the patient's suicide attempt, the patient was considered a high risk for self-harm.

II. INITIAL DIAGNOSIS:

AXIS I [psychiatric disorders]: Major Depression, Recurrent.

AXIS II [personality disorders]: None.

AXIS III [medical conditions]: Status Post Overdose.

AXIS IV [level of stress; environmental factors]: Severe: Social, Environmental.

AXIS V [global assessment of functioning; scale is 0–90]: 20

CONSULTATION AND LABORATORY DATA:

The patient was medically cleared at George Washington University Hospital. Medical records accompanied patient.

MEDICAL PROBLEMS:

As above.

CLINICAL COURSE:

The patient was admitted to the APS unit as a transfer from George Washington University Hospital, monitored for safety, seen daily in individual and group therapies. Prozac 60 mg q.d.,[daily; Remeron 30 mg increasing to 45 mg h.s at night]; Concerta 36 mg q.d., increasing to 54 mg q.d., Lithobid 600 mg h.s., Zantac 150 mg b.i.d. was prescribed.

Initially, the patient presented as depressed, but stating he was glad to be alive and had no thoughts of taking another overdose. The patient was considered to remain high risk, needing educational, supportive, pharmacotherapy, as well as gaining insight into his actions and the consequences of his impulsive behaviors. A family meeting was held with the purpose of educating family and the patient on illness, reaffirming family support and exploring discharge options. The patient did attend the educational groups, and was compliant with taking medications, gradually with noted mood stabilization. The patient was agreeing to follow up with outpatient care.

Discharge planning included returning home to live with family, attend a therapeutic educational program. Outpatient psychological testing with Alison Howard. Outpatient medication management, Dr. Salerian. Outpatient therapy, Dr. Ainsworth. The patient was denying suicidal/homicidal ideation, and was discharged on 04/02/01.

In a journal entry in April 2001, Will sums up what he sees as his many failings. He talks about missing "Gene," the elderly schizophrenic patient he met during his first hospitalization at PIW. Their brief encounter, which he describes in an earlier journal entry, becomes larger than life in his memory. I get the impression that the fleeting connection he made to Gene, comforting her and imploring her not to cry, represents a bond that he feels unable to secure with the rest of the world.

April 2001:

Recently I've found myself in some strange places. I noticed it maybe a year ago. I don't remember where or why or how, but I distinctly remember coming to a full stop at whatever I was doing and saying to myself, "Will . . . How the fuck do you get yourself into these situations?" It's a very clear memory amidst several cloudy years of my life. It's almost creepy, to me at least, that I remember so little of what happened in the months or even years around this. Thoughts pass in and out of my head and are instantly forgotten, but not this one. It's strange, but it's true. And it's not something I'm terribly happy about (as I've recently come to realize).

For a while I thought it was funny, just another way to make myself laugh. But I don't really know anymore. When I think back about the times where this thought actually applied, I realize that I laugh at my own pain more than anything. It's my own private slapstick comedy. Getting caught in my friend's car naked with a girl. Being locked in a mental hospital eating cereal and laughing at crazy people's jokes. Going to bed after taking two bottles of sleeping pills. Waking up two days later with my hands tied down and a tube in my penis. Strange situations, potentially funny, not nearly as funny when it happens to you.

I used to look back and laugh, but it's been hard lately. I try not to take myself too seriously; I've always tried not to. But then one day it wasn't as funny (not as funny to me . . . I can still turn it into a pretty funny story). I want to be good. I want to be in a position where I can't fail, not for my own sake (I am in no way a perfectionist), but for others. I left school to relieve myself of the burden of academic failure (thus letting down parents, teachers, interested relatives). I wanted to move out of the house, buy my own car, make my own rules. Slowly untangle myself from the life I lived with my family. Disconnect myself to completely rule out the possibility of failing them. I would set up my life, structure it, so that I couldn't fail. Get a low rent apartment, buy a modest car; get an easy job, something I know I could do. Something that pays, but leaves no room for me to fuck up. I love my family, but if I had the chance to leave, leave everyone I've ever known, move somewhere where they'd never find me and start over with my own life, my custom-made infallible life, I don't know what I would say. I can't say for sure if I would take it or not, but that in itself scares me. It's as if I'm in the same place thinking the same things as before this whole mess started.

I miss Gene. I don't know if I've ever cared as much about anyone as I did Gene. To know that I will never see her again breaks my heart. Maybe it's just the warped negative thinking of my depression, but I miss her a lot and I'm worried that the farther I move from the time I last saw her, I will slowly forget her.

Memo
To: Friends and colleagues
Date: April 9, 2001
Subject: Thanks to all

I wouldn't normally write a blanket thank you note like this, but I have been so overwhelmed by the kindness you all have shown during these past few weeks as I have struggled to come to terms with Will's depression and suicide attempt. I have appreciated everything you have done—the well wishes, the notes, the prayers—and the huge basket of foodstuffs delivered to the house after Will was hospitalized. You have been good friends to me and I cherish these relationships.

We are in the throes of trying to determine next steps for Will. I will be in and out of the office for the next several weeks until this is resolved, but know that I take great comfort in your support.

Gail

Will was released from the psychiatric hospital on Monday, April 2, 2001. Once Will was back at home, we pieced together a complicated schedule, so he was never left alone; Jack would take a shift so I could run out for groceries or make phone calls investigating resources for potential inpatient treatment. Will wasn't allowed to leave the house in the company of friends, only his parents. We limited his phone calls and visits with friends who came to the house. We insisted that communications with Megan be kept at a minimum (an edict her parents also issued). He was tethered to us and he resented it. He might as well have been four years old instead of seventeen. I became overprotective and fearful. Several times a night I looked in on him, just to make sure he was still breathing. I wanted to climb into bed with him and rock him as if he were a small child.

I don't think Will understood that the independence he sought when he dropped out of high school in February became untenable in our minds after his suicide attempt. *He* did not see himself in danger or at risk of another attempt—he claimed he had "learned his lesson." He was embarrassed whenever the trauma was mentioned and regarded our insistence on residential treatment as "a punishment."

Jane came home from Charleston for Easter break. It was the first time they were reunited since his suicide attempt. "I don't get it," he told Jane. "I do this one bad thing—this *one little thing*, and they're all over my case. They won't cut me any slack."

" '*One little thing*,'—that *one thing?!*" Jane shouted. She was incredulous. "Will, that *one little thing* you did—that was sooooo much worse than anything the rest of us have ever done. Will, you tried to kill yourself! *Nothing*, nothing is as bad as *that!*" Will was stung. He loved Jane. Clearly she didn't see the situation from his point of view.

Jack and I worked feverishly at this end of the continent, while Bob and Melissa scoured the West Coast to dredge up treatment facilities specifically for depressed teens. We kept striking out. Querying medical institutions over the phone often left me tangled in voice mail hell; no one seemed to offer a suitable program. Several programs we considered were not willing to take Will because of the severity and recentness of his suicide attempt. Others insisted on short-term, outpatient programs as a precondition to admission, but there were no local outpatient programs that met our needs. We were in a trick box.

After a frustrating few weeks, Jack suggested we enlist the services of a local psychiatric social worker with an advanced degree in education, who had been helpful in steering us to the appropriate educational resources for Jane when she ran into academic and emotional difficulties during her sophomore year of high school. Susan Dranitzke had been an educational consultant at one time, but by 2001 she had cut back her practice. Nonetheless, she agreed to help us.

Oftentimes the fastest route to a reputable therapeutic school is by referral from an educational consultant. In fact, many schools nowadays only admit children who have been "vetted" by an educational consultant. In the past few years educational consulting has become a growth industry, and many individuals offer their services for a fee. Many advertise in the Yellow Pages or on the Internet. By all means seek out their help, but always check credentials; ask about the types of programs they favor and expect to pay for their services just as you would pay a therapist.

Susan Dranitzke was both compassionate and effective and steered us through a complicated process requiring yet another series of sessions, more diagnostic workups for Will, reviewing reams of materials about possible therapeutic programs and filing applications to the ones we thought best matched Will's needs. Her services alone ran over a thousand dollars, and no insurance provider I knew reimbursed families for educational consultants. Likewise, none of the residential treatment options we were considering were covered by insurance.

We were shocked to discover that most private therapeutic or residential treatment programs for adolescents cost several thousand dollars a month. I despair for families and children who have no possibility of meeting the financial challenges to pay for the requisite care for their kids. They are relegated to the dregs of the mental health system—poorly managed and poorly maintained state-run facilities. Their children suffer, their families suffer—and we all pay for this heinous failure to provide adequate treatment for every young person who needs it.

Sitting in Susan Dranitzke's office following his first meeting with her, Will provided the following writing sample, at her request:

One experience which I value happened on a Friday after school last year. I was waiting for the bus on Van Ness Street; it was sunny; I was out for the weekend—all that good stuff that typically makes someone happy. So, as I waited I was looking across the street, watching people as they crossed when the light turned green and I noticed an old man. He was an old black man, probably about seventy-five years old or so, wearing a brown suit and hat, and carrying a cane. As he got closer, I heard him singing. He was singing quite loudly but I had only noticed it now because the traffic had drowned him out when he was further. I don't remember what he was singing but it was very happy and upbeat, which was reflected in his walk. He walked slowly, as if he loved being in the middle of the street and swung his cane as if that's what he had it for (carefree swinging). I wondered if he needed the cane at all. When he walked by me he didn't stop singing, walking or swinging the cane. He winked at me and kept moving.

Now, I don't know if I knew it immediately, but that old man is my hero. He does what makes him happy. I'm more envious of him than of anybody else in the entire world. I would love to have no inhibitions and be able to do what I wanted, but I think that's a right we reserve for old people and I'll have to wait.

It doesn't get any lonelier than this

'Cause I'm on this road alone

My heartbeat ringin' like a hollow drum . . .

I'm about as lonesome as a poor boy gets

And there's nothing I can do

'Cause it's dark out here

and I can't find you.

It doesn't get any lonelier than this.

from "Lonelier than This"
by Steve Earle

7

LOST HORIZON RANCH

Search for the words "troubled teens" on the Internet and a single search engine, Google, will return over six hundred thousand entries. "Boot Camps for Troubled Teens"; "Military School for Troubled Youth"; "Wilderness Therapy"; "private guidance"; "permanent solution"; "programs for defiant and unruly teens"; "tough love alternatives"; "Christian Mission therapy"; "life-changing, high-impact, residential treatment for girls"—the sheer volume of resources positing solutions is enough to propel a worried parent into orbit. The growth of the Internet has boosted humankind's ability to access information on any topic, but what does it say about our society that "troubled teens" pulls up over half a million entries?

Our goal seemed simple: we needed to find a therapeutic residential treatment program for depressed adolescents. We investigated dozens and visited three. They were all out of our area. Chestnut Lodge, a well-regarded residential treatment program in Maryland, had just closed its doors. Like many other treatment programs for the mentally ill, Chestnut Lodge had become prohibitively expensive to operate. Dominion Hospital in northern Virginia offered a short-term hospital stay and follow-up, outpatient treatment. We had already tried that. We abandoned hope of finding the right fit for Will close to home and turned our attention to residential treatment programs out of the area. On the recommendation of our educational consultant, we applied to the Cascade School near Redding, California (which closed its doors in 2004), but were turned down because Will's suicide attempt was so recent. We considered McLean in Boston, the Grove in Connecticut, Mills Peninsula in California, and six or seven more. None was an exact fit for Will. We had applications pending at Island View in Utah, and Montana Academy.

Finally we got a break: there was an unexpected opening at Montana Academy, a therapeutic boarding school for teens forty miles west of Kalispell, Montana, at the foot of Glacier National Park. The program came highly recommended by Susan Dranitzke. In fact, after we had pored over the literature on therapeutic high schools, Montana Academy was at the top of our list but initially we were told that no space was available until August.

Lucky for us, the parents of a child who had been admitted two weeks before changed their mind about enrolling their son and we were moved to the top of the waiting list. Susan faxed Will's particulars to Montana, and after a telephone conversation with the school's admissions director, Rosemary McKinnon, Bob and I hastily arranged to fly to the school to meet with the staff.

Educational consultant Susan Dranitzke's client evaluation for residential treatment placement.

I met with Will's mother and stepfather and father and stepmother on March 28th 2001. They consulted with me because their son, Will D., was soon to be released from the Psychiatric Institute of Washington where he was hospitalized after attempted suicide. I was very impressed with the four caring adults because they clearly had Will's best interests at heart. The hostility or tension, which frequently characterizes divorced and remarried families was totally absent. Clearly this is a large extended family that is able to function smoothly. There was total agreement that Will should be placed in a therapeutic boarding school even though he did not want to go away. All the parents have been quite active in Will's life and all were unanimous in their praise, appreciation, and love for him. They told me that he is "a good student with a high IQ, a wonderful person who gets along with a diverse group of adults and young people, is well-liked by all, and has no enemies." Will does not have behavior problems or substance abuse issues. He suffers from clinical depression and currently has the diagnosis of major depression from which he has suffered for several months. Several family members have also been depressed: Will's mother and his paternal aunt.

Will has had many school changes. He attended Holy Trinity in Washington DC from Kindergarten through 6th grade. He then moved to Palo Alto and went to Jordan Middle School in the fall of 1996 for 7th grade. Then Will's father (the editor-in-chief of a publishing company) and stepmother (an internet editor for a dot.com) moved to San Francisco and Will attended St. Philip's Middle School, a Catholic middle school. For High School, Will went to Sacred Heart Cathedral Prep for 9th and 10th grades, but he began asking to return to Washington DC in the 9th grade. He did return in the summer of 2000 and attended Gonzaga College High School for the first semester of 11th grade.

Will was diagnosed with clinical depression on December 11th 2000 and though his grades were good, the struggle to stay in school was too much for him and he dropped out after the first semester. The Gonzaga guidance counselor, Bill Wilson told me that "the train just kept coming down the track," meaning that the academic work load was continuous and that Will, though quite bright, could not handle the pressure while suffering from depression. Bill Wilson said that Will is a wonderful young man, who is very bright. Will was able to score well on the PSAT even when quite depressed. These scores would translate to mid 1300s for SAT's.

Will was hospitalized briefly in early January for depression and medication adjustment at the Psychiatric Institute of Washington. Then he began to work for his mother who is a director at an international humanitarian foundation, which won the Nobel Peace Prize for helping victims of landmines. Will volunteered to pay rent to his mother and stepfather. It was his intention to get a GED and go to work. Will was working and going to therapy. Then, without warning, he took an overdose of his anti depressant, Remeron. He ingested 25, 15 milligram tablets and 25, 30 milligram tablets on Sunday, March 11th. The whole family was at home at the time, including Will's stepsister Jane, a sophomore at the College of Charleston and Will's stepbrother and best friend since kindergarten, John. Will claimed that he was feeling great one minute and then a black wave of despair enveloped him.

Dr. Alen Salerian, Will's psychiatrist, feels that Will's depression is 70% biochemical and 30% therapeutic. Will is currently taking 60 milligrams of Prozac, 36 milligrams of Concerta, and 45 milligrams of Remeron and a small amount of Lithium.

Will's strengths include writing (see sample done in my office). He is very bright in all areas. He has a good sense of humor, is easy to be with, well liked by all and has never acted out. He has worked with his stepfather (an architect), at volunteer jobs including Food and Friends (an AIDs soup kitchen) and Habitat for Humanity. His weaknesses include his depression and his sensitivity to change and new situations.

When I met with Will, the first thing he told me was that he is very stubborn. He does not want to go away to school. The family told me that Will is non-committal and that it is difficult for him to say what he likes or not likes.

Will is a bright, kind and sensitive young man, who would like to be independent, but is in need of medical and therapeutic intervention for his depression. He also needs a challenging college preparatory academic program within a nurturing and intellectually stimulating environment.

Signed and dated:
April 4, 2001

Flying from opposite ends of the country, Bob and I met at the airport in Salt Lake City late Sunday night, April 23. With some unease, I left Will for the first time since his suicide attempt to visit Montana Academy, knowing that the burden to keep him safe shifted solely to Jack. But I figured Will's close and loving relationship with Jack would squelch any temptation on Will's part to give in to a suicidal mood while I was gone. And Jack was more than capable of holding down the fort.

Bob's connection was running late, but so was the Delta Airlines flight departing for Glacier International Airport in Kalispell. He appeared at the departure gate within minutes of takeoff, and at 11:45 PM, we were on our way on the two-hour flight to the northwestern corner of Montana.

There are few things as worthwhile as having a comfortable relationship with your former spouse. Despite having gone our separate ways, we were united in our love for the boys—and our turmoil over Will. Bob is patient, whereas I am impulsive; he is insightful in ways I am not. When we were together, he was always a sure-footed traveling companion, and was no less so under these circumstances. As we flew north to a place I had never heard of until a month before, to an unseen destination that held captive my hopes and fears, I drew comfort from Bob's steadfastness, knowing we were partners in this crucial endeavor.

We arrived at Glacier International Airport—a surprisingly contemporary structure with a distinctive Native American motif on display as wall art and in the gift shop—at 1:30 AM, amidst crowds of spring skiers and vacationers. What a surprise. Even at the late hour the place was bustling as drivers picked up prearranged tour groups and families greeted relatives.

Bob and I staggered out into the frigid night air to locate our rental car and began the half-hour drive to Marion. Bob drove while I squinted at the pitch-black landscape to try to get a handle on the area. There appeared to be less snow on the ground than I'd anticipated, and indeed, we were told the next day that Montana was experiencing an unusually mild winter. Trees were still bare, and wasted patches of snow mixed with mud and soot piled up on the roadside.

As we pulled into the town of Kalispell, searching for the Hampton Inn recommended because of the discount the hotel offered Montana Academy parents—even prospective parents—we were astonished to pass a brightly lit diner. It was still open for business, judging by the parking lot full of pickups and SUVs. This was too good to believe. Neither of us had eaten dinner.

We careened into Finnegan's of Kalispell, slid into a booth with red leatherette cushions, and ordered tuna melts and apple pie à la mode at 2:30 AM. I was stunned, and Bob and I saluted our good fortune at finding dinner and a great piece of pie just when and where we least expected it. Clearly, Finnegan's was the place to be when the bars closed for the night. Even predawn on this Monday morning, Finnegan's was packed. So far, everything about our expedition was a surprise. Maybe it was a good omen.

After a scant four hours of sleep, several cups of strong coffee, and directions in hand, we ventured out early to find Montana Academy and the aptly named Lost Horizon Ranch. We headed west on Highway 2 toward the town of Marion, roughly thirty-five miles from downtown Kalispell. From the highway, the town of Marion appeared to consist of nothing more than a post office, a gas station, and a convenience store, and as we continued to climb an easy grade, the landscape became rockier and more rugged. There was evidence of fresh timber logging and occasional swaths of burned-out evergreen trees, suggesting a recent forest fire.

"Jeez," I remarked to Bob as we passed through what seemed to me a blighted landscape, "this *is* remote. If we get to the end of the road and it winds up looking like the Unabomber's cabin, can we just turn around and go home?"

Bob conceded it didn't look exactly the way he had imagined it either, but we were used to warmer climates and spring doesn't arrive in the Rockies until nature has squeezed every last ounce of fortitude from its inhabitants. It was only April.

We passed a frigid-looking McGregor Lake and made an immediate turn northward and up a long and winding dirt road, which eventually gave way to a view of a tiny valley on the downhill side of a ridge. We could make out a couple of large, barn-like structures in the distance.

I felt like a New Age pioneer woman, anticipating the unknown with a mixture of excitement and wariness, trying to read the smoke signals on the horizon. We turned left onto a private dirt road and were greeted by a large hanging wooden sign atop a wooden gate announcing MONTANA ACADEMY. We had arrived at Lost Horizon Ranch.

"Don't you figure every kid who passes under that sign reads it as 'Abandon Hope All Ye Who Enter . . .'?" I wondered aloud.

The name of the ranch must have predated Montana Academy, otherwise its founders would have taken pains to inspire a more optimistic first impression with a name of their own choosing, like "Happy Dude Farm" or "Living Large Refuge."

As we approached a cluster of wooden structures—a couple of rough-hewn log bunkhouses, a reconverted barn, and a newer log cabin with a large front porch—I swiveled in my seat to peer at the animals grazing in the large pen to our left.

"What exactly do you suppose *those* are?" I asked Bob. I remember the moose at the National Zoo and I retained a clear picture of what they looked like from Rocky and Bullwinkle cartoons, but these peculiar animals lacked most of the requisite moose-like features. Whatever they were, they looked like a cross between a reindeer and a donkey, with spindly ocean coral for antlers.

We got out of the car and sniffed the air. Sunny and crisp. I wanted to take it all in so I could replay the details later in the day and paint a picture for Will, should it come to that. We made our way to the first outcropping of wooden buildings in search of the administrative office and the admissions director, Rosemary McKinnon, who had arranged our 10:00 AM appointment. I expected to see more activity, more students; we only came across a couple of boys sitting on the deck outside the kitchen door of the Admin Building, bantering and lounging in the weak sunlight; another kid shoveled gravel to make a new pathway to the log cabin dormitory some fifty yards away.

Students at Montana Academy were on "block break," a hiatus between the program's eight-week sessions. "Challenge week" followed the spring block and most of the students were off campus, engaged in organized camping trips in the Rockies or on bike trips to Moab, Utah. Those who had been in the program long enough to merit a return visit home were out of state for the week; others were spending a long weekend with families who had come to Montana to see their children. Too bad, we would not be able to sit in on classes in session or see students interacting.

Rosemary greeted us in the school's small industrial kitchen and led us to a basement conference room, where another of Montana Academy's founders, Dr. John Santa, joined her. John, a clinical psychologist specializing in child psychology and neuropsychology, along with Rosemary, a licensed child therapist with a master's degree in social work, generated a steady energy of empathetic understanding, likely acquired after umpteen interviews such as ours, with overwrought and bewildered parents of troubled teens.

Ten minutes into the conversation, I found myself stifling an urge to climb into Rosemary's lap and pour out my heart to her. She had a lovely, soothing manner of speaking; a lilting British accent retained from her childhood softened and lengthened all of her vowels. I expected her to say, "Oooh, you poooor dear." But she wasn't given either to condescension or exaggeration, and she and John Santa made it clear from the start that nothing about our recitation was unique. They had seen and heard it all. In fact, they could recite from an invisible checklist the inventory of measures taken, frantic interventions, dashed hopes, altered plans, families ripped to shreds, and so on.

As I listened to Bob recount Will's history and our unhappy dilemma, and as Rosemary and John posed their patient and insightful questions to us, I felt stirrings of hope: something might actually work out for us here. *This* might be the place. Could it be? Would they really take him? What about the severity of his suicide attempt? It was recent enough to be problematic in everyone's mind. Were they confident they could provide a safe-enough environment? An effective therapeutic program? Some measure of academic stimulation? Were they willing to take a chance?

My desperation node was operating in overdrive. "I'll bet they can smell my anxiety. Try hard not to appear unhinged," I thought. I checked myself, looked down at my hands, and resumed picking at my bloodied cuticles. "Please," I pleaded silently, "please agree to admit him."

Rosemary and her husband, Dr. John McKinnon, met while he was in graduate school at Cambridge, in the U.K., where he received a degree in economics prior to attending medical school. Dr. McKinnon was a well-regarded, iconoclastic psychiatrist with a specialty in adolescent psychiatry and with a penchant for literature and writing. In 1997 he and Rosemary teamed up with John Santa and his wife, Carol, a Ph.D. in educational psychology, after the Santas themselves spent years searching for an appropriate therapeutic setting for their troubled teenage son. Outraged by the draconian measures imposed by managed care upon doctors and therapists, the McKinnons and the Santas decided to reevaluate their careers and their lives.

Yale-trained McKinnon had practiced in a number of psychiatric hospitals for young people over the years, and in a 1999 article in *Education Week,* he summed up his concerns about where the practice of adolescent and child psychiatry was headed, railing at the constraints managed care and other restrictions imposed. He wrote:

> It was clear [to me] that it would be very hard to find an effective and dignified place to practice medicine. I decided the next place I was going to practice, *I* was going to decide the right treatment for a patient.[1]

The McKinnons and the Santas mortgaged their homes and took out a six-hundred-thousand-dollar loan to purchase the Montana property on which they quickly established a brand-new therapeutic boarding school aimed at providing an emotional growth curriculum with a strong academic component.

Montana Academy's mission statement outlines its approach to treatment:

> We seek to formulate a clear, clinical understanding of each child's developmental difficulties and to permeate our program with the appropriate responses to promote growth. Our common goal is a sustained momentum in all aspects of a child's development.[2]

They describe their two-pronged approach to learning as an "emotional growth curriculum" for kids with psychological problems. The curriculum is "grounded in practical tasks and suited to students disenchanted and disengaged from conventional classrooms."

The program "challenges students to reflect upon their personal histories" and encourages them to "make sense of parents and families." The academic program teaches students "the study skills they need to enhance learning and explore issues of personal growth." The work/study and wilderness elements of the program are designed to "link the learning process with academic content in valued community work and challenging outdoor adventure in the awesome beauty of Montana."[3]

This *was* awesome—and it was exactly the kind of program we wanted for Will.

I cannot overstate my conviction that the single most important attribute of a quality program for troubled children is its leadership and its staff. Always, *always* investigate the credentials and skills of the doctors, therapists, teachers, and counselors affiliated with the program. "Experiential" learning does not mean "experimental" learning; and "emotional growth curriculum" should never, ever entail foisting a child into the wilderness to fend for himself or herself. Trusting untried educational theories promoted by persons with little or no track record in educational development or credentials in therapeutic treatment is as sensible as confining a child to a desert island until he or she grows up.

Likewise, "tough love" or "boot camp" for teens must be weighed in the context of a rigorous therapeutic approach, overseen by skilled clinicians. A lot of people assume that because they are "big hearted" or because they "understand teenagers," they are well suited to run therapeutic programs. Not so. Unfortunately, licensing standards are not uniform and a number of programs operate with no accreditation.

The Internet is an invaluable tool. As a rule of thumb, you can expect a listing categorized as a "dot.com" (as opposed to "dot.org") to steer you to a Web site advertising the services of a for-profit business. Some are shams, and some are very effective at helping families, but it's a crapshoot. You can hire an educational consultant to help you, but if your resources are stretched, my advice is to seek out other families who have availed themselves of treatment facilities for their kids. Talk to the parents and, if possible, to the teens themselves about their experiences. The epidemic of kids in trouble doesn't bypass small towns or rural communities; it is not just something happening in the suburbs or the bigger cities. There is bound to be a family in your community who has been down this road and who can offer some guidance.

Again, the burden is on parents to ferret out the skilled and well trained from the unqualified—and you are forced to do so at a particularly stressful time in the family, when everything seems broken. But you are not without recourse—or rights: Insist on seeing the educational credentials of the program's staff and/or any published articles they may have written. Ask to speak to parents of children who have graduated from the program. You are about to make a huge investment in the future well-being of your child; it is not without risks, but you do not have to take the unnecessary ones. And finally, look for empathy and compassion in the people who run the program.*

"We have had moments deeply filled with anguish and worry," Rosemary McKinnon told *Education Week.* "This is such a tremendous responsibility. These parents are entrusting you with the most precious

---

* Both the National Association of Therapeutic Schools and Programs Web site (www.natsap.org) and Lon Woodbury's strugglingteens.com offer reliable sources.

thing they have."[4] So true. And her attitude reflects the degree of engagement and caring a parent should expect from a therapist and a therapeutic institution.

Bob and I saw all we needed to see at Lost Horizon Ranch. We were impressed. "Would it be helpful if we were to bring Will out for an interview before you decide to admit him so he could get a sense of the place and you could get to know him a bit?" I asked Rosemary.

"Oh, no," she replied. "It doesn't really serve any purpose to expose a child to this setting before they arrive. No self-respecting teen is going to be delighted at the prospect of coming here." Sound advice.

How did our lives end up at the end of that dirt road, on a ranch for sixty troubled teenagers? The scenario most definitely stretched the boundaries of my imagination. But what we saw there was heartening—a gifted and compassionate staff dedicated to working with kids in a healing, albeit remote, setting.

The working ranch offered no television, e-mail, or video games; music and movies were limited to "acceptable" genres. No provocative clothing for girls, no "gang" attire for boys. Pierced earrings and navel and nipple rings needed to be left behind, and profane and vulgar language was punishable by an immediate round of push-ups.

The kids rose at 7:30 AM, completed chores around the dorm, and after breakfast attended an individually tailored schedule of classes in the converted barn. Afternoons were devoted to individual therapy, group therapy, "experiential" classes in cooking, gardening, or woodworking, and sports. Following dinner, kids could mingle in the common areas before returning to their dorms for reading and reflection before lights out at 10:30 PM. Frequent outings—hiking, camping, skiing, ice-skating, fishing, rafting—allowed the students and staff to take advantage of the extraordinary natural wonders Montana offered.

I realize that these offerings do not necessarily hold any fascination for teenagers, but as an adult, I would trade a vacation on a Caribbean island to be able to fold myself into the safe, unfettered, structured routine Montana Academy provided. (Lights out at ten-thirty? Every moment of the day predetermined? Individual therapy? Time set aside for exercise and the outdoors? Someone else cooking hearty meals? Friends gathering to chat in the evenings in front of a giant fireplace? Are you kidding?! Add a nice bottle of red wine and bittersweet chocolate bars after dinner and I would be there in a heartbeat.)

Contact with friends and family was limited. For the eight weeks, Bob and I would only be able to talk to Will by phone once every other week, in the presence of his psychiatrist. Our first visit would follow his initial eight-week session. The program's academic track provided an accredited high school curriculum, leading to a diploma certified by the State of Montana. It offered a well-crafted curriculum, designed to integrate academics with the practical knowledge the students gained during the "experientials"—a class on physics would be conducted in conjunction with woodshop for a whimsical assignment: "After accidentally tipping over a cow, design and build an implement suitable for righting the animal."

Kids were supervised twenty-four hours a day, but there was no "lockdown." Will would receive intensive cognitive behavioral therapy, one-on-one psychiatric care to oversee his medication, and he would engage in a full sports program. And Montana Academy was coed; we could honor Will's only request: that he not be in an all-boys program.

After touring the rest of the campus, we said our good-byes to Rosemary and headed back to Kalispell for our final interview with John McKinnon. I took a final look around as we lingered by the animal pen near our parked rental car.

"What *are* those odd animals?" I pointed to the bizarre-looking creatures that caught our eye when we arrived. "Elk," Rosemary replied matter-of-factly.

The ranch also hosted chickens, cows, and horses. Students participated in the caring and feeding of the animals, as well as the communal chores, including cooking, gardening, and repairs around the property.

"Whoa! This is going to be a different experience for Will," I thought.

We hardly thought of ourselves as an "outdoors" family; we were city people. I couldn't fathom Will being enchanted at the outset by the elk grazing on the baseball diamond—or by a program that included wilderness hiking and camping, not to mention extremely harsh winters.

How ironic, given his terrifying hallucination about "bears downstairs" the morning of his suicide attempt, that we hoped to enroll him in a residential treatment program that offered an early primer on "defending yourself against encounters with bears" and outfitted all of the kids with a set of "bear bells."

Our final meeting of the trip took place in a neat one-story bungalow, the administrative office of Montana Academy, located just off Kalispell's main drag. We discerned from our conversation with Rosemary and John Santa that Montana Academy gave as much weight to the personalities, comportment, and attitudes of the parents as it did the profiles and case histories of the children when deciding which teens to admit. The philosophy suited their therapeutic practice: in order to achieve maximum benefit for the kids, the school had to be able to work with the parents. Hoping to secure Will's admission, I was anxious to "pass muster" with Dr. John McKinnon.

He strode out of his office and greeted us warmly. An imposing figure, well spoken and attentive, he put us at ease within the first few minutes. I am sure the folks back at the ranch briefed him prior to our arrival, but I was surprised he was attuned to the details of our case.

Five minutes into our interview, he probed gently, "So, who found Will the morning of his suicide attempt?"

"I did." Again, I looked down at my torn fingernails and shredded a balled-up Kleenex, trying not to give way to tears.

He paused for a moment, then offered quietly, "God, it must have been horrible for you."

For the second time that day, I felt a surge of relief, as if an invisible agent had extracted my heart from my chest and said, "Here, let me take care of that battered artifact for a moment. Let me hold it while you put yourself back together."

In the six weeks since Will's suicide attempt, no one had come close to uttering consolation that touched me where it hurt most. I am sure many people thought it—"God, it must have been terrible for her to find him that morning." But no one had articulated it until now. Someone had just thrown me a lifeline of sympathetic understanding and I was eager to grab hold.

His words hung in the air for several seconds like dust particles in sunlight. "Yes. It *was* terrible," I thought. I could finally acknowledge it. "How did it feel?" "Yes, dammit, it was the worst thing that ever happened to me." "It was ghastly"; "it was horrific"; "it was shocking to the point of nausea." I didn't have to utter these sentiments aloud. I acknowledged his words of condolence with a silent nod of assent.

On Montana Academy's Web site, McKinnon reflects,

> Few challenges have ever so fully engaged my imagination or ambition or willingness to work. This, too, has been a lucky thing . . . I like the school's students and parents and our staff. I have, at moments, lost my temper, but never have enrolled a student I couldn't like and care about. Nor do we choose students whose parents we don't like.[5]

That says it all, in my book. These people were honest, decent, and caring and put their best efforts into rethreading a loom of tangled relationships between children and parents—and between children and the wider world.

If they would have us, we wanted in. We spoke to Rosemary late in the day: it was a match. Montana Academy accepted Will, and they accepted our family. We were giddy with relief. For the first time in six weeks we were no longer in free fall. We had a plan. Everyone understood that Will posed a significant suicide risk—more so than most of the student population in the program. But they were willing to accept the risk and so were we. Bob and I left Montana feeling confident he would be safe in their care.

I was going to miss Will immeasurably, and worry is not a substance one turns off like water from a spigot, but we believed it was crucial to Will's recovery that he be in a rigorous treatment setting with other depressed teens. Up to now the sum total of his inpatient therapeutic experience had consisted of two separate hospital stays at the Psychiatric Institute of Washington, one a week long prior to his suicide attempt, and the second a three-week stay immediately following his suicide attempt. Both times he had been placed on a unit for persons with "mood disorders," none of whom was near his age. In fact, most of the patients on that unit were several years older and represented the full spectrum of mental illnesses. His ability to fit in and find common ground in that setting was a challenge. I was convinced that if he were in a setting with other teens, kids his own age, he would realize that he was not alone in his depression. Even though the issues and disorders that brought students to Montana Academy were as varied as you would find in any therapeutic setting, the tribal bond adolescents develop with their peers might bring Will to common ground. His family had not been able to keep him safe, even under our watchful care, backstopped by consistent and skillful professional help. It was time to take a different tack and embark on an all-encompassing plan.

Montana Academy was going to cost us nearly five thousand dollars a month. No insurance company on earth offered reimbursement for this kind of residential treatment program for teens. The fees, tuition, and room and board were standard for the kind of program Montana Academy offered, but on top of these costs, we had to calculate the "extras": frequent travel back and forth from Montana, additional costs for medication and individual therapy. Bob was prepared to draw down all of the savings he had put aside for the boys' college education to make this work.

When it came time to move him to Montana a few days later, Will did not put up a fight. After a brief visit with Max, Melissa, and friends in San Francisco, Will and Bob flew to Kalispell on April 29 and spent the day shopping for gear Will needed for school (insulated winter boots, polypropylene long underwear, wool hiking socks, sleeping bag, backpack, Gore-Tex pants, and a headlamp for night hiking). The two of them arrived at Lost Horizon Ranch on the last day in April. Will began school the next day.

My heart ached for Will, but for the first time in months, in those days in early May, I slept, we all slept, like dead people.

* * *

Dr. John McKinnon's missive to new parents:

A Letter to Parents: At the Start

Dear Parents,
I want to write this note to you, early in our work together, because
I know that enrollment of a child at a therapeutic school can be
stressful. I want you to know that we understand this. Perhaps, like
other parents, you feel relief to have taken action against a sea of
troubles, but it would be unusual if you didn't have strong feelings
about it. Even now, as you drive back over the ridge or read this note
at home, you may feel the car is somehow hollow, the house too
quiet. You may suffer from regrets. And I know there's a grief in this.

Meanwhile, back at the ranch, our new student will now have
just begun to absorb the message your action communicates. For
some students, parental action spells relief. For others, too immature
to see the part they have played, there is only an angry sense of
injustice. It's likely that, in the midst of all the failure and
frustration, your child would prefer, on the whole, that you feel
ashamed.

This being so, it may help if I anticipate with you the kind of
adolescent rhetoric that you may hear. There must be an infinite
number of ways to put you into conflict. But here are some of the
familiar leitmotifs:

"Mom, I don't need to be here—a little counseling, and all will
be well!"

"I am righteously baffled about what minor flaw of mine could
possibly make sense of this parental idiocy."

"I didn't realize you were serious, but hey, now I get it, so I
promise—I'll sign in blood!—if you'll just take me home I'll behave
now."

"Daddy, the boys are crazy, the girls are suicidal—so if you leave
me here with these weirdos, I'll get worse."

"Take me home now, Dad, or I'll never visit your nursing home!"

Some of you may be spared this deft rhetoric, but most parents hear some variation on these themes, which may make you feel worse, or worry your child is the only one who talks like this.

Check out with your child's therapist or team leader any complaint of staff misbehavior that upsets you . . . We'll want to know about, and address, any legitimate problems; and we can clear up distortions—our staff will tell you the truth as best they know it and investigate problems they don't already know about.

Separation may turn out to be as hard for you as it is for your child—maybe harder. Rosemary and I have all three of our daughters gone from home, as I write, and we've learned how hard this is. It helps to have contact, I think. Our staff will bring you news, in regular phone calls, and tell you, from an adult point of view, how your child is doing. Regular phone calls with your child help, of course, though too many calls, and too much news and gossip from home makes it harder to settle into the social world of the ranch. I suggest you make it plain you will reply promptly to every letter you get, but won't keep writing in a vacuum. This will encourage reciprocation, and may help bring you the contact you need.

For some parents, anxiety over separation, or guilt and shame about the events that preceded enrollment, are sufficiently painful and persistent that it's helpful to find a competent therapist to help think these matters through. Take care of yourselves. Our staff needs to concentrate on your child's adjustment at this point, so if you feel you're having trouble and want to talk this over, please feel free to call me.

Finally, I suggest you back off. Let your son settle into school, make friends, struggle with the new discipline, adjust to Thomas' cooking and learn to do the chores. Let your daughter make her own way. I know this is hard for sad parents to do. Children do bruise one another as they become acquainted; the school's rules and limits will be resented. It's likely all of this will be difficult and may provoke worries and suffering and complaints about life's unfairness. You may well hear recurrent expressions of the wish for a magical, immediate solution, for relief from the hard work.

But you should know that Montana Academy's staff and student community tends to be affectionate and attentive. We all should anticipate that it takes time for teenagers to do what you have sent your child here to do. We know this, and we also know that your child may not manage this gracefully, at first.

From now on, I ask that you speak very directly to your child's therapist about any and all of your communications with your child. This is the time, now, to build a trusting working alliance. You (and we, and your child) need this. Please tell us (e-mail may be best) how we can help you. You have honored us with the responsibility to care for your child. We look forward to working with you.

> Warm regards,
> John A. McKinnon, M.D.
> Medical Director and
> Program Director

"Well . . . that's quite some missive," I judged as I read and reread Dr. McKinnon's letter to new parents from the safe distance of home in Washington, D.C. "I'm sure we won't see much of that oppositional stuff with Will." Will's polite compliance was famous. It bordered on passivity. I figured the bulk of McKinnon's advisory was really directed at other parents, other kids. Wrong again.

To say that Will's early reactions to the program, and to his teachers, doctors, and therapists, were less than enthusiastic is an understatement. He met a few kids he liked; in fact, on his first day at Montana Academy he discovered a friend whom he had known before, Marla, a girl who attended his parochial school in San Francisco during eighth grade. What an extraordinary coincidence. But overall, he thought the program was a gigantic waste of time. We had hoped it would be otherwise.

* * *

My first letter to Will at Montana Academy:

May 3, 2001

Willo, my beloved,
By now—week one—you are settled in, wearing full cowboy regalia and wondering why you ever breathed anything but the pure air of Montana. Right? And what about those elk? Wacky, aren't they? Tell me that you've fallen in love with ranch animals.

In reality, by now, you're probably feeling pretty funky— homesick and funky. But I'm hoping you've made some friends (You're so expert at that.) and that you've been shooting some hoops, and that they can really bake a nice pie at Montana Academy and that your first night in the bunk was a restful one.

I checked the weather this morning in Kalispell and it appears that it's warming up and that the sun may be out by the end of the day. When do you get to experiment with all of your new outdoors gear? Dad said that you got a really cool new pair of hiking boots. John would be jealous. In fact, I'm not going to tell him, because he'd make us buy some for him, just so as to be fair.

Everyone here is asking about you and I am referring them to the Montana Academy Web site, so that they can see where you are. Emmylou told me that Montana is every ten-year-old boy's idea of Texas. They shot all of those old cowboy movies in Montana, probably because the Hollywood actors didn't really want all that dust up their noses in Texas. You've been to Texas. It's flat. Flat and dry. Montana is really the place a cowboy wants to be—unless he wants dust up his nose.

The beauty of this new letter-writing system is that you have to write me back. I can't imagine anything better than getting a letter from you. When you write I want to know all about the place. The kids (Are the girls as cool as you hoped?), your teachers, what you are reading, what you do in the evening, what you have for dinner— the important stuff. I would be terribly worried about you if I hadn't seen it myself and met the folks who run it. But I had such a good feeling about the place. I felt that it might become your kind of place eventually, too. Not that you want to hear that right now. So in your note you can tell me all of your complaints, too.

Last night we sent John to Whole Foods with $70 to buy food. He came back with the weirdest assortment of stuff—and he didn't even spend all of the money. That's the problem with Whole Foods in his mind: there's nothing there to buy. He bought some blueberry-flavored granola, some ground beef, three apples, some fancy cheeses and an assortment of barbecued, pre-cooked turkey drumsticks. He forgot to get juice, which is why we sent him in the first place. Now if we'd sent him to Safeway, he would have spent $30 more than we'd given him and come back with the double stuffed Oreos, but this way no one is happy.

Max is coming out for just one week in June. Jane and John will be home, too, so I expect that we'll have wild and noisy evenings keeping track of everyone's whereabouts.

Dad said that he had a really good time with you when you went to Montana and that you were in good spirits and telling lots of funny Montana jokes. (What is a Montana joke?) We were both so worried that this would be a hard transition. It sounds like you were a real trouper.

We love you like crazy, Will. We love you and miss you and I'll write again next week, and I think we even get to talk to you by phone sometime between now and then. Meanwhile, please know that I think about you all the time and wonder what you are doing this very moment and hope you are feeling brighter about your prospects on Planet Earth.

Mom

Will's first letter home from Marion, Montana, May 2001:

Mom . . .
Hi. School and everything is o.k. Miss home a lot. I'm getting my second phase thing in a couple of days. No real advantages except a

*couple of things. Actually probably a whole bunch of things. I get to go
off campus on weekends and stuff. Less boring hikes, more candy and
stuff. I'll probably be on student council because they get to go out to
some place every Tuesday and get soda and candy and cookies and
good food (it's some kind of restaurant place). Also, they don't read my
mail (they were supposed to on the first phase but they didn't even do
it then). So you can send me mail from my friends. If you talk to Maga
and Pop tell them thank you for the books. I like them a lot and am
actually reading them. Also if you could send some books up here, that
would be good. Actually, I just need more coloring books. I'm running
out of coloring books and getting tired of the ones I have because I've
already colored all the good pages. That would be greatly appreciated.
Well, this place is kind of dumb. People are nice, but there's a lot of
stupid parts. I'll talk to you soon. Love you. Say "hi" to everybody.*

Will

Bob's first letter to Will, from San Francisco:

May 11, 2001

Hey, Woo—
*Seems like a long time, since I dropped you off, but I guess it has only
been nine days. I wonder if time is passing quickly for you up in the
mountains. Mom called me right up, after you spoke to her on
Monday. She said she thought you were doing pretty well—at least
that's the way you made it sound. I hope so. I'm sure there will be
lots of times when you wonder how you ever wound up in such a
different world. Hopefully there will also be times when you see some
interesting possibilities.*

*I'll be talking to you either this coming Monday morning or the
one after that. (The school literature and Dr. Malinak's messages
don't seem to agree on whether we talk to you once a week or every
second week.) I miss hearing your voice. But I also feel certain that
you're right where you need to be for the moment.*

We got your letter yesterday. Thanks for the update on how things are going. Max and Melissa were also real interested to see what you had to say. I remember that Greg Windham had warned us, the morning you arrived at the ranch, that some kids on your team had gotten into trouble and they were deciding what should be done as a result. So you guys were put on a lockdown, eh? Must have actually been in your honor, Woo—especially the baloney sandwiches. Glad you're past that now. Glad too that there are some girls around, and at least one familiar face. What a coincidence that is.

Next time you write, let me know a few of the details of your day to day life. How has it worked out with your evening munchies, for instance? Is there a way to get a snack after taking the medications at night? Also, what time do you take them in the evening? With dinner? Or later? Do you guys do that regular reading session the way it says in the school literature? What have you been reading? Do they have good stuff in the school library? Or should I send you some books? Also, do you ever get a chance to get in any hoops? In the afternoon or after dinner? How is that court in the barn? Any home court advantage yet?

News here is pretty scarce this week . . .

I'm working really hard. Traveling a bit. Painting bookshelves at home with the game on in the background. Same exciting guy as always. Trying to make some plans for our first visit with you at the school. It will just be Mom and me, and we'll be talking it over with you ahead of time.

I think about you all the time. And lots of other folks are asking for news. You're on a forced vacation from your regular life, and I hope that you are already finding some logic in making the most of it. Do something for me . . .

Every day in your journal or someplace write down one reason why you are glad to be alive that particular day. Kind of like what we used to do at the dinner table—make everybody say one positive thing. And Max would always try to think of something about Buster and you would always come up with a joke. It doesn't have to be anything big, *by the way. Probably most days it won't be big. But you of all people could probably learn something from this. And it might be kind of interesting to see whether the things you list change as the weeks go by.*

There are lots of such reasons, by the way. Lots. And there's nothing more important than knowing what they are.

Love you a lot,
Dad

Okay, so we were forewarned the transition would be difficult, but I was unprepared for the vehemence of Will's opposition when we returned to Montana for our first parent visit in mid-June. The plan was to retrieve him from campus and take him with us "on pass" overnight anywhere within driving distance of the school—anywhere in the Flathead Valley.

Bob and I could hardly wait to see him. He and his team leader, Greg Windham, had drawn up a "pass agreement" for his overnight, a privilege afforded students who had reached "Moon Clan," the second of five developmental levels.* Will and Greg came up with three goals for this first pass, which they articulated in writing:

- have fun
- no revisiting why they sent you [to Montana Academy]
- honesty

Will, Greg, and Bob signed the statement below:

I agree to these conditions and rules, specifically and in spirit, and I agree to follow these guidelines rigorously and without putting my parents in the position of chasing me, or reminding me, or defending these rules, which are the Montana Academy rules, and not for debate with parents. I understand that if I fail

---

* Drawing on Native American imagery, the five phases of the program were Earth Clan, Moon Clan, Sun Clan, Star Clan, and Sky Clan. Successful completion of all five phases constituted "graduation" from the therapeutic program.

at this discipline and truthfulness, torments of an appropriate rigor will follow.

"Wow," I thought as I mulled over the pass agreement. "That's a little heavy . . . Torments of an appropriate rigor will follow?" Obviously, a staff member with a predilection for the medieval was having a little fun with the written rules and regulations. But we were hardly an hour into the visit and our first destination, Taco Bell for a couple of bean burritos, when I realized that we were in for a rough ride.

We had booked a hotel in Big Fork, a small resort town on Flathead Lake. We planned to have a good meal and take Will bowling. But the atmosphere between Will and us was negatively charged. Will was by turns sullen and uncharacteristically furious. He lashed out at us for sending him to Montana and asserted he was fed up with his doctor, therapists, and teachers.

"I'm getting nothing out of the place. The kids there are ridiculous." His classes were "inane" and he vowed he would "never tell Malinak [his psychiatrist] a fucking thing." On top of that: "The food sucks,"; "I'm already sick of this 'Native American' shit"; and "I hate hiking; it's hot and boring."

Oh, did I mention he was homesick and wanted to leave immediately? We argued for hours and got nowhere. At turns, we cried. Bob and I even threatened to go "by the book" and return him to campus before his allotted pass was over.

"Will, you're doing exactly what you need to be doing *right now* to get well," Bob insisted. But Will didn't buy it. The visit was a bust. (Although, he *had* accomplished one of his written goals: he *was* honest.) None of us was happy by the time it was over.

"Oh, Willy, smells like you're having brownies for dessert tonight!" I exclaimed enthusiastically as we walked through the kitchen to remand him to Greg at the appointed hour, Sunday afternoon. Will shot me a withering glance, as if to say, "Mom, you are so full of shit."

Bob and I drove away from the ranch in silence. By the time we were over the first ridge, we were both weeping.

From Will's journal, June 2001:

I am in no way a spiritual person. I have no concrete beliefs about God, the afterlife, or any of that. When I try to imagine death, I really don't know what to think. Being in Montana, there's plenty to look at. Some places I can see for what seems like miles and miles. I can see mountains and trees on those mountains and birds in those trees and a lot of other crazy shit that I never really thought I'd appreciate. When I see all of this, as strange as this may sound, I associate it with death . . . I see all those birds flying around and horses running around far in the distance and it all seems so free, so perfect and free. Maybe it's this freedom, this lack of worry and concern that ties it to death in my mind, but when I see things of such overwhelming beauty, I actually feel . . . I don't even know how to say it, connected I guess. I feel like, if I had died, I would be part of it. I don't know if I would be one of those birds or horses, but I would be part of the whole thing.

I've come to realize that I should be dead. Considering the magnitude of what I took, in addition to the tranquilizers I was given while they tried to subdue me . . . I believe I should be dead right now. I hadn't really added it all up until very recently, but I am now realizing that I really *should* have died that night. Please don't perceive this as me *wishing* I had died that night because I don't. I can say in all honesty and sincerity that the moment I woke up was one of—if not the single most—happiest moments of my life. Every day of this "second" life I stop and appreciate how incredibly fucking lucky I am, even more so recently, having come to the conclusion I shouldn't be here.

[But] the time since I woke up has been a nightmare. It has been, in all honesty, the worst [time] of my life. Weeks of throwing up out of nervousness in a mental hospital, more arguments with my parents than I remember having in my entire life, saying good-bye to friends again and again, [being] reduced to tears over something I was so absolutely sure and positive about. It was shitty, simply put, and infinitely shittier knowing it was entirely my fault. I don't really know what I want to say about it. I feel like I should apologize for it, but at the same time, my feelings are so torn about how everything was dealt with that I don't really want to. However, you should know that, as much as I might joke around and mask my feelings, it was in no way a good time and I am incredibly sorry for starting it all.

I'm driving a stolen car

On a pitch black night

And I'm telling myself

It's gonna be alright.

I drive by night

And I travel in fear

That in this darkness

I will disappear.

from "Stolen Car"
by Bruce Springsteen

8

CALIFORNIA ROCKET FUEL

In early summer, I got a call from Megan's mother.

"Will's been in touch with Megan. Apparently he called her from a pay phone when he was on a field trip." Megan's mother intercepted Will's call.

"Thanks, Virginia." When I hung up the phone, my hand was shaking. "What on earth does he think he's doing?" I wondered. Yet another wrinkle.

On a trip into Kalispell to go to the movies with his team, Will had tried to reach Megan from a pay phone. Also, we learned, he was writing to her—surreptitiously and against Montana Academy rules. Since at this stage in the program all of his incoming and outgoing mail was monitored, we were surprised that he somehow managed to smuggle letters to her.

Will, bucking the system? It was out of character for him to flagrantly challenge the rules. Maybe his behavior fell into some grand design—maybe it was a good sign he was acting out, defying the regulations, rather than drawing further into himself and sinking deeper into depression. Or maybe I was delusional for trying to put a positive spin on his actions. But I was chasing shadows; I wanted signs of forward motion, hints of progress. Not this.

Whatever Will's motivation, both Bob and I were alarmed. Bob fired off the following reprimand to Will:

Will—

Mom just called me to say that she had learned that you had been
sneaking letters out of school. And finding a way once to call up
Megan, as well. (Don't know how you managed that one.) Now, I
can well imagine why you would want—or even badly need—to try
to get in touch with your gal. But I would also urge you to think
about what that represents in terms of your commitment to the
program at school. Don't try to play around the rules. It may not
seem like it, but they have really good reasons for the way the
program is set up. It's hard being away from your friends. But you
need this time for yourself. You and your friends and your girlfriends
are great, but none of it was working well enough to keep you alive.
That is what this time is about. This is as serious as any problem in
your life will ever get. Open your eyes, Will. Give yourself a chance to
find a slightly different understanding of the world. Nothing could be
more important.

Love,
Dad

No doubt Will was hoping to forestall a permanent breakup with
Megan, but his desperate focus on the stunted relationship undermined all of our efforts to get him immersed in the program.

Show me a teenage boy who is expert at communicating emotion,
and I'll show you a kid who is about to pick your pocket, con his way
out of an assignment, or scheming for a lavish birthday gift. In therapy
Will and Dennis Malinak covered the same ground time and again,
discussing the importance of honesty and communication; honesty in
relationships and honesty in owning up to one's true feelings.

Will had spent his young life trying to please everyone, to play
the "good" kid. So when it came time to acknowledge mistakes or
shortcomings—or anger or pain—he failed and failed miserably. He
was paralyzed when it came to confessing the hurts and injuries that
pile up like landfill during the trials of adolescence.

Megan finally called the question. Recognizing the folly of holding on to a long-distance relationship as they both struggled to regain footing, she wrote him a profoundly insightful and moving letter.

Letter to Will from Megan, July 2001:

Dear Will,
Let me preface this letter with a little explanation. First, I'm sorry this is so late. Everything was sketchy with your mail and stuff and I heard you were in trouble. I'm also scared to send this off to you because you probably hate me for getting you in trouble or whatever, but it was my mom who called your mom and got the whole ball rolling, so to speak. I'm also sorry for the lack of sense this letter is going to make. I'm still a little confused as to how I feel about all this.

This isn't really a break-up letter because it doesn't really feel like we're together anymore. I'm not really zipping along in my love life now that you're gone. I just sort of put everything on hold. I'm obviously not over you in the least but I've had many epiphanies relating to our relationship.

First of all we were entirely dependent on each other. Especially in your case. You refused to talk to anyone else about your problems, and even what you told me was minimal. I feel like my presence really hindered any progress that you would have made in therapy.

I also feel like your dependence may have turned me into a stance, not a person. I think you needed me or someone there and it stopped being about me as a person. The night you tried to kill yourself we had been together for hours and I don't think you need a reminder of what we did. And during that time we were breaking up and I was seeing other people. You had to know that your trying to kill yourself would be a slap in the face. I'm not presuming to tell you that I was the only reason, but you had to know the repercussions of your actions, directly towards me at least. I don't know, it just doesn't seem like something you'd do to someone you love. Even now I still blame myself for what happened and that will probably never stop.

What I'm trying to say is that I can't go through a situation as painful as your suicide attempt ever again. I honestly wouldn't make it. I had a complete relapse when you were in the hospital. It was so scary to almost lose the most important person in my life, and especially since a lot of it was my fault. I'm not sure that I trust you not to hurt me like that again, at least the way you left me.

But I'm not ruling out the possibility that you've changed for the better. I'm just scared. I don't even know if you still feel the same way about me. And I don't know how to describe our relationship as of now. I really want to hear from you, so even if you're pissed write back. How do you feel about this relationship and me after some time away? Answer the question. Please try to communicate some legitimate feelings about everything because I'd love to sort all of this out.

You were my first real love and I'll always love you no matter what. I really hope you're doing well. And I hope more than anything that you're not just putting on your pretending to be better thing. Because that only hurts you and the people around you who love you. You have so much potential (I know how we all hate that speech.) Please think of all the possibilities you have. When things get rough (which they will) try to remember that everything will work out for the best in the end.

On a lighter note, I'm at camp right now. I'm doing really well. I haven't had any major relapses lately. The end of the school year was brutal, but it's over now so it's all good. How's everything in Montana? When are you coming back? Take your time there! I really hope you've figured out a lot of things for yourself. Write me back (if you're allowed).

Good luck with everything . . .

> *Love always,*
> *Megan*

Early August. Nearly six weeks after Bob's and my disastrous weekend visit with Will, he had not communicated with either of us in writing. I wrote in exasperation:

August 4, 2001

Will-o, you-doo-doo-head,
You can see by my salutation that I'm still really ticked-off about
your lack of letter writing. Five weeks—and not a single note. Maybe
something will come on Monday. Or maybe you just want to stay in
Sun Clan for the rest of your life.

I was in Austin, Texas this week. I don't know if you heard, but
Austin has had a run on over 100 degree-days like you wouldn't
believe. It was 107 degrees on Thursday. Totally unreal. It felt like we
were in Kuwait without the camels. Fancy air-conditioned hotels, big
cream-colored Mercedes and desert palm trees.

We're all really excited about coming to Montana soon.
Sometimes I miss you so much that it brings me to a standstill in the
middle of the sidewalk, people walking by me all around. I think
about the way you used to giggle when you were little and how much
fun you are when you're feeling well.

Max is here in Washington with his band, "Walken." They
played a very loud gig in Baltimore earlier today at a place called
"Ottobar." Right now they've all gone off to China Café for some
cheap eats—just as you'd expect.

I love you,
Mom

Megan's letter to Will from Camp Betsey Cox, Vermont, August 6,
2001:

Dear Will,
I was surprised and very happy with your letter. You really sound
like you're doing better and that's great. It seems like you're starting
to really get your shit together and I'm really happy for you. I'm so,
so glad that even though it's hard right now you're sticking with it.
I'm so proud of you.

About us getting back together . . . I don't think there's been

anything that I've thought about more in my entire life. Ideally,
being with you would be wonderful. If we really could have an open
and honest relationship all we'd need was the picket fence and yellow
lab. I just don't think we could pick it back up and have everything
be perfect. Especially since we're so far apart. If we ever want "us" to
work again it will take a lot of work from both of us that can't really
be done through the mail.

For the time being, it would probably be best if we just kept it as
friends. I would like to try again when you're home for good. (That
doesn't mean you should try to leave early . . . I'm not going
anywhere.) I just need stability and I don't think I'm ready to handle
an intense, long distance relationship. Another thing to consider is
the fact that you're probably going to go through some dramatic
changes. I don't want us to be together while you're gone and have
you change your mind and then feel bad about telling me etc. etc.

I think it would be best for both of us to wait before jumping
back into this. We need to be face to face and work it all out that
way. And everything has to be subject to a change to a more healthy
way of living. (Hmmm, I don't know if that makes any sense outside
my head . . .) Because things can't go back to the way they were.
Judging from what you said, you agree about that.

Sorry if this letter is disjointed . . . let me paint the scene where I
am . . . I'm in the infirmary for the sixth consecutive day with
bronchitis and strep throat. The camp herbalist is convinced it's
tuberculosis—it's not; she's kind of crazy. Anyway, the lone male
counselor lives in the room next to mine and I can hear some animal
rummaging around in the mess that is his room. I am very afraid to
open the door, as I anticipate being attacked by a large rat. So that's
why I am distracted. . . . sorry about the tangent.

Stepping back from everything, I still love you. But now I feel
more in need to protect myself from potentially traumatic situations
and that's why I'm waiting. Don't think that I'm saying this just to
get you off my back—I mean it all.

Please keep in touch. I want to know how your school is, what

*classes you're taking, etc. I also heard through the grapevine that
you're stuck in Moon (??) phase because you won't write your parents.
Will, Will, Will. Is that really a fight worth fighting? Your parents
might be a little weird sometimes (they all are) and you're probably
pissed at them for sending you there, but they love you a lot and only
want the best. It would be more productive if you told them all the
issues you have with them because at least then you could try to
improve your relationship. (Sorry, more unsolicited advice. Ha-ha.)*

*Again, I'm so happy for you. Keep working and fighting. I'm
sorry that you're still depressed, but eventually you will feel better if
you keep working at it. I hope everything is going well. Have you
learned how to horseback ride? Are there even horses? Write me
soon.*

> *Love always,*
> *Megan*

P.S. And for the love of God, write to your mother.

Letter from Will from Marion, Montana, mid-August 2001:

Mom . . .
*Hi. Sorry about the lack of writing and such. Bears ate my hands. I
had to wait for them to grow back.*

*It's been hard to write. Very busy. Very tired/confused. Doing
pretty well, all things considered. Feeling a little bit better. Possibly
due to recent meds. Also, possibly due to recent viewing of Bambi.
Got my camera. Taking some pictures but haven't gotten any back
yet. I'll probably get my Phase 3 on Monday. Just need to wrestle one
crocodile/lawnmower. Slay the school dragon, save the fair maiden.*

*So I'll talk to you all soon. Say hi to everybody. They claim
there's a whole assload of mail for me today. I'm on the edge of my
seat. I miss you all.*

> *Love,*
> *Will*

Note to Will from his stepfather, Jack Brady, Washington, D.C., August 2001:

Will—
Here's some insight [about bears] from my bike group—

> *Love,*
> *Jack*

MEMO:
Subject: Bear Alert

The Montana State Department of Fish and Wildlife is advising hikers, hunters, fishermen and residents to take extra precautions and be on alert for bears while in Glacier National Park area this summer. They advise people to wear noise-producing devices such as little bells on their clothing to alert but not startle the bears unexpectedly. They also advise you to carry pepper spray in case of an encounter with a bear. It is also a good idea to watch for signs of bear activity.

People should be able to recognize the difference between black bear and grizzly bear droppings. Black bear droppings are smaller and contain berries and possibly squirrel fur. Grizzly bear droppings have bells in them and smell like pepper spray.

Over time Will began to settle into Montana Academy, although he continued to voice resentment about our decision to place him there. True to his nature, he was well liked by other students, his doctors, and his teachers. I took it as a good sign when he decided to run for a seat on the student council, but he played it down.

"We get to go off campus to that diner by McGregor Lake once a week for the meetings and they've got a bunch of candy there I can buy with my allowance."

Not exactly a proclamation of grand ambition, but it was a step.

I have to believe that after three or four months, Will opened up a minimalist dialogue with his doctor and counselors that provided the underpinnings of therapeutic change, but he retained a distrust of the process and held in contempt other kids in the program who he believed manipulated the process.

From Will's journal, July/August 2001:

I guess what amazes me most (or what I wonder about or whatever) is how much dignity people are willing to give up to get out of there. Or integrity. That's probably why I don't talk. I see all these kids saying all they can hoping it'll get a ticket home. I don't want that I guess. I want to get home and all, but I don't want to be like Aaron or whatever. He seems so forced and phony. I don't want to lie my way out of here. And I think it's possible, but it almost seems like nobody here even bothers trying it. So maybe it isn't. It seems like kids here don't try to lie intentionally. They just start lying to themselves and it seems like all of the sudden they start believing it and telling it to everyone and then they go home and are comforted by the fact that no one was here to see it (except their parents, they don't even matter, they changed our diapers.) So they can just snap right out of it when they get home and no one there will even know that they ever changed. I guess Mark did it honestly. But even he didn't do it completely honest. I want to get out of here without even thinking about lying to Greg and Charles and Malinak. I just want to do it straight out. I don't want to put out a separate personality for when I'm in group or therapy or just talking to them.

I guess I have an advantage over everyone else though. Because honestly, I don't even care about clans or getting out because I always have the turning 18 thing to fall back on. Maybe that's why everyone else is so multi-sided. Aaron really irritates me in that sense. I find it so hard to believe that within a matter of weeks (days/hours?) he could go from: "I think that drugs will always be a part of my life," to being totally clean FOREVER. And he just seems too conceited about it (and everything else). Like by switching he's suddenly better than all of us. Now he no longer has to look anybody in the eye. He's one of those people who will leave here in December and I won't have to see again. It's not like those people don't exist in the real world. But they are sure as hell easier to ignore.

The biggest therapeutic challenge in Will's case was finding appropriate medication to treat his depression. For most students at Montana Academy who suffered from depression, you could trace the seeds of their illness back to dysfunctional home environments or emotional or physical abuse or stunted maturity, any one of which could seriously hinder a child's ability to succeed. The external strife in these teenagers' circumstances *triggered* their depression. In large measure the formula for their recovery consisted of providing appropriate behavioral therapy, retooling their coping skills, and boosting their ability to handle the outside circumstances. But the roots of Will's depression were largely biological and not the result of the collapse of the family, abuse, or an inability to succeed in his environment. It would take more than skilled therapy to treat his depression.

Will had been taking antidepressant medication since December 2000 without any appreciable relief. When he reached Montana Academy in May, his psychiatrist, Dennis Malinak, initially stuck with the same drug regimen: a combination of Prozac and Remeron. But by June, Dennis decided Will ought to be evincing more relief than we were seeing. He decided, and we agreed, to taper Will's dosage of Prozac and begin to introduce newer, more targeted antidepressants, either Effexor or Celexa.

Will's frustration with the medication was evident in his letters home, and in our weekly phone conversations. He started to wonder aloud if he was ever going to get better. By midsummer, Dennis confided that he too was frustrated. He expected to see Will improving gradually, but none of the pharmacological interventions were working. Bob, Dennis, and I discussed the possibility of ECT (electroconvulsive therapy), if the situation did not improve soon. Dennis broached the subject with Will; Will had no objections. He said he had "nothing to lose."

Electroconvulsive therapy's application to adolescents is controversial, although the small sample of teens that have been treated with ECT experienced the same beneficial results as adults.[1] If we were forced to consider ECT as a last resort, we were inclined to give it a chance. Dennis, Bob, and I agreed that ECT would be a last-ditch option.

Few medical issues are as controversial as the use of antidepressant drugs to treat teenagers and children—and few health care issues have the potential to arouse public hysteria.

The issue grabbed the public's attention in the summer of 2003 after the British Medicines and Healthcare Products Regulatory Agency (the U.K.'s equivalent of the U.S. Food and Drug Administration [FDA]) reviewed a rash of anecdotal evidence linking the drug Paxil to a surge in suicidal thinking and suicidal behavior among teens. The British government sounded the alarm, urging practitioners against prescribing Paxil for patients less than eighteen years of age.

The FDA, hoping to buy time for a more detailed review of the data, issued a public advisory in October 2003 designed to signal caution. The FDA's first advisory on the subject read in part:

> FDA notes, to date, that the data do not clearly establish an association between the use of these drugs and increased suicidal thoughts or actions by pediatric patients. Nevertheless, it is not possible at this point to rule out an increased risk of these adverse events for any of these drugs.[2]

The FDA's statement troubled me. It was alarmingly ambiguous. How could the government agency whose stated mission makes it "responsible for advancing the public health by helping the public get the accurate, science-based information they need to use medicines and foods to improve their health,"[3] think this clarified the issue or helped parents struggling to understand a complex medical debate that held life-threatening consequences for our children?

I wrote an op-ed piece for the *Washington Post*, criticizing the FDA, the medical establishment, *and* the media for failing to provide clear guidance to families whose children were in crisis and fueling the public's fear and mistrust of pharmaceutical interventions.

The FDA's October advisory conceded that the government needed further study of the clinical data on the drugs' efficacy and risks and offered, "As we recognize that this is a serious illness, we need a better understanding of how to use the products we have."[4]

Isn't it obvious, I argued: "Depression isn't just a serious illness. It's a *life-threatening* illness, and it's disheartening to think that so little has been done so far to sort out the confusion over remedies for our children's suffering."[5]

Shortly thereafter, I was invited to serve as the "patient representative" on the advisory panel convened in February 2004 to look at the risks of antidepressants in pediatric populations. The FDA hoped my background as an "educated consumer"—as opposed to a medical practitioner—and my sensitivities as a parent of a child with depression would add a unique perspective to the panel's composition.

In late 2003, the British government took the unprecedented step of banning the use of all SSRIs, except Prozac, for treatment of patients under the age of eighteen. Now everyone was panicking and the FDA was challenged to present a clear mission for the upcoming advisory panel.

Specifically, the advisory panel was asked to consider a spate of alarming reports transmitted to the FDA's Office of Drug Safety about serious side effects exhibited by children prescribed certain SSRIs, the newer, allegedly safer and more targeted SSRIs. The drugs being scrutinized by the FDA included Zoloft, Celexa, Paxil, Effexor, Remeron, and Serzone, as well as Prozac.

The FDA's advisory panel was asked to consider whether the United States should follow the British lead and ban or curtail the use of antidepressants in treating young people, or wait until the data could be thoroughly analyzed by an independent panel of experts at Columbia University who were tasked with doing a blind study of previous clinical trials conducted by the drugs' manufacturers.

In advance of the FDA meeting, members of the advisory panel were asked to review volumes of technical data. I spent days poring over analyses of clinical trial data (most of it far too complex for anyone without background in science or medicine). Nonetheless, I searched through the materials for the answer to the one question that bothered me most of all: Is there evidence to show that the drugs we used to treat Will's depression prompted him to attempt suicide?

February 2, 2004: the daylong FDA hearing was emotionally white-hot. Some sixty families lined up to testify in the ballroom of a Bethesda, Maryland, hotel, packed with media, government officials, and interested parties. The families hoisted placards with photos of dead children and offered personal vignettes of tragedy and loss, arguing they and their families were victimized by a heartless and greedy pharmaceutical industry, an inept and ill-informed medical community, and government agencies and lawmakers who place the interests of drug companies ahead of their obligation to protect public health and safety.

Some of the families' grievances were backed up by testimony from sympathetic doctors and trial lawyers who laid blame squarely on the FDA, charging the government agency with negligence for inadequately safeguarding our children from the adverse effects of antidepressants, and with malfeasance for basing decisions on data provided by the pharmaceutical industry. They claimed the drug companies altered or dismissed negative findings in the drugs' preapproval trials.

Presenters also attacked doctors for being seduced by the promotional tactics of drug companies whose marketing representatives urge them to prescribe newer drugs, the side effects of which have not been fully documented in pediatric patients, or for handing out drug samples without fully understanding the drugs' risks.

A handful of parents, doctors, and advocates for the mentally ill argued just as passionately about the benefits of antidepressants. Dr. David Fassler, distinguished child and adolescent psychiatrist and trustee of the American Psychiatric Association, reminded the audience that "the biggest risk for a child with depression is to be left untreated." This view was underscored by a board member of the National Alliance for the Mentally Ill (NAMI), who testified, "I, as a mother and a psychiatrist, realize that the evidence linking suicidal behavior to SSRIs is weak and I will not draw conclusions lightly based on anecdotal information and isolated case reports."

In support of SSRIs, the panel was presented with convincing evidence from Columbia University's Dr. David Shaffer, who suggested there was a link between the decline in the suicide rate among fifteen- to twenty-four year-olds over the past ten years and a greater reliance on SSRIs during the same time frame. Dr. Shaffer cited a 2003 World Health Organization study, which found a significant reduction rate (an average of thirty-three percent) of youth suicides in fifteen countries during the last decade.[6]

But these views were drowned out by the anger and bitterness of the families who lost children to suicide (and, in a few cases, to prison, for homicides committed while "under the influence" of SSRIs). Not surprisingly, their voices overwhelmed the FDA proceedings and colored the daylong debate.

The rancorous proceedings, however, underscored what I see as a more serious problem arising from a fundamental breakdown in the government machinery designed to protect the public from a market-driven drug industry and a health care system that pays more attention to the bottom line than the patients it serves.

In the United States, although Prozac is the only antidepressant currently approved by the FDA for use in treating children and adolescents with depression, doctors are permitted to prescribe any drug on the market "off label"—or without specific regulatory approval. Physicians—not necessarily psychiatrists—routinely prescribe drugs such as Effexor, Paxil, Zoloft, Celexa, Serzone, Wellbutrin, and Remeron for a host of ailments they observe in their teen patients, including anxiety disorders and attention deficit disorders, in addition to a wide range of mood disorders—such as major depression.

Sometimes a drug is prescribed after just a brief consultation with a child and parent; doctors whose schedules are constricted by the dictates of managed care cannot allocate time for close patient monitoring or observation.

We know that the first stop for a family with a child in the throes of a mental health crisis is the family physician or pediatrician; and because of managed care's prohibitive allowances for mental health, pediatric patients, whose diagnoses may be complex, are seldom thoroughly evaluated or referred to specialists. The bottom line for managed care trumps patient care, and HMOs prefer to see a child prescribed medication rather than an extended course of therapy with a trained psychiatrist or psychologist, which is far more expensive.

I did not realize we had gotten so far afield from the practice of responsible medicine. Like most parents of children struggling with a mental illness, I took it on faith that any doctor licensed to prescribe these medications was familiar with the intricacies of brain chemistry; I assumed that most doctors who see children and teens with depression designed drug treatment regimes tailored specifically for their pediatric patients. I believed that doctors matched symptoms to medication based on precise formulae, with predictable outcomes. Not true.

In 2002, an estimated 157 million antidepressant drug prescriptions were dispensed in the United States. Of an estimated 10.8 million antidepressant prescriptions dispensed to patients under the age of eighteen, pediatricians, family practitioners, or neurologists—not psychiatrists—wrote one-third of them.[7] And that is a risky approach for both young patients and their doctors.

In early 2004, product labeling or package inserts for all antidepressants carried the following:

> Suicide: The possibility of suicide attempt is inherent in major depressive disorder and may persist until significant remission occurs. Close supervision of high-risk patients should accompany initial drug therapy. Prescriptions for [Drug X] should be written for the smallest quantity of tablets consistent with good patient management, in order to reduce the risk of overdose.

It was evident, however, that few doctors, outside of psychiatric specialties, were familiar with the nuances of the drugs or their range of side effects.

In two instances cited at the February 2004 FDA hearing, teenage patients were handed a one- or two-week course of an antidepressant drug "sample" by a physician (in neither case was the doctor a psychiatrist) and instructed cavalierly to "try this for a week or two and call me back." In both instances, the children took their own lives before the sample ran out.

We will never know whether it was the result of an adverse drug reaction, lack of drug effect, or an underlying illness that led these young people to such a heartbreaking end. Likewise, I will never know if the combination of drugs or any single antidepressant medication Will was prescribed in the winter of 2001 contributed to or directly resulted in his suicide attempt. It is unlikely we will get a clear answer to this puzzle anytime soon.

Before I was named to the FDA's advisory panel, I was unaware of the process by which drugs make it onto the market. But after my exposure to the bureaucracy, I concluded that the FDA's drug approval process was inherently flawed.

With each new drug application, the FDA receives a fee of approximately five hundred thousand dollars from the drug's maker to help defray the government agency's costs of conducting the review. But I was surprised to discover that the FDA relies almost entirely upon data about a drug's safety from a single source—the drug's manufacturer (or in the FDA's parlance, the drug's "sponsor"). So, the FDA does not oversee an unfettered, government-funded drug *review* process, where, presumably, potential harmful side effects of a drug such as Paxil or Zoloft could be systematically reported, analyzed, and monitored by rigorous and independent analysis; rather, the FDA conducts a drug *approval* process narrowly based on data the drug company wants the FDA to see. And since the pharmaceutical companies consider all trial data to be "proprietary," they cherry-pick the studies that support their claims of a drug's efficacy and bury others in a drawer.

In 2001 Dr. Marcia Angell, former editor in chief of the *New England Journal of Medicine* and professor at Harvard Medical School told the NIH *Record:*

> Drug companies are exerting influence over the evaluation of their products either directly or indirectly . . . [the] FDA is beholden for its existence on companies it is supposed to regulate, and that should never be the case with a regulatory agency."[8]

In an interview in November 2002 for a documentary about the FDA's approval process, Dr. Angell asserted, "You see study after study that is really set up, designed by the company, to show what they want to find."[9] So, it is not illegal—*immoral*, perhaps, but not illegal—for a drug company to suppress or fail to disclose negative results of its clinical trials. Who knew? Not I, and I have spent the past three years scouring the literature on teen depression and antidepressant medication. As Dr. Thomas R. Insel, director of the National Institute of Mental Health, summed up in early 2004, "We have been dependent on the pharmaceutical industry to provide the answers. The questions they want answered are different than the public health questions."[10] That's putting it mildly.

Spin these observations out to their logical conclusion: drug companies are in the business of making money; the FDA is in the business of protecting the public. The two are incompatible and they have no business being in bed together.

Try to explain the dysfunctional institutional dynamic of the drug approval process to the parents of a gorgeous and vivacious young woman portrayed in cap and gown in a college graduation photo shown at the FDA hearing. Her mother, Sara Bostock, testified that Cecily became agitated and sleepless upon taking Paxil. Three weeks into a course of treatment on the drug, she stabbed herself to death late at night in the family's kitchen. Her autopsy revealed abnormally high levels of the drug in her system, suggesting that the Paxil had failed to metabolize properly.

Since we do know that drugs metabolize at significantly different rates in children and young people, and since there are few predictors of a drug's potential side effects on children, shouldn't doctors be taking greater precautions when prescribing these medications to children and adolescents than they might for their adult patients? Shouldn't younger patients—shouldn't all patients—be monitored more carefully for adverse reactions in the initial days following the introduction of a new medication?

In the midst of this debate, well-regarded author on depression Andrew Solomon wrote in a March 2004 *New York Times* editorial,

> A patient should know the risks from the start. There is a world of difference between simply believing that life has no value, and knowing that feeling that way may be a side effect of medication. Patients must be able to recognize the difference.[11]

But I argue that children and adolescents are *unable* to recognize the difference, hence it falls to parents and practitioners to exercise extreme caution, be aware of the potential and adverse effects, and monitor children and teens closely.

Members of the medical establishment fear, however, that by issuing heightened warnings about the risks associated with SSRIs and other antidepressants, physicians and parents will curtail the drugs' use, or that by sounding an alarm families with depressed children will be frightened away from seeking treatment. Their fear is not unfounded.

After my commentary appeared in the *Washington Post*, excoriating the FDA, the media, and the medical establishment for failing to provide parents with the necessary guidance, I received a thought-provoking letter from a psychiatrist practicing in a small community in Maryland. In her letter to the editor printed in the *Washington Post*, Dr. Carol Paris wrote:

> As the sole psychiatrist in full-time private practice in my county, I depend on continuing medical education programs, psychiatric

journals and consultations with colleagues to keep me up to date on the standard of care for treatment of psychiatric illnesses. I do not turn to newspapers or popular magazines. So when a parent of a teen I was treating with Paxil called to ask if I was aware of the "information" published that day about the increased risk of suicidal behavior in teens treated with this antidepressant, I was alarmed. Had I missed something in the scientific literature? The last thing I wanted was to recommend a treatment that could result in suicidal behavior in a child who hadn't been suicidal.[12]

Dr. Paris consulted a colleague who was board certified in child and adolescent psychiatry and was assured that the study widely reported in the media was flawed and inconclusive; she called her teenage patient's mother to share this information. But, she said,

I made a decision to no longer accept new patients younger than eighteen. Why? Because at this time, there is no right answer. And while I am willing to explain this to concerned parents, I am not willing to defend myself to a jury that lacks the sophistication to understand the difference between anecdotal evidence and sound scientific research.[13]

What a pity that the only practicing psychiatrist in the county felt compelled to exclude young patients out of fear of being sued, "not because," as she emphasized, "I practice bad medicine, but because I might prescribe an antidepressant and a patient might attempt suicide anyway."

At the conclusion of the FDA's February 2004 hearing, the advisory panel recommended that the FDA submit the clinical data regarding SSRIs' efficacy and safety to an independent team of researchers at Columbia University for further analysis to determine whether or not the data, once reclassified into standardized categories, would show evidence of a strong signal of suicidal thinking and behavior. Meanwhile the FDA was urged "to go ahead and issue stronger warning indications to clinicians." "*And to parents,*" added Dr. Norman Fost, a professor of pediatrics and bioethics and member of the advisory panel. I concurred.

The FDA also alerted the public to watch for specific rare side effects, including agitation, akathesia (psychomotor restlessness), and anxiety and hostility, which may be attributed to antidepressants in a small subset of patients. Reports of these side effects were at the heart of the testimony the FDA's advisory panel found particularly troubling—children and teens with no prior history of hostility or anxiety suddenly spun out of control and committed horrific acts of violence or self-destruction.

On March 22, 2004, the FDA adopted the advisory panel's recommendations and issued a new advisory calling on doctors, patients, and families to be supervigilant for worsening depression or suicidal thinking not only when a course of antidepressants is introduced, but whenever the dosage is changed. The drug companies, including the makers of Prozac, Paxil, Zoloft, Effexor, Celexa, Remeron, Lexapro, Luvox, Serzone, and Wellbutrin, were asked to add new warning labels to the packaging stating "patients being treated with antidepressants should be observed closely for clinical worsening and suicidality, especially at the beginning of a course of drug therapy, or at the time of dose changes, either increases or decreases.[14]*

By and large, psychiatric professionals support the use of antidepressants for their pediatric patients. They have witnessed the drugs' efficacy in their practices and fear that without the option of including SSRIs in a treatment regime, we would see a swift reversal of the downward trend in teen suicides. But why do the drugs' effects on adolescents vary so from the results we see in adult populations?

As we know, lack of impulse control and a proclivity for "risk-taking" behavior, attributed to an underdeveloped prefrontal cortex, are hallmarks of adolescence. Risk-taking behavior is significantly

---

* Another idiosyncrasy in the regulation of pharmaceuticals stipulates that the drug manufacturers cannot be forced to change labeling; the FDA may recommend changes in the packaging, but there is no legal requirement that they comply.

more commonplace than in either early childhood or adulthood. "[Adolescence] is a time when the brain is most vulnerable," says Dr. Jay Giedd, of the National Institute of Mental Health.[15]

It stands to reason that depressed teens may have more varied and radically different reactions to antidepressant medication than adults. But it also may be the case that, if left untreated, adolescents may suffer disproportionate damage to the areas of the brain undergoing rapid growth and change at a critical time in their development. And the propensity to engage in risky behavior during puberty should challenge us to identify every means available to ensure that depressed teens are offered all possible remedies for suicidal thinking in order to stave off suicidal behavior. I am convinced that the data we've seen to date demonstrates that antidepressants play a major role in effectively mitigating these risks in a majority of severely depressed adolescents and children.[16]

In advance of the February 2004 hearing, the FDA's point person on this issue, Dr. Thomas Laughren, wrote to the advisory panel and framed the debate succinctly:

> While the focus of the discussion at the . . . meeting will be on pediatric suicidality data, it is important to consider the effectiveness data for these drugs as part of the overall context for this discussion. Ultimately, this is a risk benefit assessment, so it is important to know where we stand on the benefit side of the issue.[17]

So true.

I appreciate that living is a risky business. There are no guarantees. And try as we might to protect our children, horrific tragedies occur. I believe that antidepressants are effective, and I feel certain that in the next few years, the evidence will continue to mount attesting to their efficacy. I am throwing my lot in with the medical experts, such as Dr. Richard Glass, deputy editor of the *Journal of the American Medical Association*, who asserts that recent investigations demonstrate that psychopharmacology has progressed "from the highly polarized beliefs of the past to assessment of carefully controlled data." In his editorial analysis of the landmark 2004 Treatment of Adolescents with Depression Study, he concludes, "As in other areas of health care, good empirical data always trumps beliefs and ideology."[18]

Knowing what I now know about the potential risks, would I still encourage an aggressive treatment regime including SSRIs to counter adolescent depression? Would I have supported our doctors' pursuit of the "right" formula for Will prior to and after his suicide attempt? Yes, I would. And I would urge parents of depressed teens to do the same, with the following caveats inspired by recent debate:

1. Become as informed as possible about the medication prescribed. If you do not understand the reason the antidepressant is being prescribed for your child or if you lack confidence in the doctor's ability to monitor your child and work with you closely during treatment, pressure the physician for more answers and a greater degree of engagement.

2. Be alert to any drastic changes in mood or behavior once your child begins a course of antidepressants or changes prescriptions or dosages. It's a monumental challenge to be one hundred percent vigilant of a child in the midst of a crisis, but err on the side of caution. Doctors and clinicians should monitor their patients routinely during treatment by insisting on seeing the patient frequently, and they should solicit feedback from parents and family about the teenager. Regrettably, the bulk of the burden falls to you, as family, to observe and report accurately any changes in mood or behavior.

I am convinced that for Will and for me, antidepressants represent the life jacket preventing us from being sucked under by depression's powerful undertow. But I also want to understand how a small number of pediatric patients exposed to these drugs experienced reactions ranging from suicide to homicide. *And* I want to know why these kids weren't being monitored more closely by the doctors who prescribed the medication. Were they misdiagnosed to begin with? Using an SSRI to treat a child with bipolar illness may indeed trigger a manic episode and, hence, lead to an uptick in suicidal impulses; psychiatrists know to stay away from SSRIs, or use them with caution when treating anyone but a person with a clear diagnosis of major depressive disorder. Were the dosages administered correctly or were they elevated precipitously when the patient failed to respond positively? And why has the pharmaceutical industry been allowed to go so long without fully disclosing the results of clinical trials—all of them?

As a direct result of the public meltdown over antidepressant medications for teens, pharmaceutical companies have come under pressure to open their trial data to public scrutiny from both the public and the medical establishment. Editors of medical journals, long regarded as the quality control engineers of the profession, have begun to require that companies publicly register drug trials at the outset as a prerequisite for journal publication, which would deter drug manufacturers from hiding the results of failed tests.

And public entities are attacking the drug companies, as well. In June 2004, New York State attorney general Eliot Spitzer accused Paxil's manufacturer GlaxoSmithKline of highlighting only the positive results of its clinical trials, while burying either inconclusive or negative results. While denying any wrongdoing, GlaxoSmithKline settled the state's case for $2.5 million in August 2004 and agreed to post test results in a comprehensive drug trial database (www.clinicaltrials.gov). Shortly thereafter, Eli Lilly, Prozac's manufacturer, followed suit. Both companies insist that all trial data will be published by the end of 2005. Other pharmaceutical manufacturers will follow suit or risk public condemnation. As Dr. Peter Honig, senior vice president of the pharmaceutical giant Merck, lamented, "Let's face it, the perceptions of the pharmaceutical industry as a whole are not healthy at this moment.[19]

Senator Edward M. Kennedy, a senior member of the Senate's committee on health, suggests that legislation needs to be enacted to force the industry into greater transparency, because "voluntary measures by companies, while generally laudable, will not produce the comprehensive

information the public needs and deserves to assess the safety and effec-
tiveness of the medicines they take."[20] We want an industry whose
research is unbiased and indisputably working in the interest of
humankind. It may be too much to expect, but as Dr. Marcia Angell
writes in her tome, *The Truth About Drug Companies* (Random House,
August 2004), "Despite all its excesses, this is an important industry that
should be saved—mainly from itself."[21]

Ultimately, whose job is it to ensure that our children are free from
harm resulting from poor medical decision-making? Given current
industry regulations, and an abysmal track record, the drug companies
cannot be relied upon to provide responsible guarantees of safety or efficacy. Does it fall to the doctors and clinicians in whom we place our trust
to "first do no harm"? Or our lawmakers, whose hefty reliance upon the
pharmaceutical industry for campaign funding casts doubt on their
objectivity to act in the best interest of the public? Or is it the responsibility of a public, taxpayer-supported FDA, whose mandate is to safeguard the public health and offer timely and critical advice to parents,
patients, and caregivers, untainted by perceptions of industry bias?

In September 2004 the FDA once more convened the advisory
panel to review the results of the Columbia University study of previously examined trial data. By that time the FDA was mired in two separate congressional investigations initiated by families of depressed
teens, who alleged that senior officials at the FDA mishandled the
internal research provided to the advisory committee in an effort to
skew the panel's recommendations in favor of the drug companies; the
FDA denied the charge. The public mistrust of the FDA, along with the
pharmaceutical industry, was running high.

Once more, the meetings were overshadowed by the anguished stories of grief and loss from families who had lost children to suicide
while in treatment with antidepressants. Once again, the members of
the advisory panel were excoriated for "having the blood of children" on
our hands. It was traumatizing enough to sit through the hearings in
February 2004; repeating the experience six months later was no easier.

The advisory panel was asked to sort out the next steps for the FDA. The FDA's Dr. Thomas Laughren once again summarized the debate: "While there remains a signal of risk for suicidality in some drugs and some trials, it is important to note that the data are not 'black and white' in providing a clear and definitive answer to the question of a link between the drugs and pediatric suicidality."[22]

At the hearing's conclusion, the advisory panel moved to urge more comprehensive labeling in the form of a "black box" warning to be placed on all antidepressant medication, and asked that the FDA provide more detailed information to guide physicians, families, and patients whenever a prescription for an antidepressant is written. They stopped short of calling for a ban on SSRIs and other antidepressants and pressed for more government-funded independent clinical trials.

On October 15, 2004, the FDA called on all manufacturers of antidepressant drugs to post black box warnings highlighting the medications' risks on their products. Along with the black box label, patients will be provided with a "med guide" outlining the drugs' risks and requirements for careful monitoring. Dr. Lester M. Crawford, acting FDA Commissioner announced, "Our conclusions are based on the latest and best science. They reflect what we heard from our advisory committee last month, as well as what many members of the public have told us."[23] I agree that the strenuous warning reflects the majority opinion of the advisory committee, but it's more than a tad disingenuous to state that the FDA's process for reviewing drug safety represents "best science." After participating directly in the process as an advisory committee member, I can attest that the atmospherics of the large public forum, with its mix of grieving families and anti-psychiatry flamethrowers, trumped any possibility of rigorous scientific debate. But the one clear message we heard from the audience at the September hearing was the more information parents get, the better—even if it comes, lamentably, in the form of a black box warning.

So now the brakes are on and only time will tell if these latest warnings will help or hinder patients. I feel certain that doctors will

no longer prescribe these drugs with the indifference to patient diagnoses and proper care evinced over the past few years. If even a small
number of children are spared because of the FDA's dire black-box
warning, then we have accomplished a laudable goal. If, however, parents or treating physicians of hundreds of thousands of kids steer clear
of antidepressants out of fear of triggering suicidal thinking, then we
are putting the millions of young people suffering horrifically from
depression at grave risk.*

At the 2004 annual meeting of the American Academy of Child
and Adolescent Psychiatry, Dr. David Shaffer reported that two as of
yet unpublished studies of adolescent suicides showed no trace of
SSRIs in the toxicology reports of an overwhelming majority of the
teens who took their own lives.[24] Is it possible that there is no causal
link between antidepressants and the depressed kids who managed to
kill themselves? Had they been on medication and simply stopped taking the drugs prior to the time of their deaths? Will these data help
resolve the safety issue in the near future?

As I have said before, depression *is* a life-threatening illness, and as
any parent of a depressed or emotionally troubled child will tell you,
access to reliable information about possible remedies and treatment
options takes on urgency proportional to the degree of your child's
suffering. Parents need as much information as they can get their
hands on, and they need to be able to access it quickly.

In an effort to stem the public's loss of confidence and on the heels
of two separate congressional investigations critical of the agency's
drug review process, the FDA announced on November 5, 2004, that it
would strengthen the system for reviewing drug safety. Dr. Steve Gal-
son, director of the FDA's Center for Drug Evaluation and Research
allowed, "Our current drug approval system has demonstrated that we

---

* An analysis of prescribing data conducted by reporter Jim Rosack for *Psychiatric News*,
September 2, 2005, reported that prescriptions of antidepressants dispensed to patients aged
eighteen and under dropped nearly 20 percent since the FDA issued its public health advisory on March 22, 2004.

don't always understand the full magnitude of drug risks prior to approval of drug products."[25] What an understatement! In an effort to reform the process, the Institute of Medicine (an arm of the National Academy of Sciences) was hired to investigate the FDA's drug approval mechanisms. I would suggest nothing short of a complete overhaul establishing a permanent and independent body that somehow untangles the influence of the pharmaceutical companies from the mission of the regulatory agency.

Until the FDA concludes a comprehensive and independent review of all the data related to both efficacy and risk, the debate over antidepressants for young people will continue to draw fire and stir the misgivings of a conflicted public. And, until the medical establishment, our government, and the insurance industry treat psychiatric illnesses as seriously as they treat physical illnesses, parents of sick children will be whipsawed by the controversy. They will be forced to wade through contradictory data and calculate the risks and benefits of antidepressants on their own. As I can attest, this is an unforgiving position to be in—especially if you are the parent who makes the wrong decision.

One day in early August 2001, I was talking to Will's psychiatrist, Dennis Malinak, about the latest change in Will's medication, and we had a collective brainstorm.

"Dennis, you know, I've just switched to a new antidepressant. I'm on Celexa and I'm taking it in conjunction with Concerta. But I still take Remeron at night."

"Right—that's the latest in combination drug therapies. People are calling it 'California Rocket Fuel'; yeah, some doctors in California have been trying it in some really impenetrable cases of depression—with good results."

"Would it make sense, do you think, to try Will on this combination? We probably share some of the same genes, would it work the same way on him?" I asked.

"Makes sense to me," he replied, and quickly adjusted Will's pharmacological cocktail. We started seeing improvements in Will almost immediately. Over the next month, as Will continued a sustained recovery, ECT was taken off the table as a possible treatment option.

* * *

Bob's letter to Will, from Arcata, California:

August 4, 2001

Hey, man—
I'm up in the town of Arcata, California spending the weekend with our friends Sheila and H.G. . . . It's a foggy, quite beautiful region right on the coast with a great many redwood forests near-by, which is this area's chief claim to fame. Naturally, there are thousands, perhaps millions of teenagers and twenty-somethings flocking up here to get their fill of the natural wonders of mountain and coast.

Another week gone. Hope you're doing well. Got a report from your mom that you had done a bit of rock climbing and some sort of downhill sports last weekend that she didn't fully understand. Apparently this was the reward for kids who had done particularly well on the most recent round of grades. So, congrats for winning the extra getaway. Hope it was fun. I'd love to hear a bit of what the rock climbing was like. Were you doing ropes and the likes? What kind of rock faces did you tackle? Was it difficult? I've never done actual climbing with ropes. I remember a few times as a kid taking on simple rock faces where you would try to make it up as far as you could go—or as far as you could keep your nerve before turning back. I remember getting myself into some places where I wasn't sure how to move either higher or how to turn back without killing myself. Although, obviously, I never did fall. I'm sure if I were back in those same places, I would see that there was never any real danger involved. But my youthful imagination made it seem pretty scary. Or, who knows? Maybe there were some precarious spots. Sometimes I watch kids doing things that, by all rights, they should never survive. Sometimes it's nothing more than jaywalking with reckless abandon through fast-moving traffic. It's a miracle that any kid survives. I'm sure I put myself in such situations growing up.

Word has it that the changes in your meds are leaving you feeling at least a little less tired—if not yet truly relieved of the heavy depression. I'm hoping that the latter will occur before long. It will happen someday. Keep remembering that. I know that Dennis tells you and probably everyone else. But we're not going to settle for anything less than you feeling okay with the world. You deserve no less, and I am absolutely confident that the day will come. Thinking of you.

Love,
Dad

Will's letter to Bob, early August 2001:

Dad . . .
Hey big guy. Sorry it took a long time to write. I've been really busy. Really tired and depressed and such. I'm actually feeling a little bit better. Possibly new meds. Lord only knows. Camping trip was slightly fun, slightly tedious, slightly boring as hell.

Movie night tonight. Watching "Coyote Ugly" (previously viewed at PIW). Never actually gotten all the way through it, or started watching it for that matter.

Letter from Megan wasn't necessarily breaking up. All very uncertain. We'll have to wait and see. I'll talk to you soon. And make a conscious effort to write more (no sarcasm).

Love,
Will

My letter to Will, from Washington, D.C.:

August 13

Dearest Woo,

Well, today I got yet another letter from you—the one about the Invasion of the Cow People and the mysterious crapper. Now you're on a roll. Keep 'em coming.

We're taking John to school next week on August 22nd. He's really excited about our being there to help him move into the dorm (not).

I'm sending you (you know I've always loved you best) my treasured collection of exotic envelopes from former Communist regimes. I would never have parted with these under any circumstances before now, but I know you're the right guy to know what to do with them.

Jack ran into Vic at Home Depot's hot dog stand—he says he's just a working fool this summer—two jobs.

Jane goes back to Charleston on the weekend and then we have no kids at home—weird! I'm trying to convince Jack to buy me a pet Iguana—something troublesome and scaly, so I won't miss those other children. He figures now he'll be able to wear his Lycra bike outfits around the house all of the time.

I love you. I love you—and I get to see you in two weeks.

Mom

Will's letter to me, from Marion, Montana:

August 17, 2001

Mom . . .

Well, not much here. School's almost over. Enjoying the benefits of Sun Clan. Haven't really seen too many of those benefits yet. I'm sure they're on their way. Get to go to movies on Monday because we celebrate the graduates and such. Haven't actually started writing friends yet. Could you send addresses for Vic, Henry, John and anyone else you can think of?

How's Max's tattoo coming? Alice mentioned something about it in one of her letters. I figure your opinion/description was probably a

bit tainted. Have to wait and see for myself. Am actually quite
relieved to get my new phase. I can have music now. I'll write to Max
and tell him to make me some tapes. I'll probably ask him about the
tattoo so as to acquire a completely *unbiased interpretation. Say*
"hi" to my buddies in the office. Tell them they can write. I'm sure
they've been holding their breath.

Love,
Will

In late August, Bob, Melissa, Jack, Max, and I spent the Labor
Day holiday with Will exploring Glacier National Park. A forest fire
raged out of control at the west end of the park, and as we drove
north and east through the Rocky Mountains, over Logan's Pass at
the summit, we could see vast swaths of lavender smoke from the forest
fire hanging over the lakes and valleys, producing the most
extraordinary visual plays of light and color I have ever seen. Will
took pictures and Max made lewd jokes and posed for a photo in
front of the National Park Service sign announcing LOGAN PASS, positioning
his body so that he covered the AN and P to spell LOG . . . ASS,
producing the trip's greatest piece of pictorial memorabilia. Max and
Will thought it hilarious.

As we pulled into the historic Glacier Park Lodge, an imposing
granite chalet at the northern end of the park near the Canadian border,
it rained ash from the fires and our eyeballs and nostrils were
stung by the acrid smell of the burn.

The fires died down and we went white-water rafting on the Flathead
River and canvassed the region for the best homemade pies.
Everyone, including Will, had a wonderful time. The trip provided all
of us a brief respite from the focus on Will's troubles and reminded us
of better times. And, best of all, Will seemed measurably better.

Letter to Will from my mom, Duff Griffith, en route to Tianjin, China,
by freighter:

August 21, 2001,

Dearest Willy,
First of all, this is not The Good Ship Lollipop. Nor is this a "sweet trip." And the next time I think about going around the world, I'll jump on the Tijuana Trolley, get off in Tijuana and drink Margaritas until the thought passes.

You probably have the only grandmother at Montana Academy who is on Pirate Watch. It used to be we would only be on Pirate Watch for a few days going through the Malacca Straits, but now you have to have everything locked up and lights off from the time you get through the Red Sea to Singapore. They [pirates] are more vicious and numerous. They even hijack ships, which aren't exactly concealable like a diamond ring or a pigskin wallet. On top of all this idiocy we have been on the ship, without getting off for eighteen days and yesterday we docked in Jakarta to unload God Knows What and pick up a load of God Knows What for Houston. But the State Department put out an official warning: No Americans should disembark in Jakarta, as leftist terrorists are out to get Americans. So we stood around and looked at Jakarta from the deck and I must admit I wasn't thrilled with what I saw and over it all hangs a pall of wood smoke–like smog.

But tomorrow we land in Singapore, which is one of my favorite spots in the whole wide world. You can walk all over the place anytime day or night safely, but God help you if you chew gum. It's my kind of town. We plan to buy newspapers, books (we are down to one 1965 Reader's Digest *condensation and one 1997* Time Magazine. *Also we are going to buy beaucoup packages of cookies and candies. I'll try to call your mom and [your aunt] Suzy . . . but sometimes it doesn't work out.*

This Muslim terrorist stuff is no joke and it's spreading rapidly. What to do?

We think about you all the time and wonder about what you are

doing and if you have taken some pictures of Montana. Do take
some in the fall. The colors should be splendid.

Give my love to everybody and special hugs for you, Sweetie,

Love,
Maga

"This Muslim terrorist stuff is no joke . . . . *What to do?*" My
mother was prescient. Who knew as the summer of 2001 wound down
that we were about to suffer a national anxiety attack at the hands of
individuals who turned the term "suicidal" on its head and used death
to make a political statement? What to do indeed.

Like the millions of Americans who struggled to figure out what
had happened on September 11, 2001, the first thing I wanted to do
was to track down my kids; I wanted reassurance that they were safe.
(They were never in any danger.) But that is what we do, isn't it? We
hear a fire engine racing down the street in the direction of our children's school and immediately our hearts leap. Our first instinct: our
children are in harm's way. We follow the siren's scream until we are
certain it isn't aimed in their direction and we hold them close in our
mind's eye until the echo fades.

I spent a year in the mouth of a whale
With a flame and a book of signs.
You'll never know how hard I've failed
Trying to make up for lost time.

When the dust in the field has flown,
And the youngest of hearts has grown,
And you doubt you will ever be free,
Don't bail on me.

River is wide and oh so deep
And it winds and winds around.
I dream we're happy in my sleep
Floating down and down and down.

And the tide rushes by where we stand,
And the earth underneath turns to sand,
And we're waiting for someone to see,
Don't bail on me.

from "Riverwide"
by Sheryl Crow

9

CALAMITY AND CLARITY

Will's birthday greeting to me, from Marion, Montana:

September 12, 2001

Dear Mom—
Happy Birthday!
   I love you a lot. Don't worry; Max is really good at music. And none of us were in any airplanes any time this week. Looks to me like everything is just fine.

Love,
Will

Letter to Will from his uncle Joe, from New York City:

September 13, 2001

Dear Will,
Will, I just had an e-mail from your dad, saying you don't mind school up in Montana too much, and you've gotten some pals. That's great news. I'm keenly interested if you like backpacking at all. When I was your age I thought it was a kind of torture old farts put themselves through, since you spent all your time looking at the trail,

making sure you didn't trip over any roots or rocks. By my sophomore year in college, on the other hand, I took a glorious backcountry backpack trip, and I was a backpacking buff for life. Next time I see you I'd love to hear about your experiences backpacking.

The bombing of the World Trade Center was so grisly and tragic, I'm not sure how much you've followed the story. I wasn't anywhere near it and never was in the slightest danger, but I did get a little catch in my throat, looking at the towers roaring ablaze with fire—in real life—so to speak, after seeing the same images on TV. I looked at the crowd looking at the towers, looked myself and was stupefied at the tragedy of it all. I then dived down into a subway, and not five minutes later the first tower collapsed. I didn't know anybody who worked up there, and felt lucky all the way around.

Today as I was teaching . . . A favorite student of mine from last year came into class late, very agitated. She had to talk so I put my ear beside her mouth and she told me her father had been working on the 97th floor of Building #2. This little girl is only 13, even though she's a sophomore in high school. She's as bright as anything, but young and sensitive and she and her mother and sister were out of their minds with worry for their beloved father. Who made it home alive. He had made it down the stairwell and crossed the plaza just minutes before Building #1 collapsed. He went directly home, his nose streaked black with smoke he'd inhaled in the stairwells. His head covered with powdered cement dust. Alive, after all their worries about him.

What happened to that little girl today? Some moron stuck his head in her face on her way to school and hollered, "Kill all the Muslims!" Hot tears glistened down her cheek as she told me this last bit: "We'd worried so much about my father, we couldn't take it, but then he came home and was all right. And now this." She had come to my class straight from a counselor, to whom she'd also told her story. She was heartbroken. It's a hard, hard world, isn't it Will?

Fortunately, from what I know of this girl from teaching her all *last year, I know she's going to be all right. Pete Hamill said (as I think I've told you before), "Being Irish means knowing the world is going to break your heart." This little student of mine didn't know that until now. But in a little while, with her loving parents and sister showering her in love, she's going to be good as new.*

If your heart is a bit broken, Will, with the struggle and confusion of wrestling with your depression, I hope it heals—at least a little bit—everyday. Your father and mother's love for you is boundless, Will. And little Kate loves you fiercely, as does Steph, and Aunt Chris and Bill. And Grandpa and Grandma love you as tenderly as they've loved me every day of my life. I'm part of this vast loving constellation, Will. I think of you and my heart leaps.

I look forward to seeing you soon, Will.

Love,
Uncle Joe

Letter to Will from Bob, from San Francisco:

September 14, 2001

Hey, Will—
Quite a wild time of it for all of us this week, what with several thousand Americans killed on their home ground. Airports closed. No stock market for now. No baseball or football, out of respect. Suddenly, all Americans are unabashedly patriotic. Tearing up at the sounds of tunes they might have joked about a week before. Irony is suddenly out of fashion. That's not as bad as it sounds. We were all getting a little heavy with it. Suddenly we're trying a lot harder to care about one another. I'm sure there are still people who are unaffected by all this, but it's a little difficult to see who they might be. I guess smaller kids might qualify.

My friend Jane in Brooklyn wrote to say they are all fine. Her son Jim (the kid who climbed all over you that time we stopped by to visit) looks at the whole event in terms of its impact on "The

Simpsons." *Sitting home for days with the New York schools closed and little but news on TV, he concluded that they must have produced most of the cartoon shows at the World Trade Center.*

Big news at home is that Max decided to drop out of Berkeley for a while. He was having a hard time getting his head back into it and he wants to work and push on his band for the time being. He may have warned you when we visited that this was a possibility. It certainly didn't spring out of the blue. I, of course, have mixed feelings. On the one hand, I think that you get a lot more out of school when you really want to be there—and I suspect that time will come again for Max. Not to say I can remember a time when Max really wanted to be in school. On the other hand, I think he's at an age where he really needs to be pushing himself in a lot of directions at once. School, music, friends—but school should be one of them for now, in my view. But this is Max's life, not mine. And it's also important that people make their own decisions.

So lots of changes on all fronts. I often feel that change is good. It keeps us fresh and on our toes. One change I know I like is that you can call us up, at least briefly, every Tuesday night. Hang in there.

                                                        Love,
                                                        Dad

Letter from Will to Bob, from Marion, Montana:

September 2001

Dad . . . Hi,
Nothing very new here. I'm reading Lonesome Dove. *It's good and I like it a lot. My friend Brad says that he read the prequel,* Dead Man's Walk *and he says I should read that first, but if I'm going to read any of them it might as well be the original one because it won a Pulitzer Prize or whatever.*

I got a letter from Uncle Joe. He had some pretty good stories and stuff about the terrorists. I read something the other day from one of the survivors of the buildings' collapse. Said he saw amongst the wreckage a body seat-belted into an airplane seat and the body of a flight attendant. Crazy stuff. Be careful out there in the real world. Crazy shit happens.

Love,
Will

Letter from me to Will, from Washington, D.C.:

September 18, 2001
Dearest Woo,
It's been so hard to write because I don't know what to say. I got your wonderful birthday note yesterday—you're so right—none of us died in an airplane crash and Max's music is good (and getting better; I understand from Dad—they're moving in a more bluesy/rock direction these days), and I am banking on everything being all right. But right now, I feel as though the world has changed fundamentally and all of our baselines have to shift, too. I am heartbroken to have you so far away. But what is most important in my life (as you know) are you and your brother. (Yes, I have to admit certain affection for "Log Ass.") And given that there's no way around that, the second most important thing to me is your getting well. That's your job right now—while the rest of us are worrying about the Taliban and whether or not we should bomb Afghanistan even farther back into the Stone Age than they already are—your job is to get well, finish high school, and get well some more.

I'm so disappointed in the world right now. I thought we were building a better life for you guys, and now it all seems to be going into the tank. It bears out the notion that the nature of war has fundamentally changed from soldier on soldier (like the good old days) to indiscriminant attacks on innocent civilians. So all bets are off. But I'm trying to focus on the small things for now—like Michael Jordan coming back to play for the Wizards, or plans for Christmas or painting new colors around the house. I can't wait to see you in a few weeks. We're planning to stay in Whitefish where we were before. We can drive to Missoula to see what it looks like, unless of course, you'd really like to spend the weekend hiking. (Ha!)

I'll talk to you Monday night. Meanwhile, know I love you like crazy and think about you every minute.

Mom

Letter to parents from the directors of Montana Academy, Kalispell, Montana:

September 23 2001

Dear Parents:
Delayed by the nation's recent tragedy we write—more or less as usual, at block end—to summarize campus innovations, to communicate policy and anticipate key events.

We were glad to reach you in the first hours of that awful Tuesday. When we gave the student body the news during Tuesday's lunchtime community meeting, we were able to tell them that you were all right. We recorded the network news, and after lunch we plugged into a monitor and VCR downstairs in the Lodge so we could share the nation's first grasp of these attacks. Then we held team groups. Afterwards, we got together again to watch a couple of hours of network feed. We watched our students (and staff) absorb the frightful news, study the facts quietly, console one another, ask intelligent questions, and we thought you would have been proud of their grace, tact and kindness. Over the weekend, we brought more recorded feed, but left the monitor downstairs, so as to preserve in the lounge and at meals a quiet space—free from the networks' shrill perseverations—for conversation.

Our Fall Workshop will take place Thursday—Friday October 25–26. We have delayed this announcement—and this letter—to be sure the airlines would be flying. They seem to be.

John McKinnon, John Santa,
Rosemary McKinnon and Carol Santa

In mid-October 2001, all parents of teens at Montana Academy arrived for a weekend of mandatory seminars and group therapy sessions at Lost Horizon Ranch. Bob, Melissa, Jack, and I returned to our now familiar haunts in Kalispell. This crop of parents arrived from all points on the map and from different socioeconomic backgrounds, and it quickly became evident that our experiences and our children were as varied as our histories.

Some of us had busted the bank to enroll our children at Montana Academy; for other families the program was an unanticipated deviation from prestigious private schooling. There were divorced couples, struggling mightily to retain a solid front for their children, and there were "intact families," whose sons or daughters had deviated from a succession of siblings who had made the transition from childhood to adulthood without incident. I only met one or two parents during all of our visits to Montana Academy I would characterize as utterly lacking in parenting skills. For the most part, a family who cared enough about a child to muster the wherewithal to enroll their teen in the program truly wanted their son or daughter to be well—happy, healthy, and well. Each of us was heavily invested—emotionally and financially—in this goal.

During the two-day parent workshop, we traded our terrible stories of out-of-control teenagers: drugs, drinking, theft, academic failure, sexual promiscuity, depression, eating disorders, and downright bad behavior, each story more awful and heartrending than the last. We resembled the dysfunctional family version of the 1950s television show *Queen for a Day*, vying for the coveted Amana Defroster Refrigerator by assembling the most heartbreaking inventory of personal statistics and putting our catalogue of woes to an audience vote.

As we revisited our personal family histories, it quickly became apparent that no matter whether our teenage children suffered from substance abuse, eating disorders, or behavioral problems, an underlying problem for almost all of them was depression. The stories were different but the constant was depression.

No family, however, had a story quite like ours, like Will's—a kid who suffered a precipitous descent into a biologically based, major depression absent all of the mishaps their own children had suffered: no declining school performance, no scuffles with authority, no transgressions involving drugs or alcohol, and no ostracism from peers— just a hot-waxed slide into the abyss of depression topped off by a near-fatal suicide attempt.

We could see our story frightened other parents ("You think your kid's in trouble, you should hear . . .") From their point of view, his illness came out of nowhere and had no bottom. I am sure some of the parents wondered if they were getting the full story. Certainly there must've been more to it than we were revealing. "Must be the divorce," or the weird extended family setup. (I admit we were a curious anomaly— two parents and two stepparents getting along and enjoying one another's company.) There had to be *something* we weren't sharing with the rest of the families.

In the afternoon of the first day's session, the parents of the eight boys in Will's team met in one of the campus log cabins normally used as a classroom. Dennis Malinak, the lead psychiatrist, who treated all of the boys in the team, and Greg Windham, the team leader, ran the group meeting. The object of the session was to foster a frank and open vetting about our sons' progress—or lack of it—at this point in the program. The group setting offered parents an opportunity to get to know one another and share our thoughts about raising our troubled children.

As anyone who has ever taken part in group therapy knows, individuals form bonds in groups, often born of shared experience. In the best of circumstances and with skilled facilitators, therapists, or clinicians, the atmosphere allows for a heightened degree of openness and revelation. Certainly, by confessing our most heinous failing—our failure as parents—and by revealing our darkest fears for our children, a bond held us, the eight sets of parents, despite our disparate backgrounds and our children's individual issues.

Will was far enough along in the program to begin anticipating his return home. Seated in a circle on hard wooden chairs, I confessed my biggest fear:

"I worry that despite all the work Will's done here, and all of the therapy and medication, that Will might make another suicide attempt, without warning . . . much like the first one."

The group fell silent. Dennis appeared to be weighing his response before voicing his opinion when one member of our group, a mother of a child in the program and an emergency room physician, threw out a flippant remark:

"Well, if someone's bound and determined to commit suicide, there's not much anyone can do about it."

The good doctor might as well have uncorked a vat of toxic waste in the middle of the classroom. I was dumbstruck. Other parents shot me sidelong glances, part empathy, part horror, before redirecting their vision to their feet. I wanted to leap out of my chair and grab the woman by the throat. Instead, I shrugged and looked at Dennis, who tried to dispel the vitriol by launching into another topic. Jack took my hand and squeezed it comfortingly, but as far as I was concerned my engagement in the remainder of the day's session was over.

The point of writing a memoir as candid and as painful as this one, and the reason I am willing to risk exposing my son, his former girlfriend, myself, and my family, is to challenge the wickedly misguided notion that (1) a person suffering from depression "wants to die," and that (2) there is "nothing anyone can do about it." Think about it: A person with terminal cancer seldom talks about wanting to end his or her life prior to the onset of pain; most want to live as long as they can pain-free. When the cancer patient says, "I want to die," don't we interpret the statement as "I want to be pain-free" or "I don't want to continue to suffer"? On the other hand, if the patient has a treatable form of cancer, shouldn't family and friends do all in their power to support a treatment regime to sustain the life of their loved one? Suicidal depression must be addressed, just as rigorously as a treatable form of cancer would be attacked by an oncologist. You will never read a suicide note that doesn't state the obvious in one way or another: "I don't want to die; I just don't want to live with the pain anymore."

At the cafeteria-style dinner served later in Montana Academy's newly constructed lodge, we sat, hunkered down like an embattled clan. Several parents approached and cautiously offered their sympathy for the callousness of our cohort's remark. But it was a low point in our experience at Montana Academy. And, placed in a larger context, it underscores the failure of the medical establishment to train its practitioners to recognize and understand depression. If an emergency room doctor could offer an opinion so uninformed and insensitive, how can we expect the rest of the population to address depression and suicide thoughtfully and with compassion? But if the first day's session was the nadir of our visit, the second day brought us profound joy.

We gathered once more in the log cabin schoolhouse late morning on the second day of the parent seminar. The region had yet to experience its first snowfall, but the temperature had dipped into the twenties overnight and the room was chilly and damp. I clutched a steamy cup of weak coffee and made small talk with the other parents, and steeled myself for the day's potential detonations.

We took our seats, and Bob, Melissa, Jack, and I arrayed ourselves in a row, designed to convey a united front. Dennis and Greg filed in and outlined the day's agenda. The eight boys would be joining us for this morning's session. Rather than being "talked about" for the remainder of the morning, they had been offered an opportunity to participate and they voted to join in. Each boy would be asked to address an unresolved issue between himself and his parents—an unspoken grievance or an apology for an incident over which he now felt remorse. Or, he could talk about his relationships to his parents, collectively or individually ("Describe a strength you admire in your father's character" or "What do you miss most about your family?" or "How do you expect to get along with your mother in the future?")

The boys ambled into the cabin. Heads down, expressions guarded or embarrassed, their eyes darted around the circle and at the wood floor, scouring the room like minesweepers hoping not to trigger an explosive charge. They sat on the floor at the base of our chairs, legs sprawling or crossed, some casually relaxing a back against a mother's leg, some purposefully resisting any bodily contact with father or

mother. The boldest, or perhaps the child the most practiced in therapeutic give-and-take (or perhaps the boy with the least to lose), spoke
up first.

Some people are good at self-examination and reflection; others
are not. In any therapeutic setting, the force of this exercise unfortunately lands heavily on individuals who are unable or unwilling to analyze their actions in the context of how their behavior affects others
and admit failings, large or small. I never cease to be amazed by parents
who do so poorly at understanding and communicating with their
children. A much older father spoke of wanting to instill in his boy an
appreciation for great literature and could not understand why his son
needed him to be more than a mentor or pedant. His son was gasping
for warmth. Another couple evinced such a poisonous rapport
between them that you worried how their son could ever return to the
family without being caught in the middle and torn apart by his parents. There were tears, bitterness, and anger; it spilled out around the
room. Round One went to the kids who had learned to frame their
actions and emotions in ways that demonstrated a real desire to break
the mold and get out from under those patterns of behavior that had
landed them at Montana Academy in the first place—with or without
the support of a sympathetic or understanding family.

I marvel that so many of us make it to adulthood. Likewise, I am
stunned by the depth of insight and empathy some parents come to
naturally. Where do these gifts come from? Are they learned behaviors
or are they innate? It stands to reason that you learn to parent from
your parents, but what I observed were families (such as ours) forced
to confront challenges our parents never imagined: the rampant
spread of illegal drugs; easy access to birth control, the sexual revolu-
tion, and a global spike in sexually transmitted diseases; the transfor-
mative shifts in technology, communications, and the economy, pitting
families and centuries-old traditions against rapid modernization. The
New World Order begins at home. We see as much disruption within
the microcosm of the family as we observe on a global scale.

As we circled the classroom, our attention leapfrogged from one

family, one boy, to another. We had been at it for two hours and Will
was the last kid to present, simply by virtue of where he sat in the circle. No doubt he had time to ruminate on an appropriate answer to
"Will, how do you characterize your parents' best attributes and what
impact have they had on you?" Four parents, all eyes and ears on him;
this was no mean feat. Will opted for brevity. Turning to face each one
of us in turn, he brilliantly elucidated characterizations of his family,
pinning a single one-word adjective to each of us:

"Dad, you're 'insight,' Melissa's 'enthusiasm,' Jack is 'humor,' and
Mom, you're 'openness.'"

His pronouncement was a stunner. It was exactly right. We loved
him so unabashedly; it seemed that all of our efforts were paying off.
He managed in a single word to recognize and acknowledge our individual strengths—and what these attributes gave him back. The
moment had required not just insight, but diplomacy and humor. He
packed it all into four words.

"Wow, Will. That was a home run!" Dennis congratulated him.
The rest of us exhaled; I reveled in the moment's pure feeling and Dennis brought the session to a close.

Letter from me to Will, from Washington, D.C.:

November 19, 2001

Woo, you turkey dude,
I spoke to Malinek today. He says he thinks you're much improved. I
sure hope so.
  And now we're about to hit the HOLLODAYS. I love the first
one: the Eating Holiday. No gifts, just more food than is right for a
starving third world country. Then the Blessed Snow Holiday. The
one where the Fairy Queen dusts everyone for fingerprints and we
make cookies shaped like little fish. Can't wait for you to get home.
John comes home tomorrow; I'm going to let him sleep in your room.
Jane comes on Wednesday. It will be good to have the children

underfoot for a test run before December, just to see how the grownups react.

I am hoping to hear from you tonight that you've made it to Star Clan. That's what you are to me. My star. (Even if you are a turkey.)

I love you,
Mom

Star Clan Assignment

1. Who am I? This question is to be answered both in a written format as well as presented figuratively through some means of creative expression—art work, collage, sculpture, poetry etc. etc. Although presented as the first question, this question should be answered last after reviewing the following questions. Please try to present your written summary in approximately one paragraph that accurately captures the central themes of your uniqueness.

2. What things do other people know about me that I have a hard time believing about myself? Why? The answer to this question may include both negative and positive traits that you have a difficult time accepting about yourself. Please use your team group to solicit feedback about yourself, both your strengths and weaknesses.

3. How has the process of therapy worked for me? The purpose of this question is for you to reflect on your stay at Montana Academy and determine exactly what has motivated you to change, and why you have made the changes in your life that you have. The answer to this question may include "pivotal moments" or a turning point that motivated you to change. Also, please examine the relationships that you have formed while at Montana Academy with both staff and peers. Have these relationships influenced you in any way and why?

4. What do I want for my future? What skills do I have that will help

me obtain these goals? What skills do I need to help me obtain these goals? Please focus on several aspects of your life including your future career, relationships, dreams, goals, etc.

5. What changes have been the most difficult for me to make while I've been at Montana Academy? How did you overcome these problems?

On December 7, Will's eighteenth birthday, my mother, Duff Griffith, was diagnosed with inoperable colon cancer. The cancer had progressed too far to treat and she would live for only four more months. It was a body blow we had not expected, in a year that had rained nothing but bad news.

I received the phone call from my father the morning of the seventh, following my mother's exploratory surgery. I made hasty plans to fly to Austin where I met with my sister, Suzy, who flew in from California. We picked up a rental car and drove in a dense black night through torrential December rain to Georgetown, Texas, a small turn-of-the-century railroad town twenty-five miles north of Austin, where my parents had settled only weeks before.

My parents loved to travel. In fact, it was the constant in their life together—and in my childhood. In October 2001, after returning from a nine-month odyssey, my mother announced their traveling days were over; they were going to find a pleasant town in which to settle down "for the duration." I found it hard to believe my folks would stay put for long (they were inveterate travelers), but it made sense to be thinking about putting down roots. After all, they were in their mid-seventies. By outward appearances, they were in relatively good health, but it couldn't hurt to be closer to family and health care options than a port of call somewhere in the Strait of Malacca.

My parents crisscrossed the country by car to locate the ideal setting: a small town with a pleasant ambiance, not too far from a major urban center—walkable, with easy access to shopping. In November, they decided they had found just the place in Georgetown, Texas. Right after Thanksgiving, three days after they moved into a lovely, cozy house with a front porch, a tin roof, and pecan trees in the yard, my mother went to a local doctor, complaining of a cough she had not been able to shake for several months. The diagnosis was rendered almost immediately and my mother began the last and final journey of her well-lived life.

I called Dennis Malinak at Montana Academy to alert him and then I broke the news to Will by phone a couple of days later, after his birthday. He loved his grandmother, who was stylish, eccentric, and opinionated but fiercely proud of her grandchildren. She catered to her grandkids' whims and lavished them with attention, maintaining a list of their favorite foods and mailing them boxes of homemade cookies on random occasions. She wrote Will and her four other grandchildren letters from all over the world describing in colorful detail the indigenous tribes of Papua New Guinea or whorehouses in Bangkok. Her oft-quoted one-time remark "I don't much care for dining with cannibals" was fodder for hilarity whenever the kids reminisced about her. It had the offbeat ring of a character given to dramatic simplification, but my mother charmed the grandchildren with her wackiness and unpredictability.

When I finally spoke by phone with Will to break the bad news, it was hard to discern his reaction. True to his poker player persona, he did not react with an outburst of emotion. He asked, "Do you think she has long to live?" and "How are you holding up, Mom?" I am sure the phone call caught him off guard, but in a year when everything in his world had been upended, this latest bit of bad news may not have registered with the impact he might have felt if his year had been going along swimmingly. I imagined he was thinking, "Oh, great . . . What next?"

But Will was now eighteen. Where he was going with his own life probably weighed more heavily than the many outside events that had penetrated his isolation over the past several months. He was old enough to "vote with his feet" if he decided to opt out of therapy, old enough to cast a vote in a presidential election, old enough to serve in the military—old enough, by legal benchmarks, to make his own decisions about all aspects of his young life.

It is an unthinking system wherein your child is depressed and suicidal and your legal dependent one day, and the very next day he is still
depressed and suicidal, but he is eighteen years old and sprung from
your reach. You lose all rights and ability to secure treatment for him
by ordinary legal means. And I was stunned to learn recently that in
some states, a child may refuse mental health intervention when he or
she is as young as thirteen years old. How did efforts to protect the civil
rights of our children become so twisted on this issue?

Throughout the fall, Bob and I strategized with Montana Academy
director John McKinnon and Dennis Malinak about the approach to
keep Will voluntarily engaged at the academy beyond his eighteenth
birthday. The school had dealt with this problem before and Dr. Mc-
Kinnon assured us that most all of the kids in the program, despite
their intention to "walk" on their eighteenth birthday, are held back by
lack of family support or the financial wherewithal to leave. In fact,
Dr. McKinnon counseled, Bob and I should make it clear to Will that if
he were to leave after he turned eighteen but before he completed the
program, he would be on his own; he would have to make his way out
of Montana and figure out the next steps, without our financial support
or encouragement. And he would not be allowed to come back
home—a classic "tough love" strategy. Bob and I outlined our resolution in a conference call to Will a couple of weeks before Christmas
break. Bob took the lead: "Will, your mom and I feel it's really important for you to finish the program. Not just for the high school
diploma, but because we think you're finally getting something out of
the therapy with Dennis and you could really make the most of the
time you have left there."

Reasonable enough. Will listened but did not respond. Bob then
let Will know that if he intended to leave Montana Academy without
completing the program, he would be on his own. Bob delivered the
ultimatum as gently as he could, again emphasizing how anxious we
were for him to stay in the program. Again, no response from Will.

No one knows exactly what he was thinking, but I know I was
wondering if I could really pull off our threat. For the past year I had

been consumed by an almost fanatic drive to put Will back together, to restore his mental health. I was tormented: Would he really walk away from Montana Academy, hike out of the remote Lost Horizon Ranch, walk the forty miles to Kalispell, in the deep cold of Montana winter? And what then? He knew he had a couple hundred dollars in savings in the bank. Would he try to access his savings and strike out on his own, like a modern-day Kerouac? I knew Will was literate enough to find this romantic model intellectually appealing. But he was just a kid, despite the arbitrary age marker; and he was a kid recovering from a serious illness. Could I really let him go down this path if he were to elect it? If he walked all the way to Kalispell, bought an airline ticket to Washington, and showed up at the front door, could I turn him away? Honestly? No way. I am thankful he never put me to the test; it was an empty threat on my part.

Will's journal entries demonstrate that he was as conflicted by this decision as we were. Sometime in late November, he wrote:

I don't know what I want to do. I don't want to graduate. So much pent up frustration and what-not behind this one. Can't read my books. All the adults and everyone want me to stay. But it's like the more they say about it, and how it's the "right choice" and all, the more I want to leave. It just pisses me off that they (or I) put myself in this position. Man, I just want to say I'm leaving and get on with shit. I don't care about school or going to college or any of that fucking mess. I just want to be out of here and on with shit. And I think the whole reason I want to go so bad is because I want to do what *I* fucking want to do. I never do what I want to do. I feel like if I go through with this shit and graduate and all that shit I'm just going to be the same sorry fucker who came in here. Always doing what everyone wants me to. But, on the plus side, everybody would be all mad or disappointed or whatever. It's not like I don't want to finish because I just don't care about anything—I just don't care about *this* thing.

Well, no—I do care. I care in that I really dislike this place a

lot and want to go home. And I'm just so goddam pissed that I'm
in here. I still hold a very strong resentment towards my parents for
being here. It just irritates me a lot. And this Spanish class shit.
They're all trying to convince me to take Spanish so that my college credits are better off so I can go to a UC [University of Cali-
fornia] school or whatever. I hate Spanish. Why don't they fucking
worry about whether or not I'll actually graduate this place and get
a high school diploma at all? Ah, I guess I'm too frustrated and fed
up right now to actually try to work this shit out, But I guess I am
running out of time.

Morning—Still [feel] the same, Dammit.

Apparently, a lot of people are asking about me or talking to
their kids about me or something. That makes me just a little
uncomfortable. I don't like being the center of attention. Especially
being all undecided or whatever. Fucking people here like me. I
kind of wish they didn't like me—at least people who I don't even
know. That like adds so much more pressure to this. I think I just
want to tell them I'm going to leave and put an end to all this business. I need to make some lists of tapes and books and games and
shit that I need (or want) to get when I get out of here. That would
take my mind off shit. Take it off the serious parts of the future. Start
paying attention to the little petty fun shit. I need to get myself out
of here so I can get myself a Super Nintendo and Super Mario
Altars. So I can play all the Mario games one after another.

Well, at least I'm in a better mood than last night. Super
Mario 3 is so much fun. I got to beat that game (get it first) when I
leave. And MDK. That was such a fun ass game. I have to get that
back when I get out.

I think Megan would be really pissed if I left without graduating. Hmmm. Surprisingly that is actually more discouraging than
one might think. For some reason I'm more concerned with that . . .
than what my parents say. Probably because I already know what
to expect from them. They can't totally reject me if I fuck up. They

have to accept me after a while. She could just totally reject it and I would never see her again. Sad. Oh, well. Just more shit to factor in—I guess I've come to the conclusion that I can recognize that staying is the smarter choice. But I can't see through my frustration and dislike for this place long enough to actually agree with and carry out that choice and actually stay. So, I guess I'm going to leave, by default. Hmmm, this should be interesting.

I really don't want to tell them this shit. That's my biggest fear through all this business. I'm so worried that it's going to be too much to say or whatever and I'm just not going to say it. That happens a lot when it comes to things that I want. It becomes too much of a responsibility or burden or whatever and I don't end up saying it or doing it and I just do what someone else wants to. This is looking to be a pretty rough one. It is all like that except times fifty because it's so important. I guess the one thing that gives me some confidence is that I know that no matter what I'm turning 18 and that's all that really matters in the final decision making. That's like, the one card that I have that nobody can dispute. So I guess that makes it different. Makes it actually my decision.

Hmmm. I don't like this one bit. This sucks a lot. Goddamn, why'd I get myself in this? Was it even my fault? I don't even know. I fucked up pretty bad. But that was a pretty direct result of depression. And that shit wasn't my fault. I can't help being sick. But it did make me fuck up pretty bad. Really bad.

As I read them now, Will's anguished musings over the decision to stay and his desire to sort out his own life do not represent anything extraordinary. In his soul-searching, he asks all the right questions, questioning his motivation and looking for a way to explain the basis of a decision—one way or another—to himself. And I think he does a pretty good job of examining the issue truthfully.

What I do find extraordinary, however, is a startling lack of maturity, which I think he managed to mask all along with a keen intellect. I don't think he presents a picture of a kid whose emotional maturity is inappropriate to his age; but I do think his reasoning underscores the argument that some, if not all, children of seventeen or eighteen years of age are ill-equipped to single-handedly make profound and fundamental decisions affecting the course of their lives.

In the end, why did he stay? I want to say it was because he deliberated his choices and determined that it was wiser to complete the program—a mature decision. In reality, it appears that in large measure he succumbed to peer pressure and that trumped all else. Typical adolescent behavior? Absolutely. But his decision was not made in a vacuum. I am sure there was an overabundance of factors we are well past taking into account.

In a journal entry written in the fall, he perceives the world outside Montana Academy to be discombobulated, as his childhood friends fall victim to circumstance or their own reckless behavior.

I heard from Megan that Vic got kicked out of school for dealing weed. I think that ends my childhood. I'm in the real life now. Vic, Henry, Enrique and I, we were best friends since forever. We were all on the basketball team in 6th grade and we won the championship. We were a crew, we were awesome. That was great. And we all ended up in high school together. And then Enrique got kicked out for selling drugs. He got in pretty bad with his foster parents and now he's living in some low-income apartments in Silver Spring with his mom. His dad died in El Salvador in the civil war. He went to a Maryland public school for a while but dropped out and is selling again.

Henry has cancer. He's had cancer since 7th or 8th grade and was supposed to die two or three years ago. His family's really poor and I don't know how they afford all his medical treatments. They didn't think he'd live very long so they went out and bought him a huge TV set with his college money (and some money from the Make a Wish thing). You would think that if a kid had cancer his parents would spoil him and be really caring and nice, but it's just the opposite. My mom says it's because they're so overwhelmed with worry and fear that they just don't know what to do. But I think they're just not really all there. They're even harder and stricter with Henry than the other kids. He's constantly kicked out of the house, staying with Vic and me.

Henry is a bad student. He has like a 1.7 GPA. His parents said if he didn't get a 3.5 by the end of the junior year they were going to stop paying for the school and send him to public school. Our local public school is a model of the unsafe, under-funded DC public school. I doubt Henry could survive a week there. He's not one to put up with tough situations. I imagine the cancer has drained him of his fight.

I didn't even last to see the end of junior year. I dropped out halfway through and tried to kill myself two months later. That left Vic. But that was enough. If Vic could graduate from a solid private high school, there's no reason he couldn't get into at least some college and we could simply follow him there. We always planned to go to Florida for college. Someplace warm and fun with lots of girls who don't wear much clothing. Someplace that wasn't D.C.

Vic was my best friend. He is from Trinidad and he's the greatest person ever. One day we were riding our bikes and he said, "Will, how long have we been best friends?" We were just little guys then. He's not white; he lives in the projects. He could be tough if he needed to, but he was never actually tough with me.

Now that Vic is gone from school, I don't know what's going to happen. It's almost as if all of us have lost it. I don't think we'll ever make it to Florida now. It's kind of sad. It's like it just gets harder all the time for all of us to get together.

When Will announced his decision to return to Montana after the Christmas break, we exulted in the news and congratulated him on his choice. The longer he was in the program, the better grounded he would be when he left. He would complete the program—both its therapeutic and academic aspects. Exactly *when* he would finish was yet to be determined, but we all agreed we were looking at one or possibly two more eight-week terms, which suggested that he would be home by early spring. Over Christmas, we would have an opportunity to gauge the soundness of his decision.

Will was due home for the first time in eight months for one week, from the twenty-first to the twenty-eighth of December. Everyone in the immediate family was coming to Washington for the holidays. After the initial shock of my mother's diagnosis, we moved forward with preparations for the holiday with a mixture of excitement and sadness.

Letter from Will to me from Marion, Montana, December 1, 2001:

Dear Mom,
Well, so I'm finally writing you. Just in time for the holidays (or something like that.) So, I guess I'll be home for Christmas. That'll be cool.

Nothing is all that new over here. I talked to you like ten times over Thanksgiving and then again on Monday. Nothing's happened since then (today's Wednesday). I talked to Phil Jones yesterday and he said all I have to do for an independent study next block is write a proposal describing everything I want to do and what books and who's going to look at my work. He said he has this big video series that I can watch [on the Vietnam war] *so that's cool. If you think of more books I should read I'll bring them back from Christmas.*

I read that book, The Sorrow of War, *the Bao Minh one. It was really sad. But anyways he* [Phil Jones] *said that based on my past academics and all that, he said it sounded very promising. He liked the idea a lot. Cool.*

Is there anything you want for Christmas? I'll probably just throw something together, make something. According to Malinak, "parents love that shit." O.K. *I'll probably talk to you next week. Say Hi to Jack. He's a good guy.*

Love,
Will

With mounting anxiety, I marked that Friday, December 21—the day the staff at Montana Academy put Will on a 6:20 AM flight from Kalispell to Washington. He would transfer on his own in Salt Lake City, and although Will was an experienced traveler, I fretted about his first venture on his own since he had been away. He had been gone for eight months. Even though I had seen him in Montana at eight-week intervals, I wondered and worried about the person he would be when he returned home.

Families are warned to expect some "backsliding" when a child returns from a residential treatment program. And in reality, this was a dry run—just a one-week trial, before the real reentry on the horizon.

I held a vivid image from Christmas the year before of Will as he lay on the couch in the living room, lethargic and brooding. He was visibly wasting; it was evident in his sallow visage and fragile-looking limbs that hung like busted twigs from his body. The rest of the kids, Jane, Max, and John, were hanging ornaments on the tree, wisecracking, stumbling over one another and occasionally poking at Will in a concerted attempt to rouse him. But he barely occupied his own frame. This December I hoped and prayed that when he got off the plane from Montana we would see signs of the "old" Will, the predepression Will.

Maybe it was a small Christmas miracle: he looked terrific when he arrived. It was hard to squelch the desire to hug him and nuzzle him constantly. Under the circumstances, it was also hard to stifle the urge to be overly cautious, overly watchful, not to analyze everything he said or did for an out-of-synch marker, or uneven response. I tried not to ask him repeatedly, "How are you doing?" or "So, how are you feeling these days?" or anything that pressed too hard on the scab of our

recent hurt and worry. And lest we forget, Will lulled us into thinking
he was well once before—with near-lethal consequences. He deceived
us before; he could do it again.

Within a day or two, we placed our worries on the back burner.
Thank God, he was much better. Genuinely, openly, markedly better. I
believe the drug regimen was finally working. Or maybe, given the passage of time, his depression was receding on its own. Perhaps he was
maturing and his hormones were settling down, or maybe he had
found a comfort level in Montana that allowed him to open up to the
doctors and therapists there, so that he was finally getting something
out of the process. We will never know for sure. But I *was* sure he was
better.

While at home, Will sought out old friends from Gonzaga and
hung out with his siblings and cousins. These reunions were bittersweet and everyone expressed relief to see Will looking so well. His
sense of humor had returned and something else: a confidence in his
demeanor, in his carriage, a vitality that had been absent for the past
two years.

Will phoned Megan soon after he returned to Washington. The
two of them agreed to meet for coffee the day after Christmas. I was
curious about their reunion and how it would unfold. By December,
Will spoke openly about his close friendships with a number of girls at
Montana Academy. But Megan . . . the intensity of their relationship
the year before, with its trauma and pain and mutual self-harm; was
there anything left between them or were they ready to jettison the
past?

A year in the life of a teenager. Adolescents are natural "rapid
cyclers"; wild mood swings are a given. With lightning speed teenagers
acquire and discard new styles, new friends, new language and behaviors. As a tribe, they remind me of the Mad Hatter at his tea party, constantly exhorting his guests, "Move down, move down, clean cups,
clean cups," in an endless effort to reinvent and renew.

The day came for their appointed reunion: Will wasn't gone for
more than a couple of hours. He and Megan met at a local Starbucks.

When he came home, I inquired, "So, how'd it go? What's she up to?" My antennae were alert to signs and signals.

"She's fine. Yeah, it was okay." Will was tight-lipped about the encounter, but I could tell from his body language their reunion held no drama, no promise, nothing disturbing or bitter. I was relieved. I hoped he was, too. I hoped they would find a way, sometime years from now, to talk about what had happened to them. But right now, I could tell, he had moved on. It was inevitable and for the best. I suspected she had moved on, too.

Megan's reflections on her first meeting with Will after his eight-month absence:

Just after Christmas, I saw Will for the first time since he left for Montana in April. I was mid-way through my junior year of high school, and I had pieced together a new life, one in which depression and Will didn't exist in the concrete anymore.

In the months since I had last seen him, he had become a concept, not a person, a connection to my illness. His phone call, asking to meet me, was jarring, despite the unchanged softness and lethargy of his speech. He casually told me that he was home from Montana for a little while and asked if I wanted to get together. I agreed on coffee, partially out of a sense of obligation to my past, partially to satiate a need for the affirmation of how much I had changed since our parting.

I took the Metro to meet him, after my mother extracted a series of promises regarding how long I would stay and where Will and I would and would not go. The familiar succession of stops brought a numbed sense of pain and a flood of memories that I fought out of my mind. I had erected rigid boundaries; this was not to be an emotional ordeal. He wasn't getting in again.

I stepped onto the platform, joined the streams of commuters, and started up the escalator. As I reached daylight, I squinted and was able to make Will out, standing hunched over a newspaper dispenser. He was exactly as I remembered him. He smiled and stood up when he saw me, I was already shaken and bared my teeth in a feeble attempt at a smile. We embraced loosely and turned to walk toward Starbucks.

Conversation didn't come easily; we awkwardly small-talked our way around discussing anything that had unfolded before our parting. I was desperately upbeat, countering his sarcastic indifference with my artificial enthusiasm. I was fiercely trying to establish distance between us, trying to show him that we were completely different people now and he could no longer affect me.

We sat at a table with our coffee, and my anxiety rose as I ingested the caffeine. He told me he was happy for me, and I pretended to swallow this at face value. I continued to babble nervously. My right arm was resting stiffly on the table, and because I was wearing a ¾ sleeved top, the largest scar was visible. In the middle of one of my sentences, Will reached over and touched the scar with his index finger, a subtle reminder of the reality of our past. I felt the blood rush to my cheeks, and not knowing exactly how to respond I reached over and fingered the pitted scar from his self-inflicted bite mark. We held eye contact for a few seconds, and then conversation halted for what seemed like an eternity. Part of me was furious at him for interrupting my efforts to maintain a contrived distance. For the most part, though, I was grateful that he introduced a touch of reality, however gritty it was, into our meeting.

Soon my allotted time with Will was up, but before we parted, he made me promise we would remain on good terms. We were officially friends again—no matter how strained our relationship was or would be for years to come.

He walked me back to the Metro station and bent down wrapping his arms limply around my body before watching me descend the escalator. All the way home my heart pounded and my breath was short. I reminded myself of all the reasons I would never slip back into who I was the year before; I was doing well in school, had another boyfriend and was rid of my depression.

It was dark by the time I got home. I tried to call friends, my boyfriend, anyone I could connect with the here and now; but everyone had gone out for the evening. I couldn't shake my anxiety over our meeting, and I had my first sleepless night in months.

You've been taken by the wind

You have known the kiss of sorrow

Doors that would not let you in

Outcast and a stranger

    You have come by way of sorrow

    You have come by way of tears

    But you'll reach your destiny

    Meant to find you all these years—

    Meant to find you all these years.

        from "By Way of Sorrow"
        by Julie Miller

10

TIME, SWEET TIME

Over the course of January and early February 2002, we prepared for Will's graduation from Montana Academy. With Will, his doctor, and his therapists, we worked up a "contract" for his release, which crafted a structure for his return home.

A "home contract" is pretty standard fare for teens returning after significant stays in residential treatment programs. Ours entailed an agreement between Will and us covering all aspects of Will's life back in Washington—curfews, responsibilities, goals for school or work, and a commitment to remain in therapy and on medication for a specific period of time.

The final document read like a lawyerly agreement between two opposing parties—hardly where you want to be with your child—but we were looking for guidelines, and the clinicians at Montana Academy, with their vast experience, maintained this was the best way to master reentry for kids returning home after a long spell in a rigorous therapeutic setting.

In fact, I think by outlining expectations in detail, a home contract gives families—and teens—something to fall back on when things don't go as planned once your child returns. Since you can count on the fact that families of troubled teens have withstood some pretty brutal encounters in the run-up to a child's institutionalization, the home contract allows parents to fashion a new way of communicating with the child and offers every member of the family a fresh start.

Bob and I made several passes at a draft home contract before settling on one that made sense to us, and to Dennis Malinak. Will was
allowed to comment on the draft before we finalized it. I offer it here as
a model:

Dear Will,
We hope to see you settle back into life at home as smoothly and as
comfortably as possible. You will have graduated high school, a time
in your life when you can reasonably expect either to be heading off
to college or into some sort of adult working life with quite a bit of
new freedom and responsibility. We're confident this will happen for
you in the months ahead and we'll do everything we can to support
you in that direction. We would urge you to take things a little
slowly, however, until we all have a better feel for how your moods
hold up away from Montana Academy.
After our discussions, here is what we've agreed upon on how
things will work:

1. *You will make a short family visit in San Francisco before settling*
   in Washington. You'll be flying to S.F. on Friday, February 21, and
   staying until the following Tuesday, February 25.
2. *You will have a meeting with Vaune Ainsworth within your first*
   few days at home and get familiar with a psychiatrist in her
   practice, who will be the one to write the prescriptions for your
   meds. As we have discussed with Dennis, we're all feeling confi-
   dent that you have a good plan for the medications, at least for
   the immediate future. But Ainsworth and this other doctor will
   be the ones to whom you can turn for whatever additional help
   you may need. Ongoing support of this sort will not be optional.
3. *You will take responsibility for keeping up with your own meds,*
   but they will be provided to you one week's supply at a time, dur-
   ing the first six months.
4. *You will start to work as soon as you can, so that there aren't a*
   lot of empty days upon your arrival. If you are able to settle in

with one of the construction jobs that Jack has been exploring, then work will start quite soon after you arrive. Failing that, we will expect to see an energetic job hunt aimed at getting you to work asap. You can always change jobs later on, but the plan is to start on something right away.

5. *You'll be expected to pay $350 a month for your room and board. This will cease should you decide to enroll in college full-time. Rent will be due on the first of the month. You'll be shooting for April 1 for your first rent check.*

6. *We want you to take it slow on the hours you keep, until you are comfortably settled in. The first two weeks, nothing after 10:00 p.m. without special permission. After that, 11:00 on weeknights and 1:00 on weekends. Hours will always be subject to conversation, while you're living at home. They will be determined in part by which other kids are at home with you. For as long as you're at home, you will need to make some concessions to the sleep patterns of your parents. On mornings when you have a chance to sleep in, nothing later than 10:00 a.m.*

7. *We are going to expect very close communication on your whereabouts for the first three months. But even after that time there will be a need to let the other members of your household know your whereabouts. It will be your responsibility to make sure we know where you are and with whom. For the duration of this contract you will be expected to carry either a cell phone or a beeper when you are away from home. (Work is the one exception.)*

8. *We will want to monitor your relationships with old friends and new for the duration of this contract. Bring home the people you spend time with. We will want to meet and get to know any new friends you happen upon, and we will want to be confident that when you're in the company of old friends they will be acting in your best interest.*

9. *During visits to California, we are going to want an open door policy whenever you are in your room during the day, whether*

*alone or with friends. You can excuse yourself to play your music
more loudly or to sleep.*

10. *No more than an hour and a half at a stretch on the computer or
    the video game consoles. And no more than seven hours total in
    a given week, unless you are working on a writing project.*

11. *Flat out no drugs. We're going to reserve the right to request a
    drug screening at any time. Refusal will be regarded as equiva-
    lent to a positive reading. You will limit alcohol use, in keeping
    with your understanding that the meds make you especially sus-
    ceptible to its effects. No alcohol period when you are planning to
    drive.*

12. *We will help you plan a visit with Maga and Pop [grandparents]
    in Texas. You can make this visit as soon as a weekend can be
    worked out with your new job.*

13. *Go to college. We're not going to beat on this idea endlessly, and
    you've made it clear that you want time to work or travel first
    and will explore college later. We understand this and are open
    to it, but don't mistake this understanding for any less concern
    that you get started on college when you're ready. We regard it as
    all but essential. We will encourage the decision to get back to
    school with financial support.*

14. *A family meeting time will be established, probably on Sundays,
    when we can update one another on how all this is going.*

15. *Consequences for the breach of the terms of this agreement may
    include loss of car privileges, grounding, or drudgery tasks.*

16. *This agreement is intended to last for six months. It expires
    August 22, 2002. At that time we can discuss whether an exten-
    sion to the agreement makes sense.*

> *Here's to the future . . . . With love,*
> *Your parents and stepparents*

Two issues in the contract stand out and merit amplification. They
have to do with friends and peers (item 8) and drugs and alcohol (item
11). Often the two go hand in hand. Articulating imposed limits on

alcohol consumption or defining a "no drugs" policy must seem shockingly obvious to parents of children who have never experimented with drugs or alcohol. But research on behavior in young people today finds that a majority of kids have experimented with both before they reach the age of eighteen.

According to data from the Center for Disease Control and Prevention, over the course of a twelve-month period during 2001,

- 56% of teens reported drinking alcohol during the previous month;
- 33% reported episodic heavy drinking during the previous month;
- 25% used marijuana during the previous month;
- 13% reported having sniffed or inhaled intoxicating substances on at lease one occasion; and
- 8% reported using cocaine on at least one occasion.

When I talk to other parents of teens, the topic of drugs and alcohol hardly ever enters the conversation, unless and until these substances present a problem for the parents of the child. This is a failing of our contemporary culture. Maybe because so many parents of my generation have personal histories replete with underage experimentation with drugs and alcohol, we turn a blind eye to our children's usage, cross our fingers, and try to rationalize it away: "They're going to try it anyway"; "It's nothing I didn't do when I was their age"; "One beer won't do them any harm."

We need to face the fact that the pass we are giving our children on alcohol and drugs *does* do them harm. The reasons we look the other way are complex. And I'm not sure what the solution is, short of a national debate on drugs and alcohol that somehow addresses the distinctions between (1) experimentation, (2) casual usage, and (3) substance abuse. I don't expect the debate to occur in my lifetime.

My real concern, however, focuses on drug and alcohol use in depressed teens. There are a couple of warnings worth reiterating.

First, teens engage in risky behaviors without regard to consequences. This suggests that a depressed teen with a history of substance abuse— or a depressed kid who uses drugs and alcohol even occasionally— runs a very real risk of compounding the problems associated with depression. Their perceptions about reality, the size and scope of personal problems, and consequences of their behavior are further occluded under the influence of drugs and alcohol.

Dr. David Shaffer, in a 1996 study of boys ages sixteen to nineteen who committed suicide, demonstrated that a full sixty-six percent had been abusing drugs or alcohol in the weeks or months prior to their deaths.[1] Since substance abuse is evident in the *majority* of teen suicides, we need to address it now. Drug and alcohol abuse do not always accompany adolescent depression, but they certainly turn up as symptoms in most depressed kids.

The second point to underscore is that a young person in treatment for depression, who is being prescribed a course of psychotropic drugs, is already under the influence of some very powerful chemical agents. Introducing illegal drugs, randomly or haphazardly—even something as seemingly benign as marijuana or alcohol—to this mix is just plain stupid, and parents need to be very wary and very aware. As difficult as it may be, it behooves us to be open with our children and address the issue of substance abuse head on.

No surprise, as the winter term at Montana Academy drew to a close, Will began to have qualms about leaving, about returning home, and he worried that his depression might return. We took some comfort knowing that he had learned a great deal about depression and we hoped he had learned a good deal about himself. If he were confronted with this illness again, we were counting on him to have the emotional tools with which to handle it, in the short- and long-term.

In the future, as with most persons afflicted with major depression, odds are he will suffer another bout. He will have to be mindful of the triggers and recognize the warning signs of his illness. He will have to know when to ask for help and allow himself to be open to receiving it. And he will have to be vigilant and take steps to avoid suicidal thinking. It's a lot to ask of anyone; I would argue that it's a colossal challenge for a young person.

On Tuesday night, February 19, Jack and I arrived in Kalispell to attend Will's graduation from Montana Academy, scheduled for 4:30 PM the next day. Bob and Melissa flew in from San Francisco and met us in Whitefish, where we checked into Pine Lodge, a now familiar haunt on the main drag leading into town, overlooking a pristine river. I wondered if I would ever go back there, to that breathtakingly beautiful part of the country. The intensity of our attachment to the northwest corner of Montana sprang, it goes without saying, from unhappy circumstances. But I had come to appreciate the clean, spare feel of the small towns and the glory of Montana's natural surroundings. Whitefish, Big Fork, Kalispell, and Columbia—all of these towns were as far from Washington, D.C., or San Francisco, geographically and culturally, as you could get.

I believe the remoteness of the place afforded added value by dislocating us from our daily routine temporarily. Drawn to this stark setting, we were forced to concentrate all of our emotion and attention on the benefits of the therapeutic program absent everyday concerns. The isolation was no accident. We had seen evidence time and again to indicate that the remoteness afforded this same opportunity to the kids in the program, as well.

On Wednesday morning, before we made our way to the ranch and the graduation ceremony, the four of us, Bob, Melissa, Jack, and I, stopped at a coffee shop we frequented on previous visits because of its excellent olallieberry popovers. I will remember Kalispell for its good coffee and wonderful breakfasts, in addition to other small treasures. Will's own fondness for pastries, pies, and donuts was legendary and he had sampled the ollalieberry popovers whenever we were in Kalispell. We bought strong coffee and half a dozen popovers for the forty-minute ride up snow-laced roads to Lost Horizon Ranch.

Finally, we were entering the home stretch. This was probably my last ride up the hill and down the dirt road to Montana Academy. I was so relieved we had made it—that Will had made it; but I also felt a blip of nostalgia. Or ambivalence. And a certain unease about what might lie ahead. Montana Academy not only offered Will an impenetrable cocoon; it provided the rest of us a respite to reflect and heal as a family in the aftermath of his suicide attempt. I wanted reassurance that when we traveled the road back to town later that day, Will in the backseat, diploma in hand, everything was going to be all right. What parent wouldn't give a limb for a guarantee of that magnitude?

Would Will miss this place? Probably not immediately. Maybe not ever. I would wager there were people, his counselors, his doctor, some of the kids, with whom he would remain in touch—at least in the short-term. But it would be hard to cast overboard the painful associations he automatically stored away for that time and place.

I have a similar reaction to the Psychiatric Institute of Washington, where both Will and I "did time." I cannot drive by the functionally ugly, brown brick structure on one of Washington's main drags without feeling little electric zaps of anxiety.

Sometimes, when I pass by in the summer, I see clusters of patients standing out in front of the building, smoking, sunning themselves, Styrofoam cups of coffee in their shaky hands. Some have that affectless, sorry gaze that never manages to alight too long on any one object, or the agitated syncopation that keeps them rocking like a metronome to an internal beat, back and forth, back and forth. I know the telltale signs by heart. I can rev up those memories in a split second. Crossing to the other side of the street, I avert my gaze as if the scene in front of PIW were the tableau of a gory accident. "There but the grace of God . . ." I imagine Will will feel that way, too.

Toward the end of his brilliant tome, *The Noonday Demon: An Atlas of Depression*, author Andrew Solomon observes:

> That is, perhaps, the greatest revelation I have had: not that depression is compelling but that the people who suffer from it may become compelling because of it. I hope that this basic fact will offer sustenance to those who suffer and will inspire patience and love in those who witness that suffering.[2]

I recall a conversation I had with a friend shortly after my first child was born. She asked, "What do you suppose he'll grow up to be?" We were sitting on the living room floor, sipping lemonade, and Max was lying on a quilt between us, eyes wide open, placid and content. I was fawning over him, drinking him in with new-mother glory. "I don't care," I replied cavalierly, "as long as he's not a dictator or a rapist." But in the back of my mind, I thought, "I want my child to grow up to be compassionate." Compassionate and caring.

Children do not necessarily come by compassion naturally. It is a virtue that needs to be instilled—or "inspired," as Andrew Solomon suggests. If Will gained anything during his many months of suffering, I'm sure he came to appreciate the many ways mental illness distills the experience of depression to its lowest common denominator, nullifying feeling and connectedness to others. But I know, from personal experience, that the process of healing requires you to take stock of who you are and where you fit in the world. This process demands a level of awareness of and attentiveness to the suffering of others.

I do not believe you can survive the experience of depression without becoming a more compassionate person. No one wants his or her child to suffer depression. None of us ever wants to see our children afflicted with any illness, setback, or trauma. Too often, however, it is out of our hands. But in the best of circumstances, we can hope our children rebound with courage, good health—and compassion.

Perhaps one of the hardest things I have had to do as a parent is roll back my expectations for my children. Everyone I know has fantasies when their kids are tiny of a grown child walking across a stage in cap and gown to receive a diploma from a prestigious school, turning to face the audience, lifting the diploma in the air, and hailing, "This wouldn't have been possible without my mom and dad!" You imagine tears of joy, your pride inflating like a helium balloon, until you virtually levitate off the gymnasium floor. Or how about the fantasy of your daughter—a future leader of America—in a beautiful long dress, shyly admiring an orchid corsage the handsome captain of the baseball team has just attached to her bodice before heading out to the prom? Dream on.

Parents need a reality check: expectations backfire. I have learned that the more tightly bound you are to the expectations you have for your child, the greater the disappointment. Parenting is a great leveler. It humbles you in more ways than I can count.

Two out of three parents I meet today tell me stories attesting to the circuitous and sometimes terrifying dilatory or unconventional ways in which their children "came of age." As my mother reminded me when Will dropped out of high school, "They all get there by different means." We are called to examine our motivation for wanting our children to adhere to the well-threaded path.

I wanted my children to experience normal, average adolescence (whatever "normal" means) because I thought it would be easier on them—and on me. But of the four children I have had a hand in rearing, two of my own and two stepchildren, all four deviated significantly from "normal" at some point during adolescence. Perhaps it is a reflection of my parenting skills rather than the choices my children made (some good, some disastrous), but as a family we didn't specialize in student-body presidents or varsity-letter athletes, science-prize winners or lead roles in the school play. For the most part, our kids struggled and stumbled, occasionally excelled, and somehow survived to become strong, capable, independent, and creative young people. Perhaps this is the *new* normal.

I never imagined seeing any of my children saddled with a debilitating mental illness smack-dab in the middle of their teens. Likewise, I do not know a single parent who anticipated having to address a son or daughter's substance abuse, sexual promiscuity, truancy, or licentious behavior. But, as our children are fond of saying, "shit happens." Embrace it. Once more, I think my mother was right when she told me, "It's how you cope . . . that measures your personal worth."

I was sorting through Will's old high school papers recently when I came across a short assignment he wrote in the fall of 2000, at the beginning of his junior year, "before this whole mess began," as he would say. His recipe for happiness? "My recipe for happiness is simply having good friends and people who care about me in my life." It is safe to say that from the perspective of his "friends and people who care" about him, he succeeded, big time.

9/20/00
Chapter 2 Ethics Assignment; Mr. Adkins
Will D.
Recipe for Happiness

Before writing this, I asked my brother what he thought the recipe for happiness is. His response was, "Knowing that I'm the greatest man alive." Obviously, he was joking, but when I thought about what he had said, (whether he realized it or not) he was right. The recipe for happiness is self-contentment. By this, I mean the peace of mind, which comes with being completely satisfied with one's self and one's situation. In order to be happy you must enjoy being the person you are, doing the things you do, living where you live, having the friends you have, etc.

As far as I am concerned, I feel that I am way too young to decide what will ultimately make me happy. At this point, my recipe for happiness is simply having good friends and people who care about me in my life. Who is to say that won't change as I grow older.

Before a roaring fire in the giant meeting hall of the main lodge at Montana Academy, Will received his high school diploma in a blue satin cap and gown, in front of family, friends, teachers, and therapists. We snapped a lot of photos and bear-hugged his teachers, doctors, and the other parents.

Three other kids graduated from the program that day, but only one, his friend Marla from San Francisco, also received her high school diploma. Even in this rarified and anomalous setting, it was a triumphant and gratifying moment. Will graduated with honors, having maintained a 3.8 grade-point average. Everyone wished him well. But our elation was short-lived.

Our last meeting with Dennis Malinak at Montana Academy later that day was wildly unsettling. We were hoping to catch Dennis for a chunk of time that afternoon, between the graduation ceremony and a dinner organized for the kids at a roadside restaurant along nearby McGregor Lake. We were expecting something along the lines of an outtake interview, some advice and guidance we could take away to cap off Will's ten-month stay . . . last words of wisdom before reentry.

Dennis was trying to sandwich a conversation with us between meetings with hyperanxious parents of newly admitted kids and preparations for the upcoming two days of parent-staff seminars. He seemed rushed and slightly edgy. Bob and I began the conversation with a recitation of our lingering concerns: Was Dennis confident that Will no longer harbored thoughts of suicide? Was the change we were seeing in Will's mood real? What about the medication? Should he continue with the drugs and/or therapy? Did he think Will would regain his footing and make the transition back home with relative ease?

The four parents crowded around the desk in Dennis's tiny office on the lower level of the lodge, looking out on a cluster of snow-topped evergreens. Dennis shifted in his office chair uncomfortably. Over the past ten months, he had spent more time with Will than any of us had, and yet, even to Dennis, Will presented a conundrum he couldn't solve. He confided that Will represented one of the most stubborn cases of adolescent depression he had ever treated.

"So are you saying he's still at risk?" I probed warily.

"I don't think so. But you know, I see him in group and individually every day for weeks and I'll be driving home from campus, from what I think was a particularly good session with Will, and I'll suddenly stop and it hits me—he hasn't said anything different from the day he came in here. I have no idea what he's thinking. And *that* troubles me."

The neurochemical roots of Will's depression were inordinately hard to reach with medication; it had taken roughly nine months to see a noticeable turnaround in his depression. Likewise, Will posed a challenge for any good therapist: he never revealed much in their sessions and was loath to share his true feelings with any one individual or in a group.

We could all agree that on the surface Will was a terrific kid: polite, easygoing, bright, and popular at Montana Academy; Dennis and others told us so. But on a deeper level, Will remained an enigma to his therapists, who hoped they could shed some light on the root causes of his depression. He had fooled us before. Would he fool us again? Will was done with the program and there were still big chunks of his persona locked in a trick box of his own making. If it was troubling to Dennis, it was gut wrenching for us.

"I believe Will's gotten as much as he can get out of Montana Academy," Dennis allowed. He conceded he was pleased the pharmacological cocktail was finally showing good results. But with a degree of candor you are rarely afforded by a physician these days, Dennis admitted he was reluctant to make confident predictions about Will's future, free from depression. It was too soon in his mind to feel assured that Will had conquered this demon.

Dennis was as compassionate and as skilled an adolescent psychiatrist as they come. He cared deeply about kids and understood adolescent boys better than anyone we had come across. But I have learned that physicians abhor broken patients they cannot mend. Given the nature of mental illness, it's much more difficult to pronounce a mind "healed" than a reconstructed kneecap. Dennis could not help this patient anymore; he had put his all into it, but as therapeutic outcomes go, he did not herald it a hundred percent success.

We had been down this avenue with Will and therapy before, back in January when Dr. Salerian first released Will from PIW, and again after his suicide attempt in March. Were Will's troubles so profound that he would go to any length to conceal them? Was his depression idiopathic, defying conventional diagnosis and treatment? Or was Will an exemplar of a subset of kids who suffer from major depression who stand apart from the rest because their illness hides behind outward manifestations of "normal"—the kid who's anxious to please, a perfectionist who conforms to the norm and tries to live up to everyone's expectations.

I don't have the answer. Perhaps I never will. But the doctors' inability to chart a clear prognosis for Will underscores just how hard it is to diagnose and treat adolescent depression. So little is known about this illness; we've barely scratched the surface since investigations into the nature of adolescent depression began in the twentieth century. I am confident, however, that medical breakthroughs are occurring at a frenetic pace, that what we know now about adolescent depression will be augmented exponentially in the coming decade, and that science will tease out all of the actors involved in depression—stress, genes, environment, diet, exercise—and add these variables to what we already know about the disease. And we can hope that by 2010 the pharmacology will be light-years beyond where it is now.

In the meantime, as a parent, I conclude where I began: you invest as much time and energy as possible mustering the information you need to serve as your child's best advocate, and then you trust in your own judgment. It is a crapshoot. And, as I have said before, the risks of making the wrong calculation are immeasurable. But until science offers more hope by way of empirically based options, a lot of treatment regimens are subject to trial and error, and the burden falls to us, the parents, for better or for worse, to seek out the best remedies for our troubled children. Do not give up.

Our final meeting with Dennis was over in half an hour. I sensed that this was not the closure Dennis had hoped for; it certainly did not play out the way we had hoped it would. We thought we would be tying up all the loose ends of this chapter in Will's life. We had asked for assurances that Will was no longer at risk for another suicide attempt; Dennis just confirmed what we already knew: there are no such guarantees. He postulated that the next decade of Will's life would be crucial to assessing whether Will's depression was idiosyncratic, perhaps just a fluke of neurological and/or biological mishaps triggered by the onset of puberty ransacking his adolescence. Or, it was possible, and, unfortunately, a statistical possibility, that his depression was chronic and that he would suffer another episode sometime in his life, perhaps with a frequency or severity mimicking my own history with the illness.

As we were getting up to leave the meeting, Dennis offered a little sliver of comfort. He proposed we use age thirty as a benchmark.

"Look, by the time Will turns thirty, he will have learned to manage the illness. Either we won't see his depression return in his twenties, or he will be able to handle it if it does." By age thirty Will may be home free. In the meantime, we have no choice but to watch him and love him. In the end, isn't that all a parent can do?

The world at large now recognizes depression as a serious illness, even though different cultures elect vastly different approaches to treatment. It is possible that Eastern traditions of healing, which emphasize the physiology of the mind-body connection, will meld with contemporary Western practice to provide new approaches; it is also possible that the global reach of pharmacology in the next decade will narrow rather than expand the exploration of remedies outside the boundaries of conventional medicine, which would be unfortunate.

In the spring of 2004, I called Dennis Malinak and Montana Academy director Dr. John McKinnon to try to get a sense of where they and the program stood with regard to the debate over antidepressant medication for adolescents. After all, a therapeutic boarding school is the perfect laboratory for close observation of the effects of medication on adolescent behavior, given the microscopic monitoring and rigorous therapeutic regime. Dennis was encouraged by the results he was getting from the pharmacological interventions for his teen patients.

"Gail, I wish we could do brain scans of all the kids entering the Montana Academy program and then again when they leave." Not only was he seeing dramatic improvements in the kids with mood disorders, but he went so far as to voice hope that antidepressants may play a role in inoculating the brain from future bouts of mental illness for young people treated at this particularly vulnerable time in their brains' development. In fact, current research is under way at the National Institute of Mental Health that may soon prove the brain's ability to override the circuitry involved in depression by introducing medication at the earliest sign of illness.

"I think this possibility holds out great promise for kids like Will," Dennis offered.

"So you don't necessarily think it's a given that he'll suffer from another bout of depression? You don't think we need to hold our breath for the next several years?" I asked.

"No, I'm optimistic that some of these kids won't see a recurrence of depression in their lifetimes."

Let's hope he's right.

Will returned to Washington in early March—a full year after his suicide attempt. He moved back into his second-story bedroom facing the street, its north-facing windows bumping up against the out-of-control blooming pear tree putting on a repeat of last year's luxuriant snow-white show. All his things were there, exactly where he had left them eleven months earlier: same khaki pants and muted plaid shirts hanging in the closet, same eleventh-grade American history and chemistry notebooks lining the bookcase, same *Simpsons'* memorabilia on top of the dresser.

To look at him in March 2002, a kid, so contained, so gentle, so seemingly unperturbed—who would guess, in this everyday setting that broadcast: "I'm just a regular kid, living this regular life," who would guess what had transpired? Who would guess that one night barely a year before he was hell-bent on self-destruction, that he had been dragged down to the lowest point in human emotion and that he had taken us, his family, with him into uncharted depths of despair.

Will had done the hard work, adhered to the structured discipline of a therapeutic program. In those first few days back home, he earnestly exuded a sense of balance and stability—and wellness—and I, just as earnestly, wanted to believe what I was seeing. He also had youth and resilience going for him. I, on the other hand, remained bereft of the self-confidence I took for granted when, five or ten years ago, I thought I knew everything about my children.

After he had been home for a few weeks, I came to the realization that Will would bounce back from this chapter in his young life quicker and with more agility than I would. And for that, I should be grateful; he's a child, and children heal faster. Did I really expect to subvert the natural law of child rearing? To be a parent is to know suffering in a boundless dimension. My scored and tested parent heart would mend slowly. It is mending still.

In the first few weeks after Will's return to Washington, Jack, Will, and I tried, with better than average results, to establish a routine. The program at Montana Academy, with its 24/7 structure and intense supervision, was relegated to his past but left its mark—initially Will was at odds with his new freedom. Although he was never much of a risk taker (let's discount the suicide attempt), he now approached the world with more caution than one would expect of an eighteen-year-old boy. But then, we were cautious, too. He stuck to the relatively early curfew without complaint and I held on to and administered his medications, doling the requisite dosages out morning and evening. I bought him a cell phone and insisted he let us know his every movement. He was compliant and courteous—almost unnaturally so.

In late March, Will and all of his cousins flew to Georgetown, Texas, for the weekend. The kids flew from as far away as Australia, New York, and California for what would be the grandchildren's final visit with my mother, who died a few weeks later on April 14. My mother was in fine spirits and was tickled to see them. They sat by her bedside, looked through old photographs of themselves and their parents, and made forays into town to sample coconut cream pie at the local diner my mother raved about. In many ways, it was a very uplifting reunion for Will, reuniting him with the extended family that he loved and who loved him.

Will flirted with and halfheartedly pursued a couple of full-time jobs and simultaneously enrolled with a temporary employment agency, which kept him working at entry-level office jobs two or three days a week, beginning in early April. He wore his khaki pants and ironed his oxford cloth shirts for job interviews. He hung out with his old friends, in particular Vic and Henry and his stepbrother, John. In his spare time, he read prodigiously, a habit left over from Montana Academy. And he wrote in his journal.

Our initial attempts to interest him in at least investigating colleges for the fall semester (though it was too late in the season to take the process seriously) failed, and after a month or two, I simply stopped raising the topic. He maintained that he was not ready to accept the discipline attending college full-time would require; I accepted his decision with resignation and hoped that he would find the idea of college appealing somewhere down the road.

As the weather got warmer and the school year for Will's friends and peers drew to a close, his buddies were following through with plans formulated over the course of the past two years. Some kids were bound for college in the fall, others were simply glad to be graduating from high school, getting jobs, and moving out of the house.

Again, I suffered minor pangs of regret that Will's launch onto the stage of adulthood had departed so radically from paths open to many of his friends. He did not have a "plan," and his lack of a plan, or his inability to articulate and follow through with a design for the future, troubled me. It troubled all of us.

As spring turned into summer, he languished, contentedly and seemingly without purpose, as he continued to search for full-time work and tackled a variety of part-time jobs. Was I putting too much emphasis on his plans for the future? He didn't seem worried, and when I would initiate a conversation on the topic, he would try to reassure me that he had things well in hand.

"No, Mom, everything's fine; I'm getting there; I'm working on . . ." Or, "I'm waiting to hear back from . . ." The object of the exercise varied from week to week.

From time to time, he entertained an earlier aspiration to pursue an apprenticeship with a union; he even brought home application forms for several job training programs. The union apprenticeship appealed to him because he figured he could draw a "decent" wage— decent enough in his mind to get a place on his own and maybe even buy a car; and if he eventually decided to pursue a degree in something like electrical engineering, the union would send him to school. Aha! A romantic blue-collar dream, but hard to fathom as a match for a kid absorbed in writing and literature, not to mention girls. There weren't likely to be many young women pursuing union apprenticeships in the electrical workers union. And, knowing Will, it was hard to imagine him being at work by 6:30 AM, lunchbox in hand, spending eight to ten hours at a job site and wrapping it all up with a couple of brews with the guys in the evening. I judged him to be too laconic and introspective to fit into the lifestyle. But I was willing to be proven wrong.

Will continued to see his therapist, Dr. Vaune Ainsworth, and faithfully took his medication, but I still worried that he had too much time on his hands. Was he drifting? Was this just a stage of recovery? I didn't know whether to cut him slack—after all, I knew better than most how difficult it is to bounce back after an episode of major depression—or to press him harder to move along. We were bound up in a tight little mother-son dance, trying to get in synch with the music for a few more months.

By late spring, Will had a new girlfriend, Sarah, a high school senior at a local Catholic girls' school, whom he met at McDonald's one night after bowling with his friends. She was a sweet, lovely young person, bound for college to study classical piano. They shared an easy affection.

Through Sarah, Will and Will's friend Vic found jobs as summer camp counselors at a nearby Quaker school—uncomplicated teenage summer jobs. Will worked with the littlest campers, who clung to him with the reverence accorded a minor celebrity. He got a kick out of his kids and entertained us in the evening with stories about his day, about a child who habitually wiped his nose on Will's sleeve or another who had an interesting way with words. The job was just what he needed. He had found a carefree niche to occupy his time for eight weeks; he earned a regular paycheck and hung out with his friends. And it got us off his back short-term. Still, no evidence he was coming closer to a "plan" for the future, but he was certainly enjoying this moment.

We reviewed the home contract in terms of bracketing his reentry and transition home. The contract was a signpost for the first six months. Presumably, if all was well, we would either abandon or renegotiate the terms, effectively prescribing whatever degree of independence we felt was his due. The end date was fast approaching: August 22, six months from the day he departed Montana Academy. He was now eighteen and a half years old.

"Okay, Will, it's showtime," I urged silently. "Time to get moving." But I could not forecast where he was headed. His girlfriend and some of his friends were in the throes of packing for college, severing ties and moving on. Will didn't seem perturbed by their imminent departures, nor did their moves seem to spur him on to a path of his own.

If a child is lucky enough to get into college and find the means to pay for it, almost everyone, young people *and* their parents, is well served by the experience. The college experience offers a young person, from roughly age eighteen to twenty-two, some tangential benefits, not all of them academic. Considering the prominent role neurobiology plays in teen behavior, I think college is an ideal place to park a young person's underdeveloped prefrontal cortex for four years. At college, kids can experiment and explore new ways of thinking and behaving away from home and parental unease. They can act out, do completely ridiculous things, engage in risky behaviors, and, as long as they remain within the confines of "acceptable" or "legal" (the terms of which are defined by their peers, the authorities, or both), you can reasonably expect a young adult to emerge at the end of the process with measurably more maturity, judgment, and aptitude for life than the person who entered.

We would be a better country if there were an established place in society for young people who are still floating, who aren't ready to move as quickly as some others right out of high school. We desperately need more opportunities that offer experience in community service programs or training in the trades. Certainly the military is an option for many, but we are just now beginning to appreciate fully that during wartime, a portion of the young people who serve will return with debilitating and long-term mental health issues that are often dismissed or inadequately addressed. Society pays in the long run for the millions of kids who have limited opportunities to extend the maturation process beyond high school.

In July, a family friend tipped us off about an opportunity worth investigating. City Year DC, an initiative of AmeriCorps, still had a few remaining openings in Washington for the program starting in late August. City Year places young people, ages eighteen to twenty-four, in public schools to mentor elementary-school kids in the basics.

The program was looking for high school graduates, with good "people skills," and it offered training in mentoring, a monthly stipend, transportation to and from the schools, a yellow jumpsuit emblazoned with the AmeriCorps logo, and a couple of thousand dollars upon completion of the program, money to be applied toward college tuition. City Year required a one-year commitment. The program sounded tailor-made for Will.

Will was intrigued and decided, after some nudging on our part, to apply. On the application he was asked to "describe a challenge you faced in your life and how you managed to overcome it." He wrote:

A year and a half ago, I suffered from severe clinical depression. I tried several medications, spent time in a psychiatric hospital, but still continued to sink lower and lower. Finally, I came to a point where I was torn between my sense of obligation to my family and friends and my complete disinterest in continuing to live my life. My depression got the better of me and I tried to commit suicide in March of 2001.

Since then, I have made an almost full recovery—I have found medications that work for me and I am feeling positive about where my life is going. It is a drastic change from how I felt before and it has taught me that absolutely no problem or negative situation is without a solution.

I looked over the answers he had typed into the spaces allocated on the application, and when I got to the line "It is a drastic change from how I felt before and it has taught me that absolutely no problem or negative situation is without a solution," my heart soared.

Will turned in his application and set up an interview with the program directors. He was accepted into AmeriCorps's City Year and was scheduled to begin his volunteer job the third week in August.

One afternoon a week after receiving the acceptance notice from City Year, I was hastily fixing dinner when Will floored me with a question.

"Mom, do you think I should look at junior colleges in San Francisco?"

My first thought was, "Huhhhh? What's up with this?" Yet another stealth maneuver from our Will? What was behind this latest turnabout in his thinking? Did the appeal of a college education suddenly smack him like a bolt between the eyes as the best possible option? Or was it a fallback for lack of direction or lack of enthusiasm for the City Year job?

"Gee, Will, are you really thinking that's something you'd like to do?" I feigned casual interest and studiously continued slicing tomatoes for a salad.

"Yeah, well, maybe. I don't know. I was just thinking . . . Maybe I could get into San Francisco State. I went online, and because Dad's a state resident, I am too, so all I need to apply, with my SATs and all, is a 3.0[GPA]. And I think the community college in San Francisco has to take me if I just show up."

"Okay, Will, let's go online and figure out what your options are."

Now we had two balls in the air: college and the City Year offer. He was going to have to make a decision. Soon.

"Willy, Willy, Willy," I whispered to myself, "where are you going with this?" He didn't exactly have a track record of reasoned decision making. For better or worse, most decisions of consequence had been made for him. And when it came to making decisions independently, his modus operandi was to dally and agonize over the choices. Or not make them at all.

A few days later: "Mom, I think I want to go to college in San Francisco. I can live with Dad and Melissa for a while and then Max and I can get an apartment. If I take classes at City College in San Francisco, it's a feeder to the UC [University of California] schools, so maybe I can do that for a couple of years and transfer."

The fall semester at San Francisco's City College began August 22. He would have to show up for placement tests on the nineteenth. We would have to move on a dime. Wow! My head was spinning.

"What's up with this last-minute change of heart about college, Will?"

He grinned and offered facetiously, "Well, I figured out—that's where all the cute girls are."

I couldn't help but laugh. We both burst into giggles and exchanged a "high-five."

What was the real reason behind his last-minute decision? I don't know. Maybe there were many reasons; it didn't matter to me. (Who could fault him for wanting to be in the company of pretty young women?) It may have been as simple as this: he was ready. Ready to move on and put the last year and a half behind him.

I was delighted that he wanted to be closer to his brother. From time to time, Will and Max had talked about finding an apartment in the Bay Area and living together. They were still extremely close and I could count on them to look after each other. He would also be nearer the West Coast cousins, aunts, uncles, and grandparents. And with his dad and Melissa there, ever vigilant, he would be secure and well loved.

With a mixture of trepidation and relief, Jack and I packed Will off to San Francisco—and off to college in mid-August. For all of us, Will's decision to attend college signified a gradual return to normalcy. A year or even six months prior, I never thought I'd be saying, "Will is headed off to college." The conventional is comforting. We had been down the road less traveled and we were more than ready to embrace "conventional." The entire family applauded this turn of events.

So what does the future hold for Will and for countless others like him?

Just as I was finishing this book, I had an opportunity to attend the annual conferences of the National Alliance for the Mentally Ill (NAMI), which was being held in Washington at the Washington Hilton Hotel, just a few blocks from my house. At the gala dinner concluding the four-day conference, NAMI celebrated the twenty-fifth anniversary of its founding. The organization has come a long way, and its membership now numbers in the hundreds of thousands; it includes families, educators, advocates, clinicians, and the individuals who struggle every day with mental illness.

The closing ceremonies were held in a ballroom resplendent with banners, and everyone was elegantly attired. We were reminded that NAMI's celebration coincided this year with the third anniversary of 9/11, and we bent our heads in a moment of silence in recognition of the innocent lives lost. I couldn't help being struck by the irony of the coincidence: each year we lose as many young people to suicide as were killed in the World Trade Center bombings. It is both a secret, hidden tragedy and public-health crisis.

In July 2003 the President's New Federation Commission on Mental Illness announced its findings after undertaking a "comprehensive study of the U.S. mental health service delivery system"[3] and issued its recommendations to the president. In its October 2002 interim report, the commissioners stated:

> The mental health delivery system is fragmented and in disarray—
> not from lack of commitment and skill of those who deliver care,
> but from underlying structural, financing, and organizational
> problems . . . The system's failings lead to unnecessary and costly
> disability, homelessness, school failure, and incarceration.[4]

Hardly a surprise.

When the commission articulated its goals for the future in the final report, it recommended sweeping changes, a "transformation," and the development of services and treatments that are "(1) consumer and family driven, not focused primarily on the demands of bureaucracies, and (2) provide real and meaningful choice of treatments, services and supports—and providers."

Two of the commissioners attending the NAMI convention gave

a briefing entitled "Using the New Freedom Commission Report to Transform Mental Health Care for Children, Adolescents and Families."[5] During the question-and-answer period that followed, two salient details emerged. When the commission was given its charge, the members were told to return with "budget neutral recommendations," meaning there would be no funding for the massive "transformation." The government's cost-cutting measures have left local and state entities short of funds required to prop up the existing system; there will be no "transforming" in the near future, as far as I can see.

The second item off-limits for the commission study was insurance parity. The administration did not want them to touch the political hot potato that would require insurers to guarantee that our children's mental health receive the same level of coverage as their physical care. So where exactly does that leave the consumer and family who is supposed to drive this stunning transformation of the mental-health system? Right back at the beginning, with no government funds to support the state, local, or federal agencies needed to simply sustain the existing system, and with no consideration to the millions of persons whose insurance won't cover their children's psychiatric care.

Our family is a member of a small percentage of the population fortunate enough to have the emotional, financial, and familial resources to steer them through this type of crisis—and for us it *still* required a titanic lift on the part of everyone involved. I am tormented by the reality that there are millions of families out there who are not as lucky as ours.

Will spent six months from the time he graduated from Montana Academy getting back on his feet. It was not a seamless transition, but overall I was guardedly optimistic that he was well again. He had been to Bedlam and exited two years later a person with a large measure of insight and compassion. Finally, he appeared to be at peace with himself. From my perspective, it doesn't get much better than that.

One sultry afternoon in August, Will and I sat in the kitchen eating lunch. The next day I would put him on the airplane headed to the West Coast—and to college.

"So, Willo, I want to ask you—in the long run, what do you think made the difference in your depression? Was it the meds, or the talk therapy, or was it being so far away in Montana? Or a little of all of those things combined? What do you think now, Will? . . . I really want to know."

He looked up from his sandwich, shifted his gaze away from me, and stared out the window at the tubs of plants profuse with summer blooms arrayed around our wooden deck. After several seconds, he turned back to me and in a matter-of-fact tone answered, "It was just time, Mom."

Just time.

Epilogue

IN WILL'S OWN WORDS

I've been asked to write an epilogue. You know, a little something to wrap it all up, one of those "what have we learned" bits. But to be honest, I don't know what to say. I'm no good at that heart-to-heart, embrace-life bullshit, and if you're reading this, odds are I don't know you.

If I were to meet each person who reads this and tell them individually what it was like to go through depression, a suicide attempt and all, I know it would change every time. All stories change even if the same person tells it. What really matters is who's listening. That makes this all the more difficult. I'm not sure I really want anyone to know my so-called story. And I'm not actually a writer. Writers know that they're going to be read. Most everything I wrote in this book was never intended for outside consumption. All of a sudden you know that people are going to read your shit and you can't think anymore.

But where am I now? Depression doesn't bother me like it used to. Maybe that's really all you need to know. I'm feeling much better. Thank you for listening. You don't need to know where I live or what I do. It's enough to know that I'm embarrassed about what happened— the suicide attempt. I hurt a lot of people, which is something that I have a particular aversion to doing. It makes me uncomfortable talking about it. And how do I convey my feelings about what happened in five to ten pages without sounding like (a) a jackass or (b) a high school motivational speaker?

These days I work and take classes at a community college; I ride the bus a lot. Most of the time when I'm on the bus I just sit there and read my books, but every once in a while I'll be too tired or just not interested and I'll just sit and watch. I like people watching. I enjoy it more than reading, and sometimes I get so engrossed that I end up sitting there way past my stop.

Twice now I've sat at my window and listened to homeless people try to harmonize with overactive car alarms. I'm wondering if it's something that I should try to sell commercially. MTV is always looking for that cutting-edge shit.

And I like sports. Most Sundays I play baseball with some of my friends and family. I'm a terrible ballplayer. In fact, most of us Sunday players are. I can run and catch well, but I'm a poor hitter and a minor birth defect left me with a pretty weak right arm, so my accuracy's nonexistent. That doesn't matter, though. I love playing baseball.

One time last summer I was on a team with a couple of my friends, my cousin, and her half-sister. We only had six players, which is just enough as long as the other team pitches to itself, and you don't mind having a giant hole in your infield (we didn't). The odds were stacked against us. The other team had better hitters and more players (seven). We never cared who we were playing against, or how good they were. We'd rather lose than split up our team to make it more even.

We took the field tentatively and we paid the price early on. Man, we must have given up fifteen runs in the first two innings. We were dropping balls in the outfield, throwing over each other's heads. On top of our ineptness, the other team had some kind of disease where they couldn't stop hitting home runs.

I'll tell you what, though, we made losing look good. We would slide into bases unnecessarily and try stupid flip plays at second base—shit like that. My friend Roberto would sing Bob Marley's "Redemption Song" every time he fucked up in the outfield. We were down by at least ten runs and it only looked like it was getting worse by the inning. But, hey, who really cares anyway? Not us.

But suddenly the tables turned. The gods of baseball (or of pity) smiled on us and we were the New York Fucking Yankees. We ended up winning by five or six runs. It was a kick. Who knew we could play if we just stopped caring? We laughed about the game the whole way home and had a few beers when we got back. A proper celebration.

That was in August of 2003. I tried to kill myself in March of 2001. Not once during that baseball game or the evening that followed did I think about depression, suicide, or how any of it had affected me in the past two years. That is what recovery means to me.

I still take antidepressant medication, and I really have no problem with it. At night, I take Remeron, which makes me very tired and very hungry in a short amount of time. Before I fall asleep I always want to eat, but much like having the munchies, and no amount of food really satisfies my hunger. The more tired I get, the hungrier I become. I find myself desperately trying to shovel cereal into my mouth, falling asleep, forgetting that my mouth is a wad of undigested corn flake mush. Very pleasant.

When I was severely depressed, the pills didn't try to kill me, I did. And there's really nothing more I want to say about that. And so what if the depression comes back? It's nothing new, right? I would be hard-pressed to handle it worse than I handled it the first time. I've pieced my sanity back together and the cracks have faded over time. If it comes apart again, I'll fix it again. But like a puzzle I've already solved, I now know where the pieces go. There's less confusion, less uncertainty, I can see what's wrong. But who thinks about that anyway? When you're happy, be happy. Don't analyze it; just enjoy it.

Now it's fall and the first cold days of the season change me. In summer, nights and days blend so seamlessly that I lose track of time. (How do people in the southern hemisphere manage to stick to New Year's resolutions?) Monday evening spills into Tuesday morning without my noticing. Next thing I know it is Wednesday afternoon and I'm still laughing about last weekend—and about baseball.

But autumn makes it very clear who's who and what's what. Night somehow pushes its way into the middle of the day. By the time I get off work I'm wondering how soon I can go to bed without feeling anti-social. When the first cold day hits my face I'm reminded of how much time has passed. I have a clock hanging on my wall and exactly once every second it reminds me how much time I'm wasting. Sometimes it feels like I'm slowly going nowhere, but, for the most part, I'm just enjoying the ride.

—*Will D.*
Autumn 2004

MEGAN'S BIOGRAPHY

Megan Mathews attends Earlham College in Richmond, Indiana, where she studies philosophy and psychology. She plans to travel, perform volunteer service, and write before enrolling in graduate school. Megan still suffers from occasional bouts of depression, but she manages her illness with medication and therapy. She and Will remain good friends and stay in close touch. They only occasionally discuss the depression that first brought them together.

ACKNOWLEDGMENTS

In the course of writing this book I was often overwhelmed by the kindness of strangers and by the generosity, time, and talent of my friends:

My hyperliterate friend and co-conspirator, author Mark Perry, urged this idea on and conned our most excellent book agent, Gail Ross, into giving me a chance. Gail and her skilled editor, Jenna Land, guided me through the terrain of seeking a publisher. During the process of writing the manuscript, I mercilessly foisted various incarnations onto friends to read and critique; I honor the magnanimity and goodwill of Susan Bachurski, Monica Baker, Bob Boorstin, Helena DeMoura, Put Ebinger, Pat and Abbey Griffin, Peter Madigan, Kevin Quigley, Peter Krogh, Patrick and Marcelle Leahy, Janice Ryan, Tim Rieser, Ricki Seidman, John Shore, Ginny Sloan, Gordon and Sharon Smith, Nancy Spielberg, Rachel Synder, Jan Stabile, David Thorpe, Henry Togna, Julia Trotter, and Loung Ung for tolerating the imposition. Thanks also to Charlotte Baldwin (mother of my stepchildren Jane and John Brady), who is not just an uncommonly good friend, but served as my technological backup, safeguarding each new draft of the book on her computer and finding me an empty office in which to write. Thanks to the folks at TSD who made me feel welcome in their midst.

I also owe a debt to the many teachers, clinicians, and doctors who helped provide a road map as we tried to find our way through the tangle of Will's illness: Vaune Ainsworth, Trish Bickford Petty, Ann Marie Crowley, Susan Dranitzke, Frank James, Rosemary and John McKinnon,

Dennis Malinak, Alen Salerian, Carol and John Santa, and Bill Wilson. Will asked that I pay tribute also to Charles Reavis and Greg Windham of Montana Academy.

Megan Mathews deserves a wellspring of good fortune for having the courage to give us a window into the world of cutting and depression as seen from the perspective of an adolescent girl. I thank her parents for their goodwill in support of her participation in this effort.

To Will's vast loving constellation of relatives, including uncles Kevin, Bill, Ken Miller, and especially Uncle Joe; aunts Mary, Chris, Michelle, and Deborah Green; Great Auntie Gail Boone and Robin; Will's paternal grandparents, Pat and Bill; my late mother-in-law, Esther Brady, and Will's cousins, Stephanie and Kate, Ben, Alice, Erica, and Patrick Maloney, we thank you for playing such a large role in our lives.

I thank my dear friends who over the years have witnessed my lowly depressions and never held it against me, in particular Margaret Cerrato, Joan Firestone, Sara and Arne Paulson, George Scharffenberger, Hattie Smith, Barbara Stone, and Mark Vermilion; and hats off to my musically gifted friends, who graciously consented to let their inspired lyrics find their way into the book; their contributions would not have been possible without the enduring friendship and many kindnesses I have received over the years from my supremely graceful and talented friend Emmylou Harris and her jewel of a mother, Eugenia.

The National Alliance for the Mentally Ill (NAMI) and Paul Murray made it possible for me to anchor funds needed to pursue this project and I am grateful for the personal attention of Darcy Gruttadaro, director of NAMI's National Action Center for Children and Adolescents. I received underwriting from longtime friends Nancy and David Donovan and through the generosity of the Shaffer Foundation. I am indebted to Wendy and Michael Appel and Ted Vecchio for their encouragement and support. Activist street-fighting hero and Nobel Peace Prize Laureate Bobby Muller gave me vision and friendship beyond measure. My irrepressible little sister, Suzy Miller, made me laugh whenever writing a book about depression became too depressing, and my dear father, Clayton Griffith (who wasn't so sure about this venture initially), helped me with a small infusion of cash in the nick of time, so I could keep writing.

Because I had never before tackled a project of this magnitude, my agent and editor pushed me to find someone in the field of child and adolescent psychiatry who could lend the book a bit of weight and legitimacy. I couldn't have enlisted anyone better than the eminent authority on teenage suicide, Dr. David Shaffer, who consented to write the foreword. I owe legions to my insightful editor at Harper-Collins, Gail Winston, who took our fragile bird of a book and gave it wings.

Thanks especially to my former spouse, Bob, and his wife, Melissa Houtte, for allowing me to expose us all without complaint. And, finally, I wish to acknowledge my husband, Jack Brady, the rock-solid captain of this family vessel, whose humor and good judgment about all things human never fails to astonish me. Obviously, I would be nowhere and no one without my children, Will, Max, Jane, and John, each of whom I believe has learned—in his or her own way—that there is no problem without a solution. To their health and well-being!

ORGANIZATIONAL RESOURCES FOR FAMILIES OF DEPRESSED TEENS

Active Minds on Campus: Active Minds on Campus is a student-run mental health awareness, education, and advocacy organization, which utilizes peer-to-peer outreach to promote its educational mission on university campuses across the United States.

    Web address: www.activemindsoncampus.org

American Academy of Child & Adolescent Psychiatry (AACAP): AACAP aims to promote understanding and treatment of the developmental, behavioral, and mental disorders which affect children, adolescents, and their families. Their series of informational pamphlets, "Facts for Families," are available online. (Also see "ParentsMedGuide" below)

    Web address: www.aacap.org

American Association of Suicidology: a nonprofit organization of mental health professionals, suicide prevention center volunteers, and survivors of suicide, devoted to educating the public about suicide prevention.

    Web address: www.suicidology.org.

American Foundation for Suicide Prevention (AFSP): a nonprofit organization dedicated to spreading knowledge about suicide and the means to prevent it. AFSP offers an excellent short video, "The Truth about Suicide: Real Stories of Depression on Campus," and a facilitator's guide for instructional use on college campuses.

    Web address: www.afsp.org

American Psychiatric Association (APA): a medical specialty professional organization of more than 35,000 U.S. and international member physicians. (Also see "ParentsMedGuide" below.) In 2005 the APA launched a new Web site, www.HealthyMinds.org, a consumer-friendly site organized by psychiatric disorder and topic information; the site offers a referral service linking patients to psychiatrists nationwide. Call 1-888-35-PSYCH.

Web address: www.HealthyMinds.org; www.psych.org

American Psychological Association (APA): a professional organization of researchers, educators, clinicians, consultants, and students working to advance psychology as a science and profession. Offers numerous educational resources and by calling 1-800-964-2000 an operator will locate your state's psychological association's referral service.

Web address: www.apa.org

Bazelon Center for Mental Health Law: a nonprofit advocacy organization dedicated to protecting the rights of children (and adults) with mental illnesses, working on issues related to incarceration and relinquishment of custody, and equal access to care and treatment.

Web address: www.bazelon.org

Breaking the Silence: an educational and advocacy organization that offers lesson plans, games, and posters directed at upper elementary, middle, and high school aged children, designed to put a human face on mental illness and address the myths that reinforce stigma.

Web address: www.btslessonplans.org

Campaign for Mental Health Reform: a national partnership of organizations representing people with mental or emotional disorders, their families, service providers, administrators, and other concerned Americans, designed to address recovery, coherence, and quality in mental health services at the national level by engaging federal policymakers.

Web address: www.mhreform.org

Centers for Disease Control, United States Government: collects statistical information regarding youth suicide and attempted suicide in the Centers for Disease Control Morbidity and Mortality Weekly Report at www.cdc.gov/mmwr/PDF. The CDC also identifies six critical types of adolescent health behavior that research shows contribute to the leading causes of death and disability among adults and youth.

Web address: www.cdc.gov

Center for the Advancement of Children's Mental Health: a joint effort among Columbia University, the New York State Psychiatric Institute, and the New York State Office of Mental Health at Columbia University, the Center aims to accelerate the acceptance and effective use of proven interventions that foster children's emotional and behavioral health by involving key community partners and stakeholders to identify and adapt science-based intervention methods.

Web address: www.kidsmentalhealth.org

Child and Adolescent Bipolar Foundation (CABF): a parent-led, web-based membership organization of families raising children diagnosed with, or at risk for, early-onset bipolar disorder. The Web site includes information and resources on early-onset bipolar disorder.

Web address: www.cabf.org

Depression and Bipolar Support Alliance (DBSA): advocates on behalf of patients and families through a patient-directed national organization offering peer support and information.

Web address: www.DBSAlliance.org

Depression and Related Affective Disorders Association (DRADA): offers educational programs and support services, including *Day for Night*, an informational video about depression for teens and their families. DRADA's adjunct Web site is an excellent resource for teens and families.

Web address: www.depressedteens.com; www.drada.org.

Families for Depression Awareness: created to support family members or friends who are caregivers to adults and children with depression and related mood disorders, and aims to help them recognize and manage these illnesses.

Web address: www.familyaware.org

Federation of Families for Children's Mental Health: a national family-run organization dedicated exclusively to helping children with mental health needs and their families achieve a better quality of life by supporting and fostering a strong educational and activist network.

Web address: www.ffcmh.org

HealthyPlace.com: self-described as the "largest consumer mental health site on the Internet," offers numerous resources and posts current developments in the field of pharmacology and treatment for adolescents with mental illness.

Web address: www.healthyplace.com/communities/depression.com

Independent Educational Consultants Association: a professional association of full-time educational consultants offering guidance and referrals.

Web address: www.iecaonline.org

The Infinite Mind: Public radio's national health and science program produced by Lichtenstein Creative Media. The weekly radio series focuses on all aspects of mental health, neuroscience, access to care, treatment advance, and the mind/body connection.

Web address: http://lcmedia.com/mindprgm.htm.

MindZone: Cope, Care, Deal: A mental health Web site for teens, developed and funded by the Annenberg Public Policy Center at the University of Pennsylvania, this interactive and age-appropriate site offers direct guidance for struggling teens.

Web address: www.copecaredeal.org

NARSAD, The Mental Health Research Association: an independent, nonprofit organization that raises and distributes funds for scientific research on psychiatric brain disorders, committed to finding the causes, improved treatments, and cures for mental health disorders.

Web address: www.narsad.org

National Alliance for the Mentally Ill (NAMI)—Child and Adolescent Action Center: the nation's largest grassroots, self-help, and family advocacy organization dedicated to improving the lives of people with severe mental illnesses. NAMI offers a wide variety of resources, including NAMI's quarterly publication, *NAMI Beginnings*, addressing issues related to children and youth with mental illness.

Web address: www.nami.org

National Association of Therapeutic Schools and Programs: a national resource for programs and professionals assisting young people with emotional and behavioral problems. Web site provides a current directory of programs and schools.

Web address: www.natsap.org

National Hopeline Network: 1-800-SUICIDE (784-2433) offers a national network of 162 certified crisis centers operating throughout the United States twenty-four hours a day. It is a program of the Kristin Brooks Hope Center, which publishes *Preventing Suicide: The National Journal.*

Web address: www.hopeline.com.

National Institute of Mental Health (NIMH): conducts research into mental illness and is a division of the U.S. National Institutes of Health, offering pamphlets and literature about adolescent depression.

Web address: www.nimh.nih.gov

National Mental Health Association (NMHA): a national advocacy, education, and support organization working to address the needs of people with mental health-related needs and mental illnesses. Web site contains valuable references and a database by region of mental health practitioners. NMHA also features Mpower—Musicians for Mental Health, a Web site specifically targeted to teens and young adults and offers good resources for college students and administrators.

Web address: www.nmha.org; www.mpower.org

National Mental Health Awareness Campaign: a nationwide nonpartisan public education campaign offering a youth outreach program of speakers and events.

Web address: www.nostigma.org

National Suicide Prevention Lifeline: providing immediate assistance to individuals in suicidal crisis by connecting them to the nearest available suicide prevention and mental health service provider through a toll-free telephone number: 1-800-273-TALK (8255). It is the only national suicide prevention and intervention telephone resource funded by the federal government.

Web address: www.suicidepreventionlifeline.org

National Youth Violence Prevention Resource Center: a "one-stop shop" for information on youth violence prevention, including suicide and self-harm, sponsored by the Centers for Disease Control and Prevention and other federal agencies. 1-866-SAFEYOUTH.

Web address: www.safeyouth.org

New York University Child Study Center: *AboutOurKids* library offers a web-based resource guide to the NYU Child Study Center offering articles and publications developed by the faculty for families and parents of depressed children.

Web address: www.aboutourkids.org.

ParentsMedGuide: the American Psychiatric Association and the American Academy of Child and Adolescent Psychiatry, in collaboration with child mental health organizations, Web site dedicated to helping patients, families, and physicians make informed decisions about obtaining and administering the most appropriate care for a child or young person with depression.

Web address: www.parentsmedguide.org

Substance Abuse and Mental Health Services Administration (SAMSA), Center for Mental Health Services (CMHS): the federal government's comprehensive source for child, adolescent, and family resources.

Web address: www.mentalhealth.org/cmhs/ChildrensCampaign/default.asp

Suicide Prevention Action Networks: SPAN USA affiliates and volunteer organizers of all ages work to promote and advance suicide prevention. Community organizers work to raise awareness about suicide in their communities and communicate with their local, state, and federal policy makers to advocate for suicide prevention.

Web address: www.spanusa.org

Suicide Prevention Resource Center: SPRC provides prevention support, training, and resources to assist organizations and individuals to develop suicide prevention programs, interventions and policies, and to advance the National Strategy for Suicide Prevention.

Web address: www.sprc.org

TeenScreen®: TeenScreen Program and the Positive Action for Teen Health (PATH) initiative creates partnerships with communities across the nation to implement early-identification programs for suicide and mental illness and promotes the benefits of mental health screening for adolescents nationwide.

Web address: www.teenscreen.org

ULifeline.org: an online behavioral support system for young adults created by the Jed Foundation and offering college-age students with links to their respective colleges' mental health centers.

Web address: www.ulifeline.org

U.S. Department of Health and Human Services Centers for Medicare & Medicaid Services (CMS—formerly HCFA): CMS administers the Medicare, Medicaid, and SCHIP (State Children's Health Insurance Program) programs for children with mental illnesses.

Web address: www.cms.hhs.gov

YellowRibbon.org: a web-and community-based comprehensive suicide prevention program offering teens peer-to-peer advice online through a team of nonprofessionals, ages thirteen and older.

Web address: www.yellowribbon.org; www.teenadviceonline.org

Youth America Hotline: affiliated with the National Hopeline Network, operates the Youth America Hotline at 1-877-968-8454, offering trained, teen-to-teen peer crisis counseling.

Web address: www.youthline.org

SUGGESTED READING
AND REFERENCES

Depression, General (Clinical guidance and memoir)

DePaulo, J. Raymond, Jr. *Understanding Depression: What We Know and What You Can Do About It*. New York: John Wiley & Sons, Inc., 2002.

Jamison, Kay Redfield. *An Unquiet Mind: A Memoir of Moods and Madness*. New York: Knopf, 1995.

Kramer, Peter D. *Against Depression*. New York: Viking Penguin, 2005.

Solomon, Andrew. *The Noonday Demon: An Atlas of Depression*. New York: Simon & Schuster, Inc., 2001.

Slater, Lauren. *Prozac Diary*. New York: Random House, 1998.

Styron, William. *Darkness Visible: A Memoir of Madness*. New York: Random House, 1990.

Depression (Child and Adolescent)

Berlinger, Norman T. *Rescuing Your Teenager from Depression*. New York: Harper-Collins Publishers, 2005.

Copans, Stuart and Copeland, Mary Ellen. *Recovering from Depression: A Workbook for Teens*. Baltimore: Paul H. Brooks Publishing Co., 2002.

Day for Night: Recognizing Teenage Depression©. Video sponsored by Depression & Related Affective Disorders Association (DRADA), in cooperation with the Johns Hopkins University School of Medicine. Vanderpool Films, 1999. To order call 410-955-4647.

Duckworth, Kenneth and Gruttadaro, Darcy. *What Families Should Know About Adolescent Depression and Treatment Options: A Family Guide*. Washington, D.C.: National Alliance for the Mentally Ill, Arlington, Virginia, 2005. Available online at www.nami.org.

Empfield, Maureen and Bakalar, Nicholas. *Understanding Teen Depression: A Guide to Diagnosis, Treatment and Management.* New York: Henry Holt and Company, LLC, 2001.

Fassler, David G. and Dumas, Lynne S. *"Help Me, I'm Sad:" Recognizing, Treating and Preventing Childhood and Adolescent Depression.* New York: Viking Penguin, 1997.

Fristad, Mary A. and Arnold, Jill S. *Raising a Moody Child: How to Cope with Depression and Bipolar Disorder.* New York: Guilford Press, 2004.

Koplewicz, Harold. *More Than Moody: Recognizing and Treating Adolescent Depression.* New York: G.P. Putnam and Sons, 2002.

Levenkron, Steven. *Cutting: Understanding and Overcoming Self-Mutilation.* New York: W.W. Norton and Company, 1998.

McCormick, Patricia. *Cut.* New York: Scholastic, Inc. 2000.

Mondimore, Francis M. *Adolescent Depression: A Guide for Parents.* Baltimore: The Johns Hopkins University Press, 2002.

Raeburn, Paul. *Acquainted with the Night: A Parent's Quest to Understand Depression and Bipolar Disorder in His Children.* New York: Broadway Books, 2004.

Electroconvulsive Therapy

Fink, Max. *Electroshock: Restoring the Mind.* New York: Oxford University Press, 1999.

Manning, Martha. *Undercurrents: A Therapist's Reckoning with Her Own Depression.* New York: HarperCollins Publishers, 1994.

Neurobiology (Adolescent)

Strauch, Barbara. *The Primal Teen: What the New Discoveries About the Teenage Brain Tell Us About Our Kids.* New York: Doubleday, 2003.

PBS Documentary series *FRONTLINE:* "Inside the Teenage Brain." Original airdate January 31, 2002.

Neurobiology

Broks, Paul. *Into the Silent Land: Travels in Neuropsychology.* New York: Atlantic Monthly Press, 2003.

Psychiatric Medication

Barondes, Samuel H. *Better Than Prozac: Creating the Next Generation of Psychiatric Drugs.* New York: Oxford University Press, 2003.

Kramer, Peter D. *Listening to Prozac: A Psychiatrist Explores Antidepressant Drugs and the Remaking of the Self.* New York: Viking, 1993.

ParentsMedGuide, a web-based resource published by the American Academy of Child and Adolescent Psychiatry and the American Psychiatric Association, 2005. www.parentsmedguide.org.

Society, Mental Health, and Adolescence

Barber, Charles. *Songs from the Black Chair: A Memoir of Mental Interiors*. Lincoln, Nebraska: University of Nebraska Press, 2005.

Currie, Elliot. *The Road to Whatever: Middle Class Culture and the Crisis of Adolescence*. New York: Henry Holt and Company, 2004.

Dudman, Martha Tod. *Augusta, Gone: A True Story*. New York: Simon & Schuster, 2001.

Finnegan, William. *Cold New World: Growing Up in a Harder Country*. New York: Random House, 1998.

Hersch, Patricia. *A Tribe Apart: A Journey into the Heart of American Adolescence*. New York: Ballantine Publishing Group, 1998.

Hine, Thomas. *The Rise and Fall of the American Teenager: A New History of the American Adolescent Experience*. New York: William Morrow & Company, 1999.

Hymowitz, Kay S. *Liberation's Children: Parents and Kids in a Postmodern Age*. Chicago: Ivan R. Dee, Publisher, 2003.

Kadison, Richard D. and DiGeronimo, Theresa Foy. *College of the Overwhelmed: The Campus Mental Health Crisis and What to Do About It*. Hoboken, New Jersey: Jossey-Bass, 2005.

Kindlon, Dan and Thompson, Michael. *Raising Cain: Protecting the Emotional Life of Boys*. New York: Ballantine Books, 1999.

Marcus, David L. *What It Takes to Pull Me Through: Why Teenagers Get in Trouble and How Four of Them Got Out*. New York: Houghton Mifflin Company, 2005.

Pipher, Mary, *Reviving Ophelia: Saving the Selves of Adolescent Girls*. New York: Putnam Publishing Group, 1994.

Pollack, William. *Real Boys: Rescuing Our Sons from the Myths of Boyhood*. New York: Henry Holt and Company, LLC, 1998.

Shaw, Robert. *The Epidemic: The Rot of American Culture, Absentee and Permissive Parenting, and the Resultant Plague of Joyless, Selfish Children*. New York: ReganBooks, 2003.

Drug and Alcohol Addiction in Young People

Maran, Meredith. *Dirty: A Search for Answers Inside America's Teenage Drug Epidemic*. New York: HarperCollins Publishers, 2003.

Zailckas, Koren. *Smashed: Story of a Drunken Girlhood*. New York: Viking Adult, 2005.

Suicide

Blauner, Susan Rose. *How I Stayed Alive When My Brain Was Trying to Kill Me: One Person's Guide to Suicide Prevention.* New York: William Morrow & Company, 2002.

Jamison, Kay Redfield, *Night Falls Fast: Understanding Suicide.* New York: Random House, 1999.

Lester, David P. *Making Sense of Suicide: An In-Depth Look at Why People Kill Themselves.* Philadelphia: The Charles Press, Publishers, 1997.

Shneidman, Edwin S. *The Suicidal Mind.* New York: Oxford University Press, 1996.

Suicide: Helping Patients and Their Families in the Aftermath of an Attempt. National Alliance for the Mentally Ill, Arlington, Virginia, 2005. Available online at www.nami.org or by calling the NAMI Helpline at 1-800-950-6264.

Suicide: Taking Care of Yourself and Your Family After an Attempt: Family Guide for Your Relative in the Emergency Department. National Alliance for the Mentally Ill, Arlington, Virginia, 2005.

The Truth About Suicide: Real Stories of Depression in College, a film from the American Foundation for Suicide Prevention, produced by Ant Hill Marketing, Portland, Oregon, 2003. Available through the American Foundation for Suicide Prevention, www.afsp.org. To order call 1-888-333-AFSP.

ENDNOTES

Chapter 1

1 American Academy of Child and Adolescent Psychiatry Teen Suicide Fact Sheet, 1998.

2 Harold S. Koplewicz, *More Than Moody: Recognizing and Treating Adolescent Depression*, (New York: G. P. Putnam's Sons, 2002), 248.

2 Ibid, 16.

Chapter 2

1 American Psychiatric Association Web site, "Let's Talk Facts . . . Teen Suicide," http://www.psych.org.

2 William Styron, *Darkness Visible: A Memoir of Madness* (New York: Random House, 1990), 33.

3 The National Alliance for the Mentally Ill (www.nami.org) has recently created an Emergency Department Resource Toolkit of educational brochures around suicide prevention describing what patients and families should expect in the aftermath of a suicide attempt. The Toolkit offers three brochures: one each for individuals who have attempted suicide, for their families, and for medical professionals who work in emergency departments.

4 Kay Redfield Jamison, *Touched with Fire*, (New York: Simon & Schuster, 1993).

5 Thomas Insel, Director of the National Institute of Mental Health, NIH, quoted in WAMU's *The Diane Rehm Show*, NPR, August 18, 2004.

6 Ibid.

7 Kay Redfield Jamison, *Night Falls Fast: Understanding Suicide* (New York: Random House, 1999), 50.

8 Kay S. Hymowitz, *Liberation's Children: Parents and Kids in a Postmodern Age* (Chicago: Ivan R. Dee, 2003), 97.

9 Rebecca L. Collins et al., "Watching Sex on Television Predicts Adolescent Ini-

tiation of Sexual Behavior," electronic abstract, *Pediatrics*, 114, no. 3 (September 2004); e280–89.

10 Ibid.

11 February 2003 survey conducted on behalf of Columbia University; findings posted on Positive Action for Teen Health (PATH) Web site, http://www.path now.org.

12 See Positive Action for Teen Health (PATH) Web site, http://www.pathnow.org.

13 National Center for Health Statistics, U.S. Center for Disease Control and Prevention, Surveys and Data, 2000.

14 *Journal of the American Academy of Child and Adolescent Psychiatry* 40, no. 7 (supplement) (July 2001).

15 U.S. Centers for Disease Control and Prevention Web site, http://www.cdc. gov/ncipe/factsheets/suifacts.htm.

16 *Journal of the American Academy of Child and Adolescent Psychiatry* 40, no. 7 (supplement) (July 2001).

17 John L. McIntosh, "1999 Official Final Statistics USA Suicide," prepared for the American Association of Suicidology, at http://www.suicidology.org.

18 Columbia University's Teen Suicide Fact Sheet, 2002.

19 National Center for Health Statistics, *National Health Statistics* 48, no. 11 (1998).

20 *Journal of the American Academy of Child and Adolescent Psychiatry* 40, no. 7 (supplement) (July 2001).

21 Koplewicz, *More Than Moody*, 246.

22 U.S. Department of Health and Human Services, "*National Strategy for Suicide Prevention: Goals and Objectives for Action*," 2001, http://www.mental health.org/suicideprevention.

23 "Suicide's Young Victims: A Chat with Teen Suicide Expert Dr. David Shaffer," ABCNews.com. online chat, March 29, 2000.

24 Jamison, *Night Falls Fast*, 90.

25 M. S. Gould, F. A. Marrocco, M. Kleinman, J. G. Thomas, K. Mostkoff, J. Cote, and M. Davies, "Evaluating iatrogenic risk of youth suicide screening programs: a randomized controlled trial," *Journal of American Medical Association*, April 2005; 293(13):1635-43.

26 David D. Shaffer, V. Vieland, M. M. Underwood, and C. Busner, "The Impact of Curriculum-based Suicide Prevention Programs for Teenagers," *Journal of the American Academy of Child and Adolescent Psychiatry* 30 (1991): 588–96.

27 Shaffer et al., "Adolescent Suicide Attempters: Response to Suicide Prevention Programs," *Journal of the American Medical Association* 264 (1990): 3151–55.

28 Recognizing that they are on the front line of child and adolescent mental

health treatment, the American Academy of Pediatrics created a task force in 2005 to get its member practitioners up-to-speed in the diagnosis and treatment of child and adolescent mental health. Likewise, Columbia University's Center for the Advancement of Children's Mental Health has undertaken to establish "Guidelines for Adolescent Depression in Primary Care (GLAD-PC)."

Chapter 3

1 "Treatment for Adolescents with Depression Study [TADS]," sponsored by the National Institute of Mental Health, June 2004.

2 Cecilia Capuzzi Simon, "On Beyond Worry," *Washington Post,* December 3, 2003.

3 C. Russell Baker, "Adolescent Depression: Signs, Symptoms and Treatments—A DRADA Meeting Review," reported in *Smooth Sailing,* the newsletter of the Depression and Related Affective Disorders Association (DRADA), spring 2004.

4 Shankar Vedantam, "Variation in One Gene Linked to Depression," *Washington Post,* July 18, 2003.

5 Caspi Avshalom et al., "Influence of Life Stress on Depression: Moderation by a Polymorphism in the 5-HTT Gene," *Science,* 301, no. 5631 (July 2003): 386–89.

6 Peter D. Kramer, "Tapping the Mood Gene," *New York Times,* July 26, 2003 (electronic version).

7 Ibid.

8 Joan Kaufman, Bao-Zhu Yang, Heather Douglas-Palumberi, Shadi Houshyar, Deborah Lipschitz, John H. Krystal, and Joel Gelernter, "Social supports and serotonin transporter gene moderate depression in maltreated children," Proceedings of the National Academy of Sciences of the United States of America, PNAS, December 7, 2004, vol. 101, no. 49, pp. 17316–17321.

9 Kramer.

Chapter 4

1 Judith S. Wallerstein and Joan B. Kelly, *Surviving the Breakup: How Children and Parents Cope with Divorce* (New York: Basic Books, 1996), 35.

2 William Styron, *Darkness Visible: A Memoir of Madness* (New York: Random House, 1990).

3 *Jacobellis v. Ohio,* 378 U.S. 184, 198 (1964).

4 Boglarka Szabo, (paper delivered at Mood Disorders Research/Education Symposium, sponsored by Johns Hopkins University School of Medicine and the Depression and Related Affective Disorders Association [DRADA], citing

1995 Center for Disease Control survey of college students over eighteen years old, Johns Hopkins University, Baltimore, Maryland, April 15, 2004).

5 Anita Manning, "Writing the ABCs of Murder," *USA TODAY*, July 2, 1992, D4.

6 Kimberly Goldapple et al., "Modulation of Cortical-Limbic Pathways in Major Depression: Treatment—Specific Effects of Cognitive Behavior Therapy," *Archives of General Psychiatry* 61, no. 1 (January 2004): 34–41.

7 John O'Neill, "Mental Health: Double-Teaming Depression," *New York Times*, January 6, 2004 (electronic version).

8 John S. March et al., "Fluoxetine, Cognitive-Behavioral Therapy, and Their Combination for Adolescents With Depression," *Journal of the American Medical Association* 292, no. 7 (August 18, 2004): 807–20. This combination treatment of medication *and* therapy ranked superior to either talk therapy alone, medication alone, or placebo.

9 *The Infinite Mind: Depression in the Brain,* radio broadcast, NPR, hosted by Dr. Peter Kramer and produced by Lichtenstein Creative Media, New York, March 31, 2004.

10 Samuel H. Barondes, *Better Than Prozac: Creating the Next Generation of Psychiatric Drugs* (New York: Oxford University Press, 2003), xiv.

11 Ibid., 134.

12 J. Raymond DePaulo Jr., *Understanding Depression: What We Know and What You Can Do About It* (New York: John Wiley and Sons, 2002), 182–89.

13 Barondes, *Better Than Prozac,* 44.

14 Ibid., 45.

15 Peter Kramer, quoted in *The Infinite Mind: Depression in the Brain,* March 31, 2004.

16 J. Douglas Bremner et al., "Hippocampal Volume Reduction in Major Depression," *American Journal of Psychiatry* 157 (January 2000): 115–17.

17 Yvette I. Sheline, Mokhtar H. Gado, and Helena C. Kraemer, "Untreated Depression and Hippocampal Volume Loss," *American Journal of Psychiatry* 160 (August, 2003): 1516–18.

18 Phillip W. Gold and Dennis S. Charney, "Depression: A Disease of the Mind, Brain, and Body," *American Journal of Psychiatry* 159 (November 2002): 11.

19 Carol Ezzell, "Why? The Neuroscience of Suicide," scientificamerican.com, January 13, 2003.

20 Max Fink, *Electroshock: Restoring the Mind* (New York: Oxford University Press, 1999), ix.

21 Ibid., 44.

Chapter 6

1 DePaulo, *Understanding Depression,* 146.

2 David Fassler and Lynne Dumas, *"Help Me, I'm Sad": Recognizing, Treating and Preventing Childhood and Adolescent Depression* (New York: Viking Penguin, 1997), 111.

3 Redfield Jamison, *Night Falls Fast,* 73.

Chapter 7:

1 Kathleen Kennedy Manzo, "Schoolhouse on the Lost Prairie," *Education Week,* August 4, 1999, cited on Montana Academy Web site, http://www.montana academy.com.

2 National Association of Therapeutic Schools and Programs Web site, http://www.natsap.org.

3 Ibid.

4 Manzo, "Schoolhouse on the Lost Prairie."

5 Montana Academy Web site, www.montanaacademy.com.

Chapter 8:

1 Max Fink, *Electroshock: Restoring the Mind* (New York: Oxford University Press, 1999), 44.

2 U.S. Food and Drug Administration, FDA talk paper, *FDA Issues Public Health Advisory Entitled: Reports of Suicidality in Pediatric Patients Being Treated with Antidepressant Medications for Major Depressive Disorder (MDD),"* October 27, 2003, at http://www.fda.gov.

3 U.S. Food and Drug Administration, Mission Statement, http://www.fda.gov.

4 U.S. Food and Drug Administration, "FDA Issues Public Health Advisory," October 27, 2003.

5 Gail Griffith, "The Fear of No Right Answer," *Washington Post,* November 9, 2003.

6 World Health Organization Mortality Database, "Suicide Rates and Absolute Numbers of Suicide by Country (2003), http://www.who.int/mental_health/prevention/suicide/country_reports.

7 IMS Health, *National Disease and Therapeutic Index,*® *Years 1988 to 2002.*

8 Rich McManus, "Abolitionist Angell Calls for Clinical Trial Reform," *NIH Record,* July 24, 2001.

9 Marcia Angell, online interview, "The Other Drug War," *FRONTLINE,* WGBH, posted June 19, 2003.

10 Shankar Vedantam, "Antidepressant Makers Withhold Data on Children," *Washington Post,* January 29, 2004.

11 Andrew Solomon, "A Bitter Pill," *New York Times*, March 29, 2004.

12 Carol Paris, "Kids, Depression and Elusive Answers," *Washington Post*, letter to the editor, November 22, 2003.

13 Ibid.

14 U.S. Food and Drug Administration Public Health Advisory, "Worsening Depression and Suicidality in Patients Being Treated with Antidepressant Medications," March 22, 2004, http://www.fda.gov.

15 Dr. Jay Giedd interview by Sarah Spinks, "The Teenage Brain," *FRONTLINE*, WGBH, January 31, 2002.

16 "Treatment for Adolescents with Depression Study [TADS]," sponsored by the National Institute of Mental Health, June 2004.

17 Thomas P. Laughren, Team Leader, Psychiatric Drug Products, DNDP, U.S. Food and Drug Administraton, "Background Comments for February 2, 2004, Meeting of Psychopharmacological Drugs Advisory Committee and Pediatric Subcommittee of the Anti-Infective Drugs Advisory Committee," memorandum, January 5, 2004.

18 Richard M. Glass, "Treatment of Adolescents with Major Depression: Contributions of a Major Trial," *Journal of the American Medical Association* 292, no. 7 (August 18, 2004).

19 Gardener Harris, "Merck Says It Will Post the Results of All Drug Trials," *New York Times*, September 6, 2004 (electronic version).

20 Ibid.

21 Marcia Angell, *The Truth About Drug Companies: How They Deceive Us and What to Do About It* (New York: Random House, 2004), 237.

22 Thomas P. Laughren, Team Leader, Psychiatric Drug Products, DNDP, U.S. Food and Drug Administration, "Overview for September 13 & 14, 2004 Meeting of Psychopharmacological Drugs Advisory Committee and Pediatric Drugs Advisory Committee," memorandum, August 16, 2004.

23 Marcia Newman, "U.S. Orders New Warnings on Antidepressant Use in Children," *New York Times*, electronic version, October 15, 2004.

24 David Shaffer, "Problems Ascertaining 'Suicidogenic' Properties of Antidepressants," paper delivered at the 2005 annual meeting of the American Academy of Child and Adolescent Psychiatry, Washington, D.C., October 2004.

25 Gardiner Harris, "FDA's Drug and Safety System Will Get Outside Review," *New York Times*, electronic version, November 6, 2004.

Chapter 10

1 David Shaffer et al., "Psychiatric Diagnosis in Child and Adolescent Suicide," *Archives of General Psychiatry*, 53, no. 4 (1996): 339–48.

2 Andrew Solomon, *The Noonday Demon: An Atlas of Depression* (New York: Simon & Schuster, 2001), 438.

3 President's New Freedom Commission on Mental Health, July 2003, http://www.mentalhealthcommission.gov.

4 Ibid.

5 Larke Nahme Huang, American Institute for Research (presentation made at the National Alliance for the Mentally Ill 2004 Annual Convention, Washington, D.C., September 10, 2004).